ULU:
Bread of Life

ULU:
Bread of Life

REFLECTIONS ON TEXTS
FROM
THE NEW COMMON LECTIONARY

B. David Williams

This book was printed in the United States of America.

The Revised Common Lectionary is a calendar of scripture readings developed by scholars, having a three-year cycle, years "A", "B", and "C". The readings for each Sunday and holy day usually include one item each from the Old Testament, the Epistles, and the Gospels, plus a psalm. The Lectionary follows the "Christian Year," and is organized around two poles: Christmas and Easter. The beginning of the year is Advent, the season before Christmas. Each year the New Testament readings center on one of the Synoptic gospels (Matthew, Mark, and Luke), and the gospel of John is read every year, especially during Christmas, Lent and Easter. Use of the lectionary ensures that the great themes of the Christian faith are addressed, and encourages a systematic approach to the use of scripture in worship. When publicized in a local church it encourages Bible reading and study.

Photographs are by the author.

Companion Publications

Companion Publications
Mercer Island, Washington, USA

To order additional copies of this book, contact:

Xlibris Corporation

1-888-795-4274

www.Xlibris.com

Orders@Xlibris.com

20023

Many years ago, in the "time before," there was a long, terrible famine in Tahiti.

The old man, Teae, a priest, gathered his people—the lean and emaciated men, the women with dried up bosoms, and the desperately hungry children.

Teae told them, "I will walk up the valley and talk to 'Te Fatu', the master of the powerful words.

The people followed him, and behind them came the skinny pigs that they had saved for the hunger of their last days.

When they reached Mount Tamanu, the center of the island, Teae told them to dig a hole in the ground, and they did.

Then Teae stepped into the hole, and implored Te Fatu, the master of powerful words. Teae stood still, his arms up. His naked chest became as tough as a big tree, and his skin changed to bark. His feet divided and took root in the soil.

His upheld arms were changed into ten branches, which became twenty, then a hundred, then many more. His hands became lovely palmate leaves, which spread throughout the branches. In the leaf clusters grew an interesting, unknown fruit.

The Tahitians ate. They were able to satisfy their hunger, and said, "It is good." This tree is known as the "**ulu**," the breadfruit tree.

The Tahitian legend of the breadfruit tree has been passed through the generations in the form of a joyful and rhythmic song.

Through techniques of food preservation Polynesians have been able to use the fruit to prevent starvation, and have used it for sustenance on their long voyages.

After the voyage of Captain Cook through Tahiti, news of the breadfruit tree spread rapidly to the English colonies, partly because it offered the possibility of feeding slaves at a very low cost. The infamous ship "Bounty," which fell victim to a mutiny, carried breadfruit plants that the harsh Captain Bligh had been commissioned to transport from Tahiti to the West Indies.

Called "uru or ulu" by Tahitians and Hawaiians, "mei" by Tongans, and "rimas" by Filipinos, stories of the breadfruit tree, ancient and modern, abound.

JEFF, LYNN, AND DENISE

Contents

INTRODUCTION

I'm convinced that the Gospel enters our experience with the most sharpness and clarity at the points of the pain and passion of our life-encounters. As a comfortable middle-class, straight, white male American Christian, I've had virtually everything to learn from the people to whom I've been "sent." Experiences in the Philippines and Pacific Islands, those while working with the World Hunger Emphasis of the United Methodist Church, and while assigned to ecumenical organizations, have had profound impact upon my faith and my approach to Bible study and worship preparation. Serving as pastor of congregations that openly welcomed gay and lesbian persons into a full participation have extended this experience.

I'm also convinced that the Gospel most powerfully enters the experience of those to whom we've been sent when it speaks practical hope to vulnerabilities and pain. At their best, and as they were intended to be, ministries of service are a vital, integral part of the task of evangelization, which not only involves preaching Good News, but BEING Good News. Preaching and "reflecting" are meaningless without serious engagement with real life!

The simplest of traditional cultures to which I was introduced have helped me in my spiritual journey. As a Filipino anthropologist friend said after spending some weeks with the so-called "Lost Tribe", the Tasaday, in South Cotabato, "We'll not realize how much we have to learn from them until we admit to what we ourselves have lost."

My friends in traditional/indigenous cultures have made me more sensitive to deeper meanings in stories and parables. Perhaps they're more aware than we so-called "educated folk" that this is how we transmit our culture and values. It's in the stories where we find the greatest richness of the Bible, in both the Old and New Testaments. Jesus constantly taught through story, parable, and metaphor. Taking a shallow, literal approach to these causes us to miss the many layers of meanings and themes which the writers intended to be addressed. While stories may not prove something, they illustrate something, and they carry their own conviction. It's up to us to incorporate them into our insight and understanding.

Hearing the stories of others has put me in closer touch with my own. May mine do the same for you!

This is not the kind of book to be read straight through in a few sittings, but one where you might "dip" and browse according to the seasons or your whims! Each reflection is a condensation of a once-preached sermon (some of them twice and thrice-preached!). There's a recurrence of some themes, but perhaps the new stories will make it worth your while!

Bible quotations are from the New Revised Standard Version unless otherwise noted.

ACKNOWLEDGEMENTS

I give thanks to God for these persons of faith, world citizens, mentors and friends, none of them neutral observers, all of them very much alive, though some have gone ahead: Rebecca Asedillo, Sinfronio "Jun" Atienza, Bill Coop, Bob Ellis, Juan Flavier, Michael Hahm, Ruth Harris, Amanaki Havea, Edwin M. Luidens, Lewistine ("Mac") McCoy, Patrick Murphy S.V.D., Baiteke Nabetari, Teofilo Pacot, Sitiveni Ratuvili, Benton Rhodes, Suliana Siwatibau, Franklin Smith, Lorine Tevi, and Jim Winkler.

The United Methodist churches that I've served in recent years in Oregon and Washington, though diverse in theology and politics, have encouraged me to be my own self and preach my convictions: Estacada UMC (The First Reconciling Congregation in the Oregon-Idaho Conference); Lincoln St. UMC, Portland; Community UMC in Sultan, Washington; First Samoan UMC of Seattle; and now Seaview UMC in Seattle, with its Tongan Fellowship. These authentic communities of faith, all "survivor" churches, have shown their courage and capacity for struggle as they raise the right questions and keep on "keeping on."

Lectionary study groups have been an abundant flowing spring of insight and stimulation. Special thanks to friends John Hasenjaeger, Rebecca Howe; David Biles and Gisela Taber; and Elois Bye, Dell Gossett, Gladys Herreid and Jan Perry Peterson.

Thanks to my partner, Susan Morrisson, who has always

encouraged me in my unusual projects. I value our far-ranging philosophical discussions.

Having a deepening sense of indebtedness to a myriad of persons, sources and resources, I sometimes wonder how many of us really have original thoughts! Chasing references through google.com has been a stark reminder of this!

Dell Gossett gave generously of her time to read the *Ulu* manuscript, and her suggestions were invaluable. Typos and other editorial inadequacies are entirely my responsibility!

Family is at the core of who I am. I'm so thankful for my late parents, Bert Williams and Dorothy Neiswanger Williams, whose love, energy, and values have resulted in a remarkable family of "caring achievers": my "sibs," Jan Roberts, Dick Williams, Marcia Ellis, and Sue Wagner, individually and together a constant source of joy and support (and accountability!) across the miles and through the years. And of course my own children: Jeff Williams, Lynn Evans, and Denise Freese, to whom this collection is dedicated.

Irrigation Agusan

1

MEMORY AND HOPE EMBRACE THE NOW

Advent 2, Year A
Isaiah 11:1-10; Matthew 3:1-12

"A shoot shall come out from the stump of Jesse . . .
He shall not judge by what his eyes see, or decide by
what his ears hear; but with righteousness he shall judge
the poor, and decide with equity for the meek of the
earth;"

Isaiah 11:1a, 3b-4a

"Repent, for the kingdom of heaven has come
near."

Matthew 3:2

As we prepare for Christmas, we wait. Do any of us like
waiting? I admit that I'm one more face in the restless crowd
looking at his watch in an impatient, Christmas-shopping world.
I recall the vivid image put forward by German theologian
Dorothy Solle in a message to the Vancouver Assembly of the
World Council of Churches: She saw thousands of people sitting
alone in their cars in a massive traffic jam on an interstate
interchange in serious need of repair, a colossal gridlock, all
participants impatient and angry, honking their horns, and

not going anywhere! And, I would guess, constantly looking at their watches. Many of them are people like me, sometimes feeling that no matter where they are, they ought to be somewhere else!

But Advent *is* about waiting. Waiting expectantly for the coming of Jesus, whatever that might mean for each one of us. Advent is the time of expectant, active waiting of a faithful church with a vivid memory of the past, and with a grasp of hope for the future. This faithfulness and hope is validated to the extent that it engages the concrete world of our "NOW"!

We look to the future and yearn for life in all its fullness. The energy of the ancient prophets flows toward us from the past, driven by their passion for the NOW. Isaiah cries out, "Seek God while God may be found; Call upon God while God is near!" NOW! John the Baptist, the voice crying in the wilderness, shouts, "Repent, for the Kingdom of God is at hand!" NOW!

The readings from Isaiah and Matthew represent a convergence of some of the most exciting Bible personalities and themes: Jesus, Isaiah, the "electric" John the Baptist. Bigger-than-life figures in times perceived as the end of the age! Super-vivid characters dealing with ultimate and final matters. But *our* time is also apocalyptic, soberingly so, for we are a generation constantly flirting with and meddling in issues that are unnervingly close to being ultimate and final matters.

As we quote the words of Isaiah at Christmas time, it's good to remember the "storm cloud" background of the times in which they were written. Isaiah and his "school" wrote from a heavy sense of crisis, danger, and judgment. He also preached and wrote from an exciting vision of possibility. The gospels consistently show how those with an emerging sense of Jesus' identity reached back to Isaiah's vision.

That's why we love to read Isaiah during Advent! That's why we dust off our old scores of *Handel's Messiah* and head for those wonderful singalong Messiah evenings to celebrate Second Isaiah's greatest "hits!"

Three themes seem especially interesting to me in these two texts. The first has to do with kings: we're given a new vision of what a king might be. The second is the idea of a natural order that is reconciled and made whole. The third is the insistent challenge that *we* are the ones who create conditions that make it possible for the messiah to come.

During Isaiah's times every king was designated a messiah, and repeatedly, as kings took their power, hopes rose for a prospective golden age. The hopes were born of the pain and anguish of crisis. We're still like that—we want our new leader, whoever he or she may be, to come to us with superhuman wisdom, authority, (and morality!) to lead us out of our morass!

Quite frankly, I'm tired of kings and regal leaders! What I've experienced, in my own country, and while living abroad, causes me to rebel against the expectation that a great and powerful king will come and save us.

The traditional, popular idea of a messiah king didn't work then, as we know from the later Isaiah materials, and it doesn't work now, as we should know from our historical experience. With great gladness we can fit Jesus into Isaiah's unique messianic vision, that of a servant king! Isaiah outlines the qualities expected of such a one supposedly worthy to govern: one who rules not by brute force, but with wisdom and understanding, good judgment and the moral energy to carry it out, with reverence and a practical faith.

Jesus of Nazareth fits Isaiah's vision. It gradually becomes clear in the gospels that Jesus knows that he fits, and he makes it clear to his disciples that he knows. In his "servanthood" he becomes the ultimate prototype servant king.

The second theme has to do with verses 6-9 of Isaiah 11, which lays out a vision of a reconciled and whole natural order. It imagines dangerous beasts living in harmonious companionship with vulnerable animals and little children . . . Wolves dwelling with lambs, the calf and the lion together, and a little child leading them. A vivid image of peace, of shalom. A world safe, happy, abundant, fair, a place of healing. A place of holiness and faithfulness. A world safe for children!

Sentimental verses, perhaps, but we dare not disconnect our hopes from the reality of our practical, everyday world. Like the reality that the intolerably high percentage of children classified as being in poverty in our country has remained relatively unchanged at about 20% since 1981 *(Federal Interagency Forum on Child and Family Statistics)*. How many things would fall into their proper place if we set ourselves to the task of making this a world safe for children and other vulnerable ones among us.

Whether or not lions and lambs will ever be brought together in MY barn, Isaiah tells me that a radical change in human existence as we have known it will have to occur when the world is transformed according to the values of the realm of God, a natural order that is reconciled and made whole.

The third area of interest has to do with John the Baptist, "the voice crying in the wilderness." Years ago Methodist Bishop Gerald Kennedy preached on the theme "A Wilderness Crying for a Voice!", and don't we have one of those?! John the Baptist's task was to confront the conditions that make it difficult for the King to come.

Striking here is John's sharp condemnation of those who claim they are born of Abraham. Quite frankly, I see this as a warning for us church people! The axe is laid to the root, it says in Matthew 3:10. Our roots do not count here. In this we stand before God naked and alone. John called not just gentiles to repentance, but Jews themselves. *All* are confronted. Yes, especially I, an "O.K." guy: I'm white, American, male, presuming to be a serious Christian, middle class, straight . . . . Watch out, spiritual danger!

John proclaims that new things are happening! We are warned that we cannot fall back on the roots of tradition. "Bear fruit that befits repentance!" The Gospel is *new* wine, for new wineskins, and we must ever guard against stifling prejudices and judgments. There's no basis for thinking that John would be any less critical and challenging of religious institutions and practices today, including, and especially, those bearing Jesus' name.

I would not like to live with the difficult person, John the Baptist. Yet Jesus demanded to be baptized by him. When we engage ourselves in the work of John the Baptist, preparing the way for Jesus, in that way do we participate in the baptism of Christ.

Advent assures us that God can bring new things out of our wildernesses. Even those precious things which we might suppose have died, if we stubbornly insist upon remembering them, can sprout and bring forth new life. So we cling to memories of Isaiah's magnificent vision, we hold fast to our eternal yearnings, and we engage our active love with the real world of the NOW.

2

COMFORT FOR THE EXILES, CLASS OF 2003

Advent 2, Year B
Isaiah 40:1-11; Mark 1:1-8

"As it is written in the prophet Isaiah, 'See, I am
sending my messenger ahead of you, who will prepare
your way; the voice of one crying out in the wilderness:
"Prepare the way of the Lord, make his paths straight.'"

Mark 1:2-3

"Comfort, O Comfort my people, says your God."

Isaiah 40:1

The Advent theme of exile assaults me as I face the reality
that in the year 2003, *I* live in a world of exiles. I live in a nation
that may well be in exile from its own soul. You and I live amongst
a wandering people, many of whom are in exile from their
truest and best selves! We may well be members of a church
that is in exile from its covenant.

Unless the Gospel is Good news for the exiles, class of 2003,
it is not really Good News.

My most stunning experience of exiles was when as the
Coordinator of the Church and Society Program of the Pacific

Conference of Churches I led a World Council of Churches' team to Kili, a tiny, isolated island in the Marshall Islands. We visited the people of Bikini, who had been moved from their peaceful, spacious, home atoll in 1946 so that our government could test nuclear bombs. Some of them had pressed their fervent desire to return to Bikini, but radiation levels were so high there that they were not allowed to do so. We saw them as a sad, vulnerable people. One night they sang us a plaintive song about how much they missed their island home. It made me cry.

In our lesson from Mark, John the Baptist proclaims the advent of a new order. Mark is a no-nonsense writer as he quickly builds a frame of reference for the story of Jesus, the one who comes to "save." The entrance of John is sharply jolting. In my mind's eye I see a wild-eyed man wearing a camel's hair cloak with a leather belt around his waist, a character surviving on the meager fare of the desert: locusts and wild honey. Mark immediately builds a sense of expectation, and one after another example comes forward as to how the ancient prophecy is fulfilled. Every setting is filled with symbolic meaning. Mark's gospel sets a rapid pace and moves quickly, relentlessly, to the main thrust of Jesus' ministry.

Mark uses the word "gospel" in his very first line. In no uncertain terms he defines Jesus as "the one who brings Good News." Mark serves notice that the comfort which is being announced is essentially a declaration of challenge to the political and economic culture of the empire; and to the religious establishment, the priests and the scribes, whose power in the society was derived from controlling the temple.

The new order which John proclaims is not going to arise from within the centers of existing power relationships, but will come from the margins of society. Third World Christians who are hard-pressed politically and economically are very quick to grasp this, and they eagerly, and theologically, connect it with the prophetic voices of the Old Testament like Isaiah.

"Comfort, O comfort my people, says your God. Speak tenderly to Jerusalem, and cry to her that she has served her term, that her penalty is paid, that she has received from the Lord's hand double for all her sins." *Isaiah 40:1-2*

It is in the more complex forms of writing like this where we lose so much meaning in translation. Poet Robert Frost once said that "Poetry is that which is lost in translation."

The American poet Paul Zimmer tells of how one of his volumes of poetry was translated into Japanese. "That book was dedicated "to Sue with love," he said, smiling at his wife, Sue. "But when the book arrived, I showed it to a Japanese friend. He happened to open it up at the dedication page which read, when retranslated into English, 'To press a lawsuit with love.'"

The Bible is an example of how we lose much in translation. The biblical material about John The Baptist is such strong stuff that we have to work hard to earn our understanding. Isaiah is also a case in point, as it has a historical background so rich and complex that adequate translation is very difficult. Fortunately, Chapter 40 of Isaiah carries virtually all of the essential elements of the entire message of the prophet Isaiah and his school: confidence in the presence and power of God to save; the prophet's recognition that the people depend upon God; the admission that the judgment which has fallen on God's people is fair; and the announcement of God's victory, as Isaiah sees it, for all the world.

Verses 9, 10, and 11 say that Zion herself, these exiled people, will be the herald of the good news to the surrounding cities of Judah. All of Judah, devastated through the years of exile, will now see the new hope of God's blessing and favor.

What *are* the extreme stresses and hurts to which Isaiah addresses comfort and deliverance? Exile for them meant being torn away from their beloved home. It meant the destruction of Jerusalem, their sacred city, symbol of the spiritual and political power of their nation; identity crisis, loss of power, loss of hope. It meant being stuck in Babylon (yes, Iraq, just a few miles south of Bagdad!). It meant despair, giving up on God. Isaiah insists that amid the ruins of the broken vows of human covenants stand the dependable promises of God, who does not abandon us.

Back to the exiles, class of 2003. Consider the incredible number of uprooted persons in our world today. If the Good News of Christmas has continued relevance, it is for these ones. These are the first in line as ones for whom the message of comfort and deliverance is meant.

Comfort for the refugees! Worldwide, there have never been so many. Comfort for the homeless, victims of the complex interrelated causes of homelessness, and for those who have lost their jobs and may even be going into exile from their professions.

Comfort to those of the economic underclass of our society, in exile from their wallets! Despite our affluence, we have a large and growing sector of people who by all essential definitions are a less-developed nation in our midst.

Comfort to our elderly in nursing homes. Granted, there are many fine nursing homes, and nursing homes are an important option in our culture, but too many of our elderly exist in exile, somewhere, in exile from their children and grandchildren, from their homes, alone with their memories. All-too-often they're in exile from their own minds, mellowed out on medications.

Comfort to the ethnic minorities of our land, who are experiencing more hate and discrimination than they did 20 years ago.

Comfort for those we have defined as being "different," including persons of same-sex orientation, who have been forced to flee from their own selves, from a complex identity they did not choose, but which they are growing to understand, accept and respect. Surely the comfort and deliverance pronounced by the prophet Isaiah is for them, too.

The comfort and deliverance of Christmas is for battered women and their children, exiles in their own homes, or driven from their own homes. May God bless them and the caring ones who give them shelter and comfort.

If any of these exiles are bitter and unable to trust in the comfort and hope proclaimed by comfortable churches at Christmas time, should we be surprised? Comfort does not simply mean to express sympathy. It means to *stand close to*, as a way of giving strength. "Fortify" is the root of the word. Baskets for the needy once or twice a year won't cut it.

Just as Lent is a time of preparation for the passion and resurrection of Christ, Advent is a time of preparing to receive Jesus, a time for self-examination and repentance. Those who look toward Jerusalem and the Easter beyond have to pass through the wilderness, a journey of repentance. Those who long for Bethlehem and the shining star of hope had better take up their shovels to help "make straight the highway," the way through the wilderness for the exiles to return to their land!

Fiji

3

O LOVE THAT WILL NOT LET ME GO

Advent 3, Year A
Isaiah 35:1-10
Luke 1:47-55

"Then the eyes of the blind shall be opened, and
the ears of the deaf unstopped; then the lame shall
leap like a deer, and the tongue of the speechless sing
for joy. For waters shall break forth in the wilderness,
and streams in the desert . . ."

Isaiah 35:5-6

Advent is a time of preparation, watchfulness and mindful
waiting—not easy in an instant gratification culture! I love the
great themes of Advent, the season of celebration of God's
fierce love, which despite our wanderings and stubbornness
and inattention, simply refuses to let us go.

One thing that the birth in Bethlehem teaches us is that
God's grace often appears in our midst in unanticipated ways.
Advent waiting takes place, biblically and today, in the
wilderness.

I know jungle, and I know wilderness. I have lived there,
literally and figuratively. We live in a hurting wilderness heavily

populated with hurting people. The voices of Advent are the voices of biblical and contemporary figures who know pain, frustration, and hurt, and who do not cover it over, but are willing to say it, because they have hope.

The "community of hurt," which is a community of memory and of hope, is willing to cry out, and it knows *where* to speak its grief, because it remembers the One, our loving creator, whose outcomes are no longer in doubt for us. We are its representatives and its members.

Is this image of a hurting people in a hurting world "too much?" I don't think so. In Advent we must move back and forth between the poles of hurt and hope. We can not have one without the other.

In our culture, speaking hurt is sometimes considered subversive. Yes, because when we do we're saying that things as we presently find them—not only in our personal lives, but also in our town, in our nation, and in our world, are not the way that God intended them to be.

In Advent, especially in Advent, we proclaim that we are open and ready for a new order. Not the "New World Order" of certain presidents and the World Trade Organization, but another. In his marvelous book, *Prophetic Imagination* (Philadelphia: Fortress Press, 1978), Walter Brueggemann says:

> "What we ready ourselves for in Advent is the sneaking suspicion, the growing awareness, the building restlessness that this weary world is not the one God has in mind. God will work another world. God will do it soon. God will work that new world according to the person and passion of Jesus. God will work a world precisely for those who are ready and able to relinquish the old one."

That's great news: The world that God has in mind is far better—more caring, more fair, and more peaceful—than the one we presently see!

Advent poses sharp questions for us about our own personal selves, and about our world, and Advent asks us if we are bold enough to speak our longing for newness. It asks if we are ready for a newness to be given. Our lifeline from the old to the new is the Love that will not let us go!

Isaiah takes courage for the future, insisting upon a God who works for those who wait: those who know the name of God, who remember God's past action; and who understand their need for God. That *should* describe the church!

Our lesson from Luke 1, "Mary's song of praise," has probable roots in the Old Testament (Hannah, in Genesis 29 and 30; Deuteronomy 10:21; II Samuel 16; Psalms 25:18, 103:17, and 111:9). It's one of the most revolutionary of gospel passages, and I constantly encountered reference to it in the 1960's and 1970's in "people's" Bible study groups in The Philippines:

> "My soul magnifies the Lord . . . . he has looked with favor on the lowliness of his servant . . . His mercy is for those who fear him from generation to generation. He has shown strength with his arm; he has scattered the proud in the thoughts of their hearts. He has brought down the powerful from their thrones, and lifted up the lowly; he has filled the hungry with good things, and sent the rich away empty . . . . *Luke 1:47, 48a, 50-53*

The early church was a struggling church, but it lived expectantly. Each morning, literally, the "faithful" looked for the return of Jesus. Nearly two thousand years later it's harder to do that, and we eagerly grasp assurance in Jesus' statement that we "will not know the times nor seasons" *(Acts 1:7)*. What we *can* say is that we're willing to be waiting in an active, participatory way for the new creation which God is working.

We *can* say that we intend to "live the hope"—participating in the shaping of the future in line with the values of the "realm" of God.

Surely it means helping to strengthen the increasingly fragile bonds of community and refusing to surrender our God-given human image in the face of an ever-more-impersonal, computer-driven information age.

Could it mean being willing to openly face the new possibilities and the new dangers of bio-medicine, and to participate actively in examining the difficult but terribly serious issues facing bio-medical ethics, being willing to listen as well as shout?

Could it mean to more squarely face the issues and questions that face humanity in relation to not just possible, but probable environmental catastrophe which will occur if we do not change some of our practices?

Could it mean to be willing to work seriously to find better ways to sit down and talk together, at home, locally and globally, to resolve bitter conflicts before the entire world becomes a "Holy Land" battle ground?

It's not easy to be a waiting people in a turbulent, confused world. One time when I was in Newport, Oregon, I found myself sitting on the long breakwater giving thanks that I didn't have to maneuver my sailboat from the rough ocean into the harbor there. I watched a buoy at the entrance of the channel getting hammered by the waves, often completely covered over. But when the waves subsided, there it was, bobbing upright again, right where they belonged! I knew that this was happening day after day, and month after month. And it didn't sink, because it's made of stuff that doesn't sink, and it doesn't get blown away, because it's connected to a chain that goes down to solid rock.

That's a great image, because that can be *us*, as we wait. And our chain is the love which will not let us go!

God's steadfast love and faithfulness is something more than a theological phrase or a biblical doctrine. It's a loving, saving power working in our lives every day. As you wait for Christmas, as you prepare for it, notice the many ways in which God's faithfulness has made itself known in *your* life.

May you have peaceful, joyous waiting, full of meaning and hope!

4

"UPSIDE-DOWN"

Advent 4, year C
Luke 1:47-55

"He has scattered the proud in the thoughts of
their hearts. He has brought down the powerful from
their thrones, and lifted up the lowly; he has filled the
hungry with good things, and sent the rich away empty."
Luke 1:51b-53b

The world of Christmas is quite upside down. The high are
brought low. The low are exalted. The Messiah comes not as a
knight in shining armor, but as a baby born in a feed box for
cattle. Born of the peasant woman whose name was Mary. And
according to Matthew and Luke, Mary was a maiden, a woman
who had never known intimacy with a man.

To do the most important thing, God uses nobodies from
nowhere: Isaiah. Mary, a very young peasant maiden, and her
husband, Joseph, a carpenter. A "mountain man," John the
Baptist, announces that the Messiah is coming, and that *he,
John, is not the one*—it is someone else! How many leaders do
you hear that from today! "Take a look at me friends. I am *not*
the one you are waiting for!"

There's a delightful custom of teasing among Filipino pastors. Sometimes, when one of the pastors would do something noteworthy, to keep them humble, friends would say, "Are you the one we've been waiting for, or should we look for another?"

The gospel stories tell us that poor people, shepherds in the field, were the first to know about Jesus' birth. The rich and the wise then came and kneeled before the humble manger. The one in that manger was later to teach that the last will be first, the first will be last, poor is rich and rich is poor, and weak is strong. Trust and truth, not force and bluster, save us. He pointed us back to Isaiah, who said that those who are crushed would be healed. Slaves would be freed, prisoners released. Debts would be canceled. The weak would be empowered, and the strong are warned. Israel's hopes and longings would be fulfilled.

St. Paul says in I Corinthians 1:25: "God's foolishness is wiser than human wisdom, and God's weakness is stronger than human strength."

We don't have to worry about how the star of Bethlehem could have "happened." We don't have to have an astronomy explanation, or to count how many angels sang out in the sky the night that Jesus was born, or how the three wise men were able to find him.

What we *do* need to pay attention to is that the kinds of relationships pictured in this "first Christmas world" are diametrically opposite the customs and values of the wider world, the world we live in.

Humble Mary is the mother of Jesus! Our text is one of my favorite passages—the Magnificat, or Mary's son: "My soul magnifies the Lord, and my spirit rejoices in God my Savior, for he has looked with favor on the lowliness of his servant" *(Luke 1:46-48a)*. Many Roman Catholics use this prayer at evening throughout the year. Here we see a beautiful image of acceptance of God's will: "Let it be done to me according to your word." For Catholics Mary's sincere trust and faithfulness is the image of an ideal Christian.

But Mary's song goes beyond the theme of obedience, because in it, and it's reminiscent of the prayer of Hannah in I Samuel 2, we hear themes that are quite political, if we take them seriously: This God who "stoops" to work through a lowly peasant maiden has turned things upside down, lifting up the poor, the oppressed, the enslaved. And "God has scattered the proud in the imagination of their hearts."

Are you looking for someone to rescue us? The voice of Christmas says, "Don't look to the courts of kings and queens, look among the slaves. Don't look to the capital city, Jerusalem, look to Nazareth! Look to Sultan, Washington or Estacada, Oregon.

It could be that we're not really quite ready for Christmas. We love the wonderful classical music settings for Mary's song, like the ones by de Lassus, or Palestrina. Mozart also composed one. But why is it that as people who are basically comfortable economically we're so reluctant as to pick up the *practical* message in Mary's song? Probably because we live in a time very similar to the world of the first Christmas!

The Good News of the first Christmas came at a literally *terrible* time, the time of Herod the King. Herod was a puppet king for Rome. He murdered anyone who stood in his way, even killing one of his wives and two of his sons. Into the worst possible atmosphere, in the midst of the most depressing, despairing of times, was Jesus of Nazareth born! The gospels frame Jesus' life with Herod in the beginning, Pontius Pilate at the end, and Roman colonial Palestine as the backdrop.

And our time is no picnic. This year, despite a negotiated settlement in Albania, despite a reduced national deficit, despite the fact that the U.S. economy is roaring (*Guess when I first wrote this!*), or despite the fact that the Republicans still control Congress or that there's a Democrat in the White House, or despite the fact that Seattle has a new baseball field, or despite the fact that the Huskies and the Seahawks are winning again), I think it is not a misstatement to say that this Christmas the star of Bethlehem will shine on more poverty, more suffering, and more conflict than this world has ever known.

There's a beautiful poem by Madelaine L'Engle, that I saw on a Christmas card:

That was no time for a Child to be born,
In a land in the crushing grip of Rome.
Honor and truth were trampled by scorn—
Yet here did the Savior make His home.
When is the time for love to be born?
The Inn is full on the planet earth,
And by greed and pride the sky is torn—
Yet love still takes the risk of birth.

In the days of Herod the King, Mary and Joseph made their way to Bethlehem. There a child was born. Angels sang, and a brilliant star lit up the night sky. In the upside-down world of Christmas, in the midst of the worst possible days, God takes a risk and gives us a festival of hope.

In the midst of your own struggles, despite whatever it is that's dragging you down, in your personal life and in the life of our world, whatever crushing burden, whatever pain and sorrow afflict your heart, the Good News of Christmas has something for *you*. In the midst of the times when life is most difficult, God's Good News is that the light still shines in the darkness, and the darkness can not put it out.

The whole world seems to be fascinated with Christmas, and one might wonder why. Some have said that Christmas is for children. Maybe it's because they so easily respond to joy, and reflect joy. Thank God for the joy of children. It's true that our "inner child" especially relates to Christmas, and leads us to Christmas.

Or is it just because of time off from work, and the festival atmosphere? I like to hope that it's more than that. Meg Greenfield, a columnist for *NEWSWEEK* wrote:

"The non-Christian world envies and covets Christmas, wants to participate in it, is forever seeing just how close it can come to this particular experience without threatening the imperatives of its own religion. The non-Christian world is bent on universalizing the reach of Christmas."

Yes, Christmas is for the whole world, our whole crazy, upside down world!

It's hard to trust in what we cannot see, especially when those around us seem to believe in the survival of the fittest and that those who finish the game with the most toys win. How *do* we trust in God's promises that it is not riches and power that will save us, but faithfulness and righteousness?

Whatever darkness lies around you or beside you or even within you, wrap yourself in the warm, festive hope of the good news of the crazy-upside-down world of Christmas!

Brahmapura River, Bangladesh

5

FOLLOWING STARS

Epiphany, Years A, B, and C
Isaiah 42:1-7; Matthew 2:1-12

"In the time of King Herod, after Jesus was born in
Bethlehem of Judea, wise men from the East came to
Jerusalem, asking, 'where is the child who has been
born king of the Jews? For we observed his star at its
rising, and have come to pay him homage.'"

Matthew 2:1-2

It was well past midnight when the tiny bright light
appeared in the distance. Max Webster and I had gone for an
afternoon sail in his outrigger canoe out on the Lingayen Gulf.
The wind had been brisk, and when I, then a total novice, had
taken the helm, instead of letting out on the sheet in a strong
gust, I had hauled it in. We capsized. Quite an accomplishment
in an outrigger canoe. The mast was sticking straight down in
the water!

Both of us being strong swimmers, we readily dismantled
the sail and got the canoe upright. We finally succeeded in
bailing out the water, but only after the wind had stopped. It
was then that we realized that we had neglected to bring a

paddle (please don't say it), had brought only a bamboo pole for the shallow waters near the shore. So, taking turns, we paddled towards Anda Island with the pole. Fortunately, the sea was calm as night came upon us. But it was the time of month when there was no visible moon whatsoever, and in the near total darkness we couldn't see well enough to set an accurate course.

Until the light appeared. We hoped that it marked the place where we wanted to go, that it might be a friend who had noticed that Max's canoe was still out, but whatever light it was, with the slender bamboo pole we paddled straight towards it. A few hours later, dead tired, we reached the "pantalon," where Frank Calicdan sat patiently with his bright Petromax kerosene pressure lamp. Our outing was purely recreational, virtually empty of meaning. As far as I know, our situation was not life-threatening, though under some circumstances it could have been quite dangerous. But, still, that light was good news!

The Star of Bethlehem is full of meaning, and is great Good News. It marks where we want to go. Today we celebrate Epiphany, which means "sign," or manifestation, and is the commemoration of the appearance of the star of Bethlehem and those who followed it. Our lessons during the season of Epiphany beckon us to follow it, and use various kinds of "signs" as themes.

Matthew's gospel is where we read the interesting account of the wise men following the star. But let's not forget that according to the gospels there were many who came to see Jesus, not just "the wise men." Mark doesn't say that there were three of them, or that one of them was black, or that Matthew knew their names, despite all that we've learned from church Christmas pageants! That's O.K.—what we *think* we know about the three wise men is compiled from various traditions.

There seems to be some disagreement as to whether or not these three men were kings. Even though we like to sing "We Three Kings of Orient Are," they were probably not kings. They were probably Babylonian astronomers, but we don't even know that for sure. Anyway, there are some traditions about them, but these are not based on scriptures. Legends say that their names were Gaspar (which means "white"), Melchior (which means "light"), and Balthasar (which means "the Lord of the Treasury"). Some years ago I visited the Cathedral in Cologne, Germany, which claims to have their skulls, deposited in the "Chapel of the Three Wise Men." I don't find this helpful.

What *is* helpful is the food for thought that this ancient story gives us. For example: The Wise Men traveled far. The saving purposes of God are now clearly, irrevocably, extended beyond the Holy City, beyond the power of Rome, beyond the Jews, beyond the United States of America, beyond white people, beyond nice and acceptable people, beyond "cool" people, beyond the United Methodist Church, beyond all of these human-made boundaries. The light is given to the whole world, for all the people. The light is OUT THERE, and deep down inside, breaking through darkness, through boundaries.

Those who responded to the witness of that star were obviously seekers; they saw the star as a sign, and they reached out to it; they were stretching for something; they were living not only in their present world of food and drink and their possessions and all their pleasures, but were after something more.

It's fun to try to imagine the people who traveled to Bethlehem because of that star. They must have been a unique and motley lot, having had enough sense of awe and mystery to make the journey! Whatever the reason, the wise men followed it, too. I'm glad we call them "wise."

What were they looking for? For sure they weren't looking for a learned book; or a cute gadget that would make their friends go "wow"; or a psychological theory that they could use to analyze the people around them! Or a special health food that would cure their ailments. I doubt that they were looking for a political system that would bring liberation: justice and peace for all—though I would have liked that very much.

They were almost surely looking for some*one*. A person. Maybe they were surprised that the person turned out to be a child. In any case, biblically, and in everyday life now, we consistently see that God's grace is mediated through *persons*.

They carried gifts, each one having a special symbolic meaning, each gift considered precious. Are there special gifts among us?

The star of Bethlehem beckons us to get involved, each in our own way. Not that the all-sufficient Creator needs us, but that it actually gives God joy to be in relationship with us, and to have us as co-participants in the creative and transforming process. The idea that we're called to follow a star is an important one, because some of us have a low opinion of ourselves and the significance of things that we might be able to do.

I recently spent a day in a hospital for some tests, and was surrounded by some of the most amazing instruments and devices. I marvel at all of that equipment, but, you know, it's nothing without persons to use it, to mediate the technology for us, to interpret the information, and if they have no interest in us as persons, it can all be rather unhelpful and even be dangerous!

In a school we need the books, the equipment, the facilities, and it's a real problem when we don't support our schools adequately with those things—but all of that is worth very little without caring, competent teachers. All the books and computers and other teaching aids in the world are not going to save a neglected child! Needy children are helped by persons who care and voices that say "I love you and want to help you. I am willing to listen to you. I am willing to be involved with you." Support public education!

The ministry of the church boils down to people. The star calls us to be the persons who reach out to folks a lot like our own selves—with their troubled consciences, their forgetfulness, their stubbornness, with hands that seem stained and cut from this peculiar world, seeking restoration and forgiveness, longing for someone to listen, looking for new life, new possibilities, longing for new integrity and wholeness. Answers for these longings are more than new systems, new moral codes, new theories, though God knows we need better ones of those too! What is needed is *persons* with new visions, who are willing to follow stars.

Do you have a star to follow? Where do you see it? Give it a name—what will you call it? Do you have a gift to bring? What is your gift? Name it! Do you have a road to travel? Put it on your map!

It isn't always easy to follow a star. The Hale Bopp star was an easy one. We simply strolled down to the Mercer Island I-90 "lid" one evening and looked up! The three wise men had to stop what they had been doing, had to interrupt their routine for months, possibly even years, and had to risk something new. They had to travel into strange new territory. But they did it. We're talking about change, and change is difficult.

As dark as this world can be, it still has many beacon lights, signs of hope, and guides for our way. Maybe you're one of them!

6

A MOST PECULIAR NATURE

Epiphany 1, Year A
Isaiah 42:1-9

"I am the Lord, that is my name; my glory I give to
no other, nor my praise to idols. See, the former things
have come to pass, and new things I now declare; before
they spring forth, I tell you of them.

Isaiah 42:8-9

When I lived in Papua New Guinea, one of my friends, Bernard Narakobi, a devout Roman Catholic, the first fully accredited Papua New Guinean lawyer and later a PNG Supreme Court justice, asked, *"Why did God make mosquitoes?"* He noted that missionaries are troubled by the existence of mosquitoes because so many of their friends had died of malaria. "But," he said, "We Papua New Guineans might well say that God made mosquitoes so that our country would not be totally overrun by missionaries!"

William Willimon, Dean of the Chapel at Duke University, tells of a retired theology professor acquaintance who says, "When I get to heaven, if I get to heaven, I'm going to stand before the throne of God with a cancer cell in my hand and say, 'Why, why?'" He mentions a little book entitled *Children's Letters to God*. One of the letters was by a little girl named Norma, and she wrote, "Dear God, did you mean for giraffes to look that way, or was that an accident?"

Willimon says that when we get right down to it, most of us have some kind of quarrel with God. (*Pulpit Resource,* Jan 13, 2002)

This doesn't mean that we're angry with God, though it's probably honest to say that from time to time most of us do have some sort of anger toward God. That's O.K., it's important to work through it, and if you have doubts that this is biblical, read the brilliant story of the book of Job!

What Willimon meant was that we act as though we're dissatisfied with the way God really is and what God really does (you might have your own special words for God). We project onto God the way we wish that God was, which is usually a version of ourselves!

If we're honest enough to admit it, we're puzzled and perplexed by the way God is in the world; by what God chooses to do; and how God chooses to do it. We ask, Why do we have Giraffes and mosquitoes?!"

Isaiah gives us the Hebrew vision of who God is and how God acts in the world, and often this action is contrary to what we would expect or like. As the psalmists have said, God's thoughts are not our thoughts, and God's ways are not our ways. Thank God.

In Isaiah 42, the prophet, in the first of the servant songs, probably written just as the Hebrew people are about to come home from Babylon, and worried that the people may have forgotten who God is, reminds them. A servant of God is proclaimed, a servant with power, with God's attributes, or characteristics, who is a gentle servant:

> *"A bruised reed he will not break, a dimly burning wick . . . he will not quench. He will faithfully bring forth justice. The servant, God's chosen, will bring forth new things."*

The related Epiphany reading for today in Matthew tells of the baptism of Jesus, a powerful experience complete with the spirit of God descending like a dove. It's the Bible's way of reminding us that, truly, here is the Messiah, the chosen one of God!" But almost immediately, we learn that this is not necessarily the Messiah we expected. We did not expect to get rescued by one so humble, so pure, so totally giving.

And we did not expect to have our practical, everyday "style of living" so put into question: our attitudes, our habits, our cultural training, if you will.

Not to mention our impatience! Oh, so God is going to establish justice? Well then, why doesn't God get at it, *right now*, in this terribly messed-up world?

And then the Bible reminds us: he will come not as a mighty conqueror but as a gentle rural fellow, gardener and carpenter, and lamp lighter. "A bruised reed . . . he will not break. A dimly burning wick . . . he will not extinguish."

Thank God for that, because most of us *are* bruised reeds, feeble burning wicks: imperfect, vulnerable, and incomplete. So we have a God who has chosen to take the form of a servant, to become vulnerable on our behalf, even to the extent of death on a cross. A most peculiar nature.

How in the world can this work? How is the frail, vulnerable servant described by Isaiah and embodied by Jesus to do any practical good? Just suppose that the pattern that the servant follows is the very same pattern that God wants for the world. Suppose the servant embodies in his or her life and work God's way of dealing with what's wrong with us and the world.

I was in a seminar once with a gentle, extremely intelligent pastor from the Methodist Church in Ghana. He made the comment, "if you want to find God, look for a coincidence!) In our Seaview Bible study group Gladys Herreid said, "How do I know that prayer matters? Not only because it matters to me personally, but because when I pray, coincidences happen!" It must matter to God!

The Bible pictures a God who does *not* stand on the sidelines. We're especially interested in that as we ask people to pray for us.

Why did God make giraffes, and mosquitoes, and cancer cells? And earthquakes, and Tsunamis, and why does God allow war, and famine? And accidents? I don't really know. And we really don't know about the accidents that *didn't* happen. What I *do* know is that God has created an awesome orderly creation full of mystery and surprises. Our feeble minds have a hard time grasping the complicated ways of God's creation. We have to learn to live with that. I have no doubt that God can micro-manage creation if God so chooses, but I'm not convinced that God needs to!

What I *do* believe is that God has created us as an integral part of creation, not to be dominators; has created us for relationships, with our neighbor and as neighbors with all creation. I *do* believe that it gives God joy to be in relationship with us, and that it makes us whole to be in relationship with God.

This is possible only if we are free beings. True love requires freedom to love, both in the love between humans and in our love for God, but this is exactly what God has given us. Entering into loving, caring relationships entails risking vulnerability and loss, and this is exactly what God has done.

What is most troubling about the reality of our world, of creation, is that so many of the God-intended relationships have been broken. This is not God's failure, but ours. The destruction that human beings in their tragic use of freedom wreak upon each other is an attack upon God's creation.

I spent most of my childhood and teen years either living on a small farm or working for neighboring farmers during the summer. So I have some vivid images of newly born farm animals. I heard it said (with newly born farm animals) that "Only a mother could love something so ugly!" I find this deeply theological, and underscoring a wonderful feminine image of God!

When a cow delivers a calf, it is wobbly and spindly and slimy wet. Baby chicks are unbelievable scruffy. Only a mother would take them under her wing! Baby pigs are pretty cute when they're born. It's later on that only a mother could love them. Puppies are pretty ugly when they're born, with their eyes closed and their high-pitched grunts.

Aren't we like that? We, too, are a work in progress. But God does reach out to us, does love us, does forgive us, ugly though we can be at times (and I'm not talking about a nose or pimples)! One thing we know about God is that it gives God joy to be in relationship with us, in spite of us!

A most peculiar but wonderful nature.

La Union, Phillipines

7

THE GEOGRAPHY OF ETERNITY:

FROM VOID TO VOID AND EVERYTHING

IN BETWEEN AND AFTER!

Epiphany 1, Year B
Genesis 1:1-5; Psalm 29; Mark 1:4-11

"In the beginning when God created the heavens
and the earth, the earth was a formless void and darkness
covered the face of the deep, while a wind from God
swept over the face of the waters."

Genesis 1:1-2

"The voice of the Lord is over the waters; the God
of glory thunders, the Lord, over mighty waters."

Psalm 29:3

The famous economist, E.F. Schumacher, who wrote the
book *Small is Beautiful,* shared this item:

One day a philosopher was out walking in the woods, and
came face to face with a figure bathed in a radiant beam of
light. He thought this must be none other than God. As he
had spent a lifetime pondering God's existence, the

philosopher was only temporarily awed. "You are the Lord, I presume."

"Yes," said God, "I am."

"Well then, my Lord, I wonder if you would be good enough to answer a few simple questions that have been troubling me for some time."

"Certainly, my son."

"Is it true, Almighty, that what is for us a million years here on earth is for you but the merest moment?"

"Yes," my son, quite true."

"And is it also true," the philosopher went on, "that a million dollars here on earth is for you nothing but a paltry penny?"

"Also quite true, my son."

The philosopher paused only a moment. "Then, I wonder if it would be possible for you, if it is not too much trouble, to give me a penny?"

"Why certainly, my son," said God. "Just wait here. I'll be back in just a moment!"

How difficult it is for us to wrap our puny minds around the idea of eternity. The inspired writers of The Bible knew this, but they still tried, and they've given us a great blessing with passages loaded with powerful metaphors.

We start with Genesis: "In the beginning— . . . the earth was a formless void. How do you give a name to a formless void? How do you identify nothing?!! And darkness covered the face of the deep. Now we've got "the deep." And then a wind from God swept over the face of the waters. Wind. Which we cannot see— we can only see the results of wind! And then there was light. And then it was given value: "God saw that the light was GOOD." How would it be if it were always dark? Or if it were never dark?

Psalm 29 says that "The voice of God is over the waters, the God of glory thunders." Energy! Power! Majesty! "The voice of the Lord breaks the Cedars!" God makes Lebanon skip like a calf, the voice flashes forth flames of fire, and shakes the wilderness, and strips the forest bare. The Lord sits enthroned over the flood. The concept of creation continues to expand.

I can't help but think of the striking, poetic passage at the very beginning of John's gospel: "In the beginning was the Word. And the Word was with God, and the Word *was* God." Word is capitalized. In the Greek language, Logos represents not only the Word, but the *meaning* behind the word, or the *idea* behind the word. Creation began as a precious idea in the mind of God! Even before the void! Even before the darkness.

When I first read the texts for today I wondered, "Why do we have this thing about John the Baptist again? It seems like we've been hammering on this all through Advent, and now we have it again. In Mark 1 here's John the Baptist, just as we saw him in Advent. The key moment is when Jesus is baptized by John and comes up out of the water. Out of the water! Does this mean he came out of the void? Was this a whole new beginning for creation? "And as he (Jesus) was coming up out of the water he saw the heavens torn apart and the Spirit descending like a dove on him, and a voice came from heaven, "You are my Son, the Beloved; with you I am well pleased."

The New Testament writers struggled to adequately express what they thought was so totally remarkable, even radical, the coming of Jesus in the midst of God's drama. The Mark passage for today is a good example of the intensity of the Gospel of Mark. Frederick Grant, in *The Interpreter's Bible*, notes that Mark uses the word "immediately" 41 times! But we, too, live in tense times! Maybe we need a few more people now who have John's style!

Seeing this in relation to the theme of creation as presented in the Genesis reading is an opportunity to be reminded of the connection between the creation and our Baptism, which proclaims the new creation in Christ Jesus.

So what's new? I get asked regularly what I think is happening to the church. What I think about the church is that it is changing shape, and that I want to be a part of the *new* shape! Somewhat like our wanting to be an "authentic church, here at Seaview." The church is changing shape, and our lives are constantly changing shape. There are new kinds of "shoots" springing forth, and there is pruning taking place. It's a journey. It's what's happening on the way to eternity!

Our reading in Mark 1 brings us to "The New Creation." That ritual where we put water on people and say some nice words, Christian baptism, is about our being included in the new creation.

Baptism is symbolic of repentance and new life. Repentance means, basically, "a new mind." Turned in a new direction, re-connected with eternity, if you will.

Do we need repentance? The whole matter of dealing with the reality called "Sin" took on more powerful meaning for me when I visited China in 1976. The political education and "self-criticism" there were extreme, and at that time the party line was that if they kept up their very radical political education effort, someday the selfishness and the anti-social conduct would be reduced to a level where it would no longer be a problem. They were terribly worried about the whole cluster of tendencies that they called selfishness and greed—which we know is at the core of our idea of Sin, and they were working very hard to deal with it.

As a Christian I was struck by this, because I think that the Chinese were definitely on to "The Problem." But Christians traditionally haven't believed that we can finally "stamp" it out. Experience shows that it's a *continual* presence for each new person that is born, and with every person on earth for their whole lives, and that it's through a continuing process of repentance and renewal that we deal with it.

It seemed ironic to me that the Chinese were taking Sin very seriously and had the wrong answer, and Christians have the right answer, but many of us aren't taking the question seriously!

I think of this when I follow a car that has a bumper sticker that says, "Teach Peace!" I agree, and I do want to see more teaching of the basic elements of peace-building, non-violent conflict resolution, and emphasizing values like cooperation and understanding. I'm a strong supporter of peace curricula, and peace studies. I have helped teach them.

But when it comes to the crunch, I know that what *I* need, what *you* need, what we all need, is some sort of transformation experience, and the admission that we have a persistent, powerful tendency towards selfishness, willfulness, and self-absorption. We need help! The basic attitude of repentance and humility is what is so desperately needed in this conflict-weary world of ours, and that's what makes it possible effectively to lift up the biblical vision of shalom.

Because of the colossal human problem of narrow self-interest, it is *accountability* which becomes the means of grace enabling us to function. Because we live in a world of broken-ness, it is *accountability* that provides the possibility of curbing the power of rich over poor, and which makes democracy and humane society possible. It's interesting that those who best understand issues of accountability (you know, the ones who hire the most accountants!), who devise the most clever schemes to avoid accountability! This illustrates the point!

Repentance and renewal have everything to do with our coping—struggling with the continuing, everyday experiences such as depression and death, and the problems of loneliness, stress, confusing situations, and relationships that threaten to undo us. Luke wrote lines in Acts 19:1-9 (another lectionary reading for today) showing disciples moving from repentance to power. Christian theology says that you and I started our lives pre-void, a treasured idea in the mind of God! In the "Now" we're invited to be a part of the unfolding new thing! We don't have to wait a million years, and we're not waiting for a measly penny! We join the faithful people of God, past, present, and future, on the epic journey from the void to eternity.

8

EPIC CALLS AND THE SIMPLE 'YES' TO LIFE

Epiphany 2, Year B
I Samuel 3: 1-11; John 1:43-51

"Now the boy Samuel was ministering to the Lord
under Eli. The word of the Lord was rare in those days;
visions were not widespread . . . . Then the Lord said to
Samuel, see, I am about to do something in Israel that
will make both ears of anyone who hears of it tingle . . . .
As Samuel grew up, the Lord was with him and let none
of his words fall to the ground. And all Israel from Dan
to Be'ersheba knew that Samuel was a trustworthy
prophet of the Lord."

I Samuel 3:1, 11, 19-20

About the time I felt called to ministry, while a freshman in
the College of Agricultural Engineering at the University of
Illinois, someone told me about the farm boy who while
cultivating corn one fine summer day, looked up and saw a
cloud formation that appeared to have the letters "G P C."
He'd been thinking about where his life was headed, and with
a start realized that these letters might represent a call: "Go
Preach Christ!"

So he finished college and went to seminary. But after preaching his first sermon assignment in the homiletics class, his professor, knowing about his call, said, "Son, I think that the 'G P C' must have meant "Go Plant Corn!"

There are many stories in the Bible about God calling people and the diverse circumstances in which they were called. Rebekah of the Old Testament was drawing water at the city well at Nahor, when she heard God's call. St. Paul was on the road to Damascus.

There are fascinating examples of calls since Bible times: St. Augustine was out working in the garden. C.S. Lewis, who wrote *The Screwtape Letters* and many other wonderful books and theological essays, was riding in the sidecar of his brother's motorcycle. Martin Luther, I have read, was sitting on the toilet in his monastic cell when he heard God's call. That's what I read.

Today we look at Samuel's call: he was young; he had few outstanding qualifications. He was called during a time not known for its dramatic manifestations of God; in fact, the text says that Samuel didn't even yet know the Lord!

And in John Jesus calls his disciples: His first question to them is very sharp and specific: "Who are you looking for?" His promise *("You will see greater things")* points to a remarkable experience ahead! Jesus "invited" persons who were quite ordinary, and who were right there.

As for us, we know about "calls." Phone calls. We have call waiting—we can put off calls; call screening—we can refuse to talk to the chosen ones with whom we don't want to communicate; and we have call forwarding so that we won't miss calls! We have cordless phones, and one of my favorites, the "phoneless cord!"

I've noticed a tendency to see "Christian callings" in terms of a narrowly spiritual, traditional discipleship, or in terms of talking or listening to God. Quite frankly, if someone were to walk up to me today and say that they had just been talking to God, and that they have an answer for me that came straight from God, I'd be pretty leery, and even might consider them nuts. In my opinion some of the most dangerous persons in history have been individuals who either thought they were God or who thought that they had a special private line straight to God!

Let's try to break through some of the traditional images and see how this theme might speak to our whole life—to see discipleship not only in terms of being "fishers of persons," but also in terms of living out a greater "Yes" to life.

We're *all* called, in one way or another. God does call us, if not through clouds or a voice in the sky, then through the countless signals and open doors that would evoke a response. It's a beautiful thing that life tends to seek us out—if we don't build a shell around ourselves. God tends to seek us out, and sometimes life hits us over the head! Each day, unless we're particularly withdrawn, we have the opportunity to be responsive, even by questioning or resisting. A part of our call is simply to be human, in the fullest sense of being created according to an image in the mind of God.

It has been pointed out that biblically, and in terms of real life experience, God often calls us to do the very thing we have said we would never be caught dead doing; God often calls us to do the very thing other people are better at doing than we are; and God often calls us when and where we least expect it!

Samuel got called. Andrew and Simon Peter got called. It would be interesting to hear how you may have sensed a "call:" a call that you thought was an invitation to a higher level of living or a fuller measure of being and feeling; a feeling that you are special (I think this is an important one!); a more deeply rooted faithfulness and obedience to your professed values. How did you respond?

I've had numerous people tell me with a clearly detectable sadness, after my missionary presentations, that when they were young they had experienced some sort of call to be a missionary—but had never become one. And (of course!) always wondered how their life might have been different. And this is ironic, because I had become one—I had said "yes," to a call, but had never really seen myself as a preacher or a missionary type, and had simply leaned forward into it saying, "who, me?"

Dag Hammarskjold, in his famous book, *Markings*, said about his call:

> "I don't know who—or what—put the question. I don't know when it was put. I don't even remember answering. But at some moment I did answer 'yes' to someone—or something—and from that hour I was certain that existence is meaningful and that, therefore, my life in self-surrender had a goal."

I became a lay missionary, and then an ordained minister, but what I now think is that our "yes!" to God is not necessarily a question of "institutional" discipleship. The important thing is that we become warm, caring, open persons, creatively responding to the Spirit of God working in the world. And every one of us can be this and do this as ordinary people! That would make us extraordinary people!

Some would suggest that, fundamentally, this is what our best spirituality would be all about: Our saying "Yes!, God, here am I! Saying "Yes!" to life. "Yes, I am willing to try to be responsive, to be a good listener! I will keep trying to say 'Yes!' to Love. To Truth. To Fairness. To Forgiveness. To Possibility."

Too many people are on a fierce quest for certainty. These folks are unusually open to having someone tell them just what to think or do, open to receive calls that are the "wrong numbers." It's sad to see churches that try to lay down a path of certainty with a rigid authority. How much of God's "creative freshness" will they miss?

We can't deal with the call to life if we insist upon keeping our spirituality on the back burner. In 1949 William L. Sperry wrote a book entitled *Jesus Then and Now*. I read where someone ordered it in a store, and when he filled out the form transposed the title as *"Jesus Now and Then."* That's part of our problem!

There's a great passage in Deuteronomy, which says:

> "I call heaven and earth to witness against you today that I have set before you life and death, blessings and curses. Choose life so that you and your descendants may live!" (Deut. 30:19)

May you be able to see more of life's open doors, and may you have the courage to walk through them.

Local Band, Tonga

9

NO EXCUSES REQUIRED

Epiphany 2, Year A
I Corinthians 12:1-11; Luke 14, 15-24

"Now there are varieties of gifts, but the same Spirit;
and there are varieties of services, but the same Lord;
and there are varieties of activities, but it is the same
God who activates all of them in everyone."

I Corinthians 12:4-6

"Then Jesus said to him, 'Someone gave a great
dinner, and invited many. At the time for the dinner he
sent his slave to say to those who had been invited,
"come; for everything is ready now." But they all made
excuses.'"

Luke 14:16-18a

Excuses are perhaps the most common of human actions
and reactions. Excuses start in The Bible at the very beginning,
where Adam says, "That woman you put here with me gave me
the fruit, so I ate it;" and the woman said, "The serpent fooled
me, and I ate."
Gospel-writer Luke makes a great use of excuses to make

his point about commitment: in The Parable of the Great Dinner, he tells of the invited guests who could not come. One had bought a piece of land, one had bought five yoke of oxen, one was just married. And earlier he had told about the man who said, "Jesus, I'll follow you anywhere, do whatever you want me to—but first let me go bury my father." Actually, I think that all of these are pretty good excuses! You can see where I am!

Those who have served in the military and those who have grown up in large families usually have some hilarious stories about excuses. About the "Yes, but" people!

Richard Lederer, in a book called Anguished English, has a chapter listing excuses parents have written to schools explaining their children's absence:

"Teacher, please excuse Mary for being absent. She was sick and I had her shot. (signed) Mary's Mom."

"My son is under doctor's care and should not take P.E. today. Please execute him."

"Please excuse my son's tardiness. I forgot to wake him up and did not find him until I started making the beds."

"Please excuse Ray from school. He has very loose vowels."

Funny. But we might stop and consider the excuses people make to God. St. Paul's letters to the Corinthians are fascinating because Paul was so worried about their excuses and petty bickering. In fact, he changed his travel plans at one point and actually waited until he had an answer from them to one of his letters. As it turned out, they still loved and respected him, and he felt great relief. So he felt free to write this letter, which is full of advice and guidance. What a character is Paul, with his humility and boasting, all in the same sentence!

It's hard for us to imagine what a leap it was for some of the early Christians to integrate into the new church community. First Corinthians 12:3 is a clue—it talks about people who "curse" Jesus. In those times curses and blessings were very commonplace, and this new faith, Christianity, at times experienced the full fury of pagan curses!

But Paul also addresses issues that we still experience in churches, like people feeling that what they do is more important than what someone else is doing! He assured them that all of these gifts are important. No excuses necessary.

Paul can get pretty confusing sometimes, but he really had a grasp on how people of different backgrounds, talents, opinions, interests, could attain remarkable unity. This is possible, Paul realizes, because diversity is a gift of God. Just as our strengths are made perfect in our weaknesses, our unity is made more perfect in our variety and difference. Paul was very democratic in his thinking here. Every person has a special contribution. The church is not a bottle of homogenized milk, or a puree of cooked vegetables run through a blender. We are more like a wonderful salad, where we keep our unique identities, but in relation to an integrated whole.

Perhaps like the difference between a choir where everyone sings the same notes and one where there is harmony—different notes that blend together. We might get pretty bored if everyone always sang the same note. When we first arrived in Fiji, and went to the big Fijian Methodist church in Suva, the hymns, while in the Fijian language, were often familiar tunes for us, but there was a rather interesting difference in the sound. Finally we figured it out: The people loved to harmonize so much that almost no one was singing the tune!

It is in the dissimilarities, even the dissonances sometimes, in the church, that we find the vitality and aliveness. It is the mix of sounds and the clash of interpretations that testify to the richness of the church. The multiplicity of spiritual gifts moving in the midst of the church is a sign of health, not disease. "I can't carry a tune!" (a great excuse. But no excuses are required!)

While we don't ask for trials and tribulations, and misfortunes and thorns in the flesh, and sickness, and the loss of loved ones (and it is my fierce conviction that God does not will that these happen to us), when they do come, *and they will come*, we have the opportunity to further grow and develop. Not, perhaps, in the way we thought we would grow, but in ways that we never dreamed were possible. Strength made perfect in weakness!

I supposed that we've all heard stories about persons who stammered terribly but who worked with it and became eloquent speakers.

Did you know that when Wilma Rudolph, the great Afro-American Olympic runner was a little girl she suffered a terrible condition that left her legs disabled? They thought that she might never be able to walk again without help. She had a great excuse! But she overcame adversity, became a great runner, and more importantly, became a great human being!

Helen Keller was born deaf and blind, yet went on to develop her outstanding gifts of intellect and feeling, and her remarkable ability to communicate with others. She might have had a reasonable excuse!

Stevie Wonder, though blind, became a world-renowned pianist-singer. He might have had an excuse!

An awkward, shy, Eleanor Roosevelt used her privileged position to advance the causes of less fortunate people. She might have had an excuse!

The Bible repeatedly shows how strength can be made perfect in weakness! No excuses required! What can we do? What can we be?

I kid you not, and you probably won't believe me: I did not deliberately time the use of this text to coincide with our nominations for leadership positions in this church!

I've enjoyed watching my three granddaughters and how they love "playing grownup." I can just see them now, rummaging through their carton of dress-up clothes from Aunt Marcia, and coming up with some fantastic outfits with which they play "house" and other creative scenarios. The sky's the limit on their imagination! Amazing how children see with fresh eyes, attempting great things in their play, not worrying about being correct.

Jesus turned water into wine. Consider how God can make very ordinary persons like us become something special. It doesn't mean that *we* will be able to turn water into wine, or that we'll be able to change pennies into silver dollars. It does mean that we can turn a life "empty" of meaning into a fullness of relationships, loyalties, values, and commitments. We can't escape our "holy possibilities" with the excuse that we're too ordinary!

St. Paul celebrated that people who do things differently, and who have very different capabilities and talents, and even people with weaknesses, who disagree about many things, may set aside their excuses and work together for the good of humankind and the glory of God!

10

GOD'S FIERCE WILL TO SAVE

Epiphany 3, Year B
Jonah 3:1-5, 10; Mark 1:14-20

"The word of the Lord came to Jonah a second
time, saying, 'get up, go to Nineveh, that great city, and
proclaim to it the message that I tell you. So Jonah set
out and went to Nineveh, according to the word of the
Lord."

Jonah 3:1-2

I'm a saver, and while it's handy to have a supply of *stuff* to
· dip into while doing those projects, it really makes life tough
when you go to move.

My Mom was a saver. String. Glass jars. She couldn't bear to
throw away glass jars. Paper bags, then when they appeared,
plastic bags. Her cupboards were crammed with plastic bags,
all neatly folded, ready to be used again. It got to be a real
pain, doing dishes for her, because we had to wash the plastic
bags as well as the dishes (She was a "Depression Mom")!

You should see our baby books. The stuff she saved: our
drawings, our letters, little snippets of hair.

I shouldn't make fun of her, first of all because she loved

us so much, and she was a wonderful mother. And secondly, because I've got the "saver virus," too. I simply refuse to throw away hardwood scraps, like maple, or oak, or walnut. I keep walnut scraps the size of a deck of playing cards! And little scraps of steel. Those are for my "projects." So I save. Someday, when I have to move, I'm going to need lots of help.

Our Bible shows us again and again that God is a saver. God is a saver that even makes savers like me look like a punk! God hates to throw out people. In the Bible, God keeps giving people another chance.

There's a difference here. I'm probably a saver because, being a depression baby, I'm anxious about the future. God saves people because of a deep, unconditional love. The story of Jonah and the whale is a classic. Even people who know very little about the Bible are familiar with Jonah. He's always a colorful character, especially with his very human tendency to turn away from what God wants him to do, and his very human comment, "I just wanna die!"

Some have pointed out that this has got to be the funniest book in the Bible, bar none. One of the things that makes Jonah such a hilarious work is that it is not actually a book of prophecy in the classical Hebrew sense, but rather a lampoon of classical prophecy. If you doubt this, read chapter 3, verses 7 and 8, where the repentant king of Assyria commands that even the animals in the kingdom must fast and wear sackcloth, along with the humans, as a sign of repentance!

In Mark we have more of the "call to discipleship" material, where Jesus is calling his fisherfolk followers to make them fishers of people. The underlying idea for both of these texts is that God has this fierce will to save the people.

Yes, God is consistently shown in the Old Testament as the stern judge, but the bottom line is forgiving love. Yes, we human beings are foolish, willful, self-centered. We seem hell-bent to bring about our own destruction. But deep down, we are structured for relationships—meant to live in a redemptive relationship with the Ground of our Being, our Creator, our

Father-Mother God. In the words of St. Augustine, "O God, our hearts are restless until they find their rest in Thee."

Yes, when we look around us we see violence and unfairness, abandonment of moral and spiritual values, cancerous corruption. We see the wicked prosper. But our faith tells us that redemption and healing are the final word. That's why we call ourselves "Easter people."

Jonah found it tough to accept that God wanted to save the people of Nineveh, and he didn't want to go there. When God told him to go east, he went west. When God called again, he took a boat to get away from God. Finally after God clubbed him over the head with a storm at sea and had him swallowed up in the belly of a whale, Jonah submitted to God's will. He didn't get away, because of God's fierce will to save him and to save Nineveh.

Jonah's not your ordinary cowpoke here. According to the story, Jonah owned 7,000 sheep, 3,000 camels, five hundred yoke of oxen, and five hundred donkeys. That's what it says. (Haven't I told you a million times not to exaggerate?!)

Jonah finally did what God said. The story says that the people of Nineveh turned from their violence and their evil ways, and God did not have the heart to punish them. Then Jonah had a temper tantrum—he had wanted them punished (How many of us have sat in church wishing that a certain someone else were there to hear the sermon, or were about to reap consequences of their evil ways?!). But it was God's desire that they be saved. God loved the people of Nineveh, and God loved Jonah. That God had changed God's mind was not an issue. That God remained faithful to God's plan to save was the important thing.

How would this read in our own time? Did God want to save Adolf Hitler? We'll never know—Hitler and his team most likely put themselves so far out of reach of God's grace that they could no longer connect with God. How about Saddam Hussein? There are strong feelings in our land about these evildoers, feelings like those that drove Jonah.

In Mark's lesson maybe the disciples had been listening to Jesus for a long time and had already given it a lot of thought. Maybe they were going through a midlife crisis and were ready to try anything. Maybe. Maybe Mark is just telling the barebones of what happened, and not giving us a lot of background. Maybe. What we do know is that Mark considered this a pivotal moment. It surely reflected his sense of urgency that all people should know that the kingdom of God was at hand.

What in the world does that mean? Is this kingdom the "pie in the sky bye and bye" place? I hope so, because I like pie in the sky bye and bye.

But in my book it's also that real world place, that space, where God's will is done, where the whole truth is told, where forgiving love is truly practiced, and where redemption is taking place. What space? Geographical space: in the world, in the U.S.A., in farms and fields and factories and neighborhoods and in the oceans and in the forests. In Washington state (or maybe even in Washington D.C.), in the community called "West Seattle." In the Seaview United Methodist Church.

In what space? In the time space of John the Baptist. In the time space of Jesus, of Martin Luther, of Billy the Kid and Billy Graham, of 9-11, in the time space of right-now-2003.

What space? Relationship space—that space where we see human relationships: children to parents, parents to children, spouse to spouse. The relationship space between politicians and people.

What space? Economic space. The space between dollar bills and hungry people. The space between jobs and human energies and skills.

These are the kinds of space where the saving action of God is carved out, nurtured, enjoyed, defended.

In both Jonah and Mark we see a consistent thread of judgment as a result of choices. The kingdom of God involves choices. During a flight from Chicago the flight attendant asked if I would like dinner. "What are my choices?" I asked. "Yes or no," she said! In a way, the Kingdom of God is like that. We can pray "Thy kingdom come, thy will be done," or we can pray, "Thy kingdom can just stay at a distance, thy will be too tough!"

The time is fulfilled. Mark saw Jesus coming in the "fullness of time," the ripe moment. It surely was. A perfect time for Jesus' word to be dispersed. The Roman highway system was in place. People could travel, more freely than they can now. Pax Romana—law and order enforced by imperial Rome in even the most remote colonies. A common currency and coinage. The Jews had dispersed all over the known world of that time, forming fertile seed plots for the planting of the gospel. Greek language and culture and the excitement of discussing philosophical ideas was widely experienced. It was a perfect time. Tom Seaver, the legendary baseball pitcher, once asked Yogi Berra, "What time is it?" Yogi replied, "You mean now?" The text in Mark says, "NOW!"

What about that word, "Repentance?" Something in us recoils when we hear this word, but it's a good word. Tacky highway signs and non-communicators on soap boxes may have immunized us with small doses of this word until we're unable to appreciate its importance, as we're called to reexamine and re-orient our lives. Turn around! Turn back! The wonderful thing about this word is that it unlocks the possibility that we may participate in the redeeming activity of God. In Jesus' teaching, repentance means turning toward a God who has already turned toward us and who wants to include us in the plan.

The other day I found myself wondering, "Is God's creation biased towards healing and reconciliation, or is it going the other way?" Our bodies, and even the earth have a remarkable capacity for healing, which is truly a gift from God. Yet there is cancer, and yet we see damage being done to the earth which may for all practical purposes be irreversible. My faith answer to this tough question is that, yes, God's fierce will to save makes creation lean toward healing and wholeness. Admitting that my answer *is* a faith answer, I will try to live as though this were truly so! Perhaps this will help to make it so.

Jesus was an incredible-but-credible manifestation of God-with-the-fierce-will-to-save. Our tradition holds that Jesus washed dirty feet, fed hungry mouths, healed sick limbs, opened blind eyes, cleansed leprous skin, spoke with a sad woman at the well, and shared a difficult word of truth with a rich young man. Jesus spoke about lost sheep, lost coins, lost people. Jesus said, in effect, "Follow me, and get found."

11

FIGURING OUT WHO'S IN CHARGE

Epiphany 3, Year B
I Corinthians 1:10-18; Matthew 4:18-23

"And he said to them, follow me, and I will make
you fish for people. Immediately they left their nets
and followed him."

Matthew 4:19-20

I saw a wonderful item about a new immigrant to our
country who was impressed at what he was seeing in the
American supermarkets. He wrote a letter back home, saying,
"On my first shopping trip I saw powdered milk. All you do is
add water and you get milk. On my second trip I saw a package
of powdered orange juice. All you do is add water and you get
orange juice. On my third trip to the supermarket I saw this
can of baby powder. Now, is this a great country, or what?" *(from
Laron Hall, quoting Bill Ritter)*

He'll probably make a very loyal citizen, and First loyalties
are very important to governments. As an American living
overseas I learned in no uncertain terms that The Government
of The United States of America does not like it when its citizens
flirt with issues having to do with loyalty—like getting involved

in politics or applying for citizenship in another country, or voting in another country. While in 1986 Congress amended citizenship law to make it more liberal concerning such acts, dual citizenship countries usually deal with you as though you were their citizen alone, and sometimes require a renunciation of all other citizenship. We're still involved in a lengthy trial of John Walker Lindh, who actually took up arms against his own country. His idealism notwithstanding, he now finds himself in a very tight spot.

Do you folks get a lot of phone calls from people who are trying to sell something? The lead-in lines usually give them away immediately. The one I really like is, "Are you the head of the household?" When they ask that I often answer, "I really don't know." So they try asking it another way. What they really want to know is, "Who is in charge here?"

I enjoy Susan's sharing at the end of the day about her teaching, and one occasional topic is "6th grade boys," an interesting group! Boys trying to get themselves in charge of the class (this does seem to be more of a boy thing than a girl thing) and teachers trying to keep control!

All through the ages Christians have had to deal with claims for their loyalty. One of the most well-known examples was Sir Thomas Moore, who in conscience refused to bend to the will of the King. His words: "I am the King's good servant . . . but God's first."

Of course, there are loyalties, and there are loyalties! Loyalty to spouse and family is good, but then we consider the Mafia. Loyalty to one's religious faith is supposedly good. Then we look at certain cults. Some say that "you can't go wrong by trusting in Jesus." We notice, however, that there are those who go around shouting, "Jesus, Jesus," and yet do things that are absolutely contrary to Jesus' way.

In his first letter to Corinth, St. Paul is asking about loyalties. Here's a young church that is divided, with some Christians claiming their first allegiance to Apollos, some to Cephas, some to Paul, some bragging about who baptized them, thinking that this may have given them a greater blessing than someone else!

On the matter of baptism Paul does them one better, with some really impressive name-dropping. And then he says, "So what!" He speaks of some of the persons of Corinth that he has baptized. There were some very prominent persons mentioned here, and we know them from other sources. Crispus was identified as an official in the synagogue (Acts 18:7-8). Gaius later hosted Paul and a group of believers in his large household (Romans 16:23); Stephanas was a leader in the Corinthian assembly and maintained a wealthy household well-stocked with servants (1 Cor.16:15-18). And then he says, "So what?" It is God who is in charge, and we find our unity in Christ, who is "God-with-us." I think of some great Bible passages about loyalties:

> in Exodus 32 Moses berated his people for worshipping the golden calf.
>
> At one point Jesus said, emphatically, that unless we "hate" (which in a more accurate translation means "unless we *love the less*,") our own families, our mothers, our fathers, our brothers, our sisters, we will not enter God's kingdom. Blessed is the family where this is not an issue.
>
> James thought that our tongues threatened to be in charge! In the letter of James we read: "Every species of beast can be tamed, but no one can tame the tongue!"
>
> The writer of Revelation admonishes the churches, seeing apathy as being in charge: "I know your works— you are neither cold nor hot! So because you are lukewarm, I will spit you out of my mouth!"

Our culture is too often in charge. Many of us feel a cultural struggle more clearly at Christmas time as we try to hold and protect our own Christmas as a religious observance. Martin E. Marty, in *The Christian Century*, shared this little item: "In

Baltimore, the Handel Choir performed *The Messiah*. The program printed that in the third part the soprano would sing, 'I know that my reindeer liveth!' (instead of the intended 'redeemer.') At last, a role for Rudolph in a Christmas pageant!"

So we have to choose whether we'll be directed and shaped by our culture, or follow our calling as a people of faith. How *will* we demonstrate to the world that we are the loyal people of God, and how will we do it in such a way that we don't presume to be more righteous, more worthy, than everyone else?

The ongoing challenge is to discover and rediscover the mind and spirit of Christ. Often this is fairly clear, and sometimes it's not. If Jesus-values are to direct us, then we must continue to clarify them, and then live them. This involves going to church, but is far more than going to church. Lawrence Peter said, "Going to church doesn't make you a Christian any more than going to a garage makes you a car!" And yet—it's hard to imagine being on this challenging journey as a lonely, isolated individual.

Until recently having a boat, I was quite exposed to the thinking of the nautical world: the captain of a boat is *in charge*. What a great entrée for a power trip! After all is said and done, the captain is responsible for all that happens, good and bad! I have mixed feelings about that, because I'm a firm believer in democratic concepts. On a boat in a storm, however, decision-making by a committee might not be such a great idea. The point here is simply that choosing one's captain, one's primary loyalties, is important.

And so for a nation. Note this prayer by Abraham Lincoln that is eerily apropos in 2003:

> "O, God, we have been recipients of the choicest blessings of heaven. We have been preserved these many years in peace and prosperity. We have grown in numbers, wealth and power as no other nation has ever grown; but we have forgotten God. We have forgotten

the gracious hand which preserved us in peace, and multiplied and enriched and strengthened us; and we have vainly imagined, in the deceitfulness of our hearts, that all these blessings were produced by some superior wisdom and virtue of our own. Intoxicated with unbroken success, we have become too self-sufficient to feel the necessity of redeeming and preserving grace, too proud to pray to the God that made us. It behooves us, then, to humble ourselves before the offended Power, to confess our national sins, and to pray for clemency and forgiveness." *(Abraham Lincoln, cited in* Between Heaven and Earth, *ed. by Ken Gire, Harper, San Francisco, 1997)*

As we worship, we acknowledge who is in charge, as we praise, confess, give thanks, and proclaim. We rediscover with our hearts and our minds that our central task is to be faithful to the One who created us, redeems us, sustains us, and loves us in spite of ourselves.

Tarlac, Central Luzon

12

CONGRATULATIONS!

Epiphany 4, Year A
Matthew 5:1-12; I Corinthians 1:18-31;
Micah 6:1-8

"When Jesus saw the crowds, he went up the
mountain; and after he sat down, his disciples came to
him. Then he began to speak, and taught them, saying:
"Blessed . . .""

Matthew 5:1-3a

Blessed are the poor? Blessed are those who mourn? Hello?
Saying "Blessed are the poor" sounds a bit like the pastor
who was invited to preach to a group of inmates at a state prison
and began his sermon with the greeting: "Well, it's nice to see
so many of you here."

The "beatitudes" (from the Latin word *beatus*, meaning
happy, fortunate, blissful) are another example of the crazy
upside-down world of the gospel, which has always been a
challenge! During Jesus' time there were often magicians and
entertainers roaming the countryside, and people would
gather around them expecting a show. a miracle, something
exciting. But Jesus tended to shy away from miracles, and we

can easily infer from a reading of the gospels that he had mixed feelings about dramatic displays of the power of God. He was more prone to giving lessons, and this passage is about a sermon with a twist presented to a crowd.

Sometimes we get new energy and insights when we try new words in a text. Let's try a substitute for the word "blessed." How about "congratulations?" I've seen translations that actually translate the passage in Matthew in this way.

My old edition of *The Interpreter's Bible*, which was copyrighted 45 years ago, has some interesting comments about the word "blessed" along this very line. It says that the Greek word (*makarios*, with the root word *makar*) used here denoted the highest stage of happiness and well-being. For the Greeks this meant a happiness such as the gods enjoy, and it is used to represent the Hebrew word *ashre*, which is often used as a word of congratulations to humans, though not applied to God.

It's the same Greek word used in Luke 1:42, which has Elizabeth exclaiming to Mary, "Congratulations to you, among women, for blessed is the fruit of your womb."

And it's used again in Luke 11:27-28, when a woman in the crowd said to Jesus: "Congratulations to the womb that bore you and the breasts that nursed you!" But then Jesus said, "Congratulations rather to those who hear the word of God and obey it!" Well, let's see how it might sound:

> "Congratulations to the poor in spirit, for theirs is the kingdom of heaven!"
>
> "Congratulations to those who mourn, for they will be comforted."
>
> "Congratulations to the meek, for they will inherit the earth!"
>
> " . . . . Congratulations to you when people revile you and persecute you and utter all kinds of evil against you falsely on my account. Rejoice and be glad, for your reward is great in heaven, for in the same way they persecuted the prophets who were before you." Congratulations!

What *is* the lesson? This passage is very rich, and it is really difficult to do it justice in just one reflection. I've known ministers to preach a series on the beatitudes, going on for weeks! But let's try to get at the heart of it.

We can have no doubt that Matthew was NOT saying that God will be happy if people are poor, or hungry or thirsty, or if they are persecuted. There is a deeper teaching here. These people whom Jesus was addressing were what some have referred to as "The righteous poor." In Jesus' language, Aramaic, the word used is "Amha-aritz." It means: the good people of the countryside: basically honest, having good will toward others, peasants who were hardworking, who knew how to struggle but were economically poor. Jesus consistently took sides with them!

One of my commentaries points out that an interesting thing about Matthew's version of the beatitudes is that it utilizes materials not found in Luke, and that he uses grammatical forms that make the lesson more "active."

These are forms that pose a vision of *doing* rather than sitting passively waiting for the end of the age. The material from Matthew's "M" source would have Christians *showing* mercy, *pursuing* God's will, *making* peace, or even *suffering* persecution for *doing* God's will. Matthew's version of the beatitudes is for *acting* Christians *bringing* the end of the age by *doing!*

But even if doing is the intended goal of Jesus' sermon, it is clear that the doing must be characterized not by pride, but by a spirit of humility and peacefulness, regardless of the cost.

In the spirit of the greater biblical witness, NOT congratulations to you if you are making yourself into a human doormat, or wallowing in self-flagellation. Yes, congratulations to you if you are engaging in active redemptive love, at personal cost, standing for what you believe. In a world that seems to recognize only brute strength and power, let us keep on saying "congratulations" to those who with dignity and purpose turn the other cheek.

Congratulations when someone listens carefully to a person with whom they disagree. Congratulations when someone offers a prayer of grace and blessing for a so-called enemy.

Today, on Superbowl Sunday, yes, congratulations to the winner. But even more congratulations to the ones who play fair and clean, and who help opposing players up off the ground. Congratulations to the players (and fans!) of the winning team who say to their opponents, "Congratulations! You came this far, and you were a worthy contender." Congratulations to the losing players who go to the winning players, and say "Congratulations!"

And to those who taunted their opponents, or who gave no recognition whatsoever of their opponent's effort and run off to the locker room to pop their Champagne corks—you may have won, and you may be famous, but you are not to be congratulated.

"Congratulations!" when you experience anew the astounding truth of St. Paul's claim in I Corinthians, that divine foolishness is greater than human wisdom, and such foolishness frees us to mourn, to be merciful, and to make peace.

The divine foolishness frees us to love justice, to show kindness and to walk humbly with God, as set forth in Micah. Micah has been called by some scholars "the Hebrew Beatitudes," because, like the beatitudes of our lesson today, Micah offers a series of short lines that contain great truths and challenges for our behavior. It's easy to let these lines roll off our tongues. It's hard to live them every day.

We generally honor the signs and wisdom, in Paul's words, "of our age." We are drawn to power, not weakness. We're attracted by beauty, not lowliness. We value material wealth rather than the righteousness of which the prophets speak.

Congratulations, to you, my friends, if today's lessons help you to get disengaged from a "winner-take-all" culture and see the very different success model pictured in all three of these passages.

13

THE PROBLEM OF LOVING IN GENERAL

Epiphany 4, Year A
Corinthians 13:1-13

"And now, faith, hope and love abide, these three;
and the greatest of these is love."

I Corinthians 13:13

The young couple was out for a walk when they decided to sit on a park bench and rest. After a long pause, she asked, "Do you think my eyes are like the stars?" "Yeah," he replied. "And do you think my teeth are like pearls?" "Yeah," he said. And do you think my hair is like spun gold in the moonlight?" "Yeah," he repeated. "Oh, Joe!" she exclaimed. "You say the most wonderful things!"

Paul's song of love is not about the young couple on the park bench. It's not about romantic love, the love all wrapped up in itself, which under the right circumstances may be a wonderful gift. No, we're talking about unconditional, unselfish love which the Hebrews and the Greeks and other societies have identified and have given their own special words for, the kind of love which we have become convinced describes the very nature and character of God. Love best understood as a verb, not as a noun!

I Corinthians, chapter 13 contains the best-known words that Paul wrote, and is surely the all-time favorite passage for Christian weddings!

A practical guide it is, helping us to address our persistent tendency to love "in general," as compared with loving *specifically and in particular* each next person we meet.

When we recall just what kind of city Corinth was, the meaning of Paul's letter becomes even more clear. There in that tumultuous, cosmopolitan city was a new experiment in friendship and caring and getting along with one another being undertaken by an emerging faith community. Paul is pleading with the struggling Christians at Corinth to give love a chance!

I've been privileged to see Corinth with my own eyes. It's a relatively quiet town now, and there's a modest canal. In St. Paul's time this was one busy place! Some anthropologists number the population at the time of Paul, including its two ports, at about 600,000.

The main point here for understanding Paul's letter is that Corinth was a bustling city, with people from all over the known world. It was a major center for the Roman government, so rolled up in one it was like a primitive Fort Brag, a Hong Kong of trade, and in terms of sports was like ongoing Olympic Games! For lust and license it would make today's Las Vegas look like Wheaton College! The phrase "To live like a Corinthian" meant to wallow in immorality.

The patron saint of Corinth was Aphrodite in her see-through nightie, the goddess of love, with her temple attended by a thousand prostitutes. Wicked Ale and Red Hook? According to the Corinth Department of Tourism on its current web site, in one small area, historian-diggers have discovered thirty-three taverns!

Roughly 30 years after the crucifixion of Jesus, Paul carried his faith to this wild and crazy place. Within eighteen months a thriving community of Christian converts could be found there. Five years later he wrote them a vigorous letter because he was so upset with them. In this first letter to the Corinthians, written while he was in Ephesus, Paul really lets them have it! Chapters 1 through 12 "covers the waterfront," and he tries to set them straight on one matter after another.

Chapter 13 is the high point. It's prefaced by the last verse of Chapter 12: "But strive for the greater gifts. And I will show you a still more excellent way." And then we have Paul's remarkable "Song of Love," which has probably been analyzed and expounded upon by scholars and preachers in as great detail as the beatitudes.

This is in a mode that might have been very appealing to non-Christians. It is practical and not "churchy," and there is no mention of Jesus. Yet we know that Paul was addressing a Christian community, and that the church has always accepted this as a profoundly Christian writing.

It addresses, in effect, a key challenge of loving, which is, the problem of loving in general and not in particular. Perhaps as in the words of a child deeply moved by an experience of acceptance: "I love EVERYBODY!"

I was struck recently while re-reading The Brothers Karamazov, Dostoevsky's classic, at the words quoted by "The Elder" for the rich lady questioning her own faith:

" . . . . 'I love mankind,' he said, 'but I am amazed at myself: the more I love mankind in general, the less I love people in particular, that is individually, as separate persons. In my dreams,' he said, 'I often went so far as to think passionately of serving mankind, and, it may be, would really have gone to the cross for people if it were somehow suddenly necessary, and yet I am incapable of living in the same room with anyone even for two days, this I know from experience' . . . . 'In twenty-four hours I can begin to hate even the best of men: one because he takes too long eating his dinner, another because he has a cold and keeps blowing his nose . . . . (furthermore) 'It has always happened that the more I hate people individually, the more ardent becomes my love for humanity as a whole.'" *(Dostoevsky, Fyodor,* The Brothers Karamazov, *translated by Richard Pevear and Larissa Volokhonsky, New York, Vintage Press, 1991, p. 57)*

It strikes me that this is a deep truth in the same way that believing in general *(it doesn't matter what you believe, as long as you believe something)*, or praying in general *(God bless everybody!)*, or forgiving in general *(without dealing with the poisons of specific resentments)*, or caring about the environment in general *(but not wanting to recycle or turn off lights, or use the car less)*, "loving peace" *(but not wanting to do the tedious work of building peace)* all of these may, in fact, be rather empty of meaning.

As we savor again this inspired poetry in First Corinthians we consider how it might help us to love each person we meet, which is often quite challenging. I don't think it's *bad* to love *in general,* but how much more sound theologically and how much more effective it is to manifest our love specifically, concretely, in real situations with real persons!

In verses 4 through 7, where it tells us that love bears all things, do we have a set up for co-dependency? If you're familiar with Paul's writings, you can't think that! Love has to absorb a lot of stuff. Love is willing to struggle, and willing to wrestle with complicated questions and avoid simplistic, rigid, judgmental answers. Love is willing to speak the truth.

Throughout the Hebrew scriptures God is characterized as "steadfast love." In the New Testament God IS love, and love is the energy of God, and love is stronger than death!

All around us and in our midst are persons, rich and poor alike, beautiful and plain, who seem to be bundles of restless, unfulfilled yearnings. Maybe the answer to their yearnings will be a complicated one. But love will be a part, it "simply" will. People will find their peace that passes all understanding not by being loved in general, but through specific, practical encounters involving unconditional, forgiving love.

14

LOVE AS A MODE OF KNOWLEDGE

Epiphany 4, Year B
I Corinthians 8:1-13

"Food will not bring us close to God. We are no worse off if we do not eat, and no better off if we do. But take care that this liberty of yours does not somehow become a stumbling block to the weak."

I Corinthians 8:8-9

In St. Paul's time many people still worshipped pagan idols, and it was common for the meat left over from the sacrifices to be used at social occasions. It was also sold in the local marketplaces. Scholars say that many of those who were new in the faith would continue to socialize with those of their own family and their friends who still followed the pagan practices, and would partake of this meat left over from the sacrifices. Whether or not a Christian should eat such food was a hot topic! I won't tell you about some of the things that I've eaten, in the Philippines and in New Guinea! That could be a hot topic, too.

We, too, live in an age where people talk about food constantly—what we should eat, what we shouldn't eat! I would guess that probably no other society on the face of the earth has so many people who know their cholesterol count (or think they know!) People struggling to find their next meal must talk about food a lot, and we people who have too much food do seem to talk about food a lot. The modern day meaning of "backslide" has little to do with religion—it simply means to go off one's diet!

In this interesting passage from I Corinthians, Paul confronts an issue that's difficult to explain, and he knows that it is difficult, and he plays a "balancing act," which is about the best thing that he could do. He's urging the followers of Jesus to see that there are many questions where you simply can NOT get black and white answers, and he suggests, in effect, *that Christians learn to trust love as a mode of knowledge.* His ethic: try to practice thoughtful consideration of the many factors that affect our relationships. Even though there are things that we might do which are quite empty of moral significance in and of themselves, we might do well to voluntarily avoid doing them so as not to confuse or cause harm.

There was another dynamic here. Paul had some fierce opponents called "Gnostic Christians." "Gnosis" is the Greek word for knowledge, and these Christians believed that they had certain "special knowledge" and knew certain secrets that would guarantee their salvation. Claims of privileged knowledge proved to be very divisive in the early church, and I think we could honestly say that they still do!

Paul worried about this. In verse 1 of Chapter 8, as well as in Colossians II and I Timothy 3, he speaks of the dangers of being "puffed up" with pride. He says that in contrast to knowledge, which puffs up, love *builds* up. Paul develops this carefully and extensively later in this letter, in chapters 11 and 12. Love, and not secret knowledge, is the special way in which Christians are to "know."

It is our hearts that offer us the synthesizing ability through which we integrate all that we know. It is love that enables us to bring together the many competing values and claims that divide our minds.

The bread of which we partake this day might be a good example: We know about bread, especially freshly baked bread. Our five senses tell us about that. It feels hot, smells good, sounds crunchy-soft, looks like fresh-baked bread, and tastes great (is it less filling?). So we know about bread!

But there's far more to bread than that, and our hearts know it. Coming *home* to hot bread on a cold day is comforting, satisfying, reassuring and carries a sense of being loved. We know about the bread that unites us at this table, and that we kneel, literally, this day, with millions of people of faith, desiring new life and claiming God's forgiveness; grasping unity, hope, and a common vision. Beyond our intellectual understanding of this, it is our hearts that know it, because love is the mode of knowledge for these very special kinds of things.

Nearly every day we have to make choices where the issues are complicated, and there's no easy answer. Life is not black and white, but white and black and gray and many colors. It might be nice to have a religious leader who will give you clear, definitive answers! Like Paul, in this case, I don't like to do that. I prefer heart-knowledge. It presents us with a greater test, a greater responsibility than law-knowledge, because it demands that we look outside ourselves into other hearts.

Paul dismisses the ethical importance of what the Corinthians have been eating. His real issue with those whom he challenged had to do with freedom and love, and not meat. As for "knowledge" about such things, this is subsumed under the question of "love." Our love for God, for others, and even for our own well-being comes under this. It is love that brings our divided minds together and enables us to know.

Mindanao Sunrise

15

REGARDING SALT-FREE DIETS

Epiphany 5, Year A
Matthew 5:13-20

"You are the salt of the earth; but if salt has lost its
taste, how can its saltiness be restored? It is no longer
good for anything, but is thrown out and trampled
under foot."

Matthew 5:13

Salt-free diets are not easy for a family like mine. I can
remember family and friends sitting down for a meal, and even
before tasting their food picking up the salt and pepper shakers
to put a generous shot of seasoning. That made the cook feel
really good!

Dad often kept a bucket of black walnuts on the workbench
in our basement woodworking shop in Illinois, and next to it
there would be a hammer to crack the hard shells on the anvil
of the vise, some 10 penny finishing nails to pick out the meats,
and a jar lid with salt in it. We would remove the walnut meat,
then lick it, dip it in the salt, and eat it. Yum. Real salty! Did
you ever do that? It slows down the woodworking projects, but
we weren't in a hurry.

And I remember that as a little boy, when out walking in the pasture, I'd come upon the block of salt that was there for the cows to lick, and I'd get down on my knees and have a lick myself. It never occurred to me that the cows' tongues were any less clean than mine!

Salt-free diets are extremely important for some people, and I don't want to discount them. We know that some people must be very careful about their sodium intake. I go easier on the salt than I used to, and I season my food with stuff other than salt. But I'm glad that I don't have to go on a salt-free diet. Yet.

Today's lesson from Matthew immediately follows the beatitudes, and is still a part of the Sermon on the Mountainside. Matthew seems to be warning the early followers of Jesus about being neutralized, of becoming too comfortable in their faith. After the series of "blesseds," they're cautioned that they might be made irrelevant. One wonders if the gospel writers, as they wrote these accounts, had thought that the church, though keeping the appearance of being the people of God, had lost the bite, the energy, the flavor that they were meant to have? The example is pointedly personal, but is also clearly corporate.

We're still in the period called "Epiphany," and the theme is still "witness." The scriptural expectation is that *we* become the epiphany, or the sign of encouragement and hope, of vitality and energy to those around us. So Matthew gives us the metaphors of salt and light.

These days we tend to think of salt mainly as a flavoring for food. Our use of it in this way is so common that it's in just about everything we eat. If you're on a salt-free diet, you have to be quite careful, because substantial amounts of salt are in most processed foods.

It's important to look back to the culture of Jesus' day and try to imagine how salt was used, because Jesus' use of salt as an image here may be richer in meaning than might first appear. It's also possible to read more into it than was meant!

Salt was a precious commodity that served a variety of really important purposes beyond seasoning. It was considered of such value that people were sometimes paid their wages in salt. Clearly, they used it in barter trade.

Since ancient days salt has been known to give long life to the things that it permeates. Some of the Old Testament prophets used salt as a symbol of God's eternal covenant with the Hebrew people, in some places calling it the "covenant of salt." (Lev. 2:13; Numbers 18:19; II Chronicles 13:5) So it was recognized as a preservative. Before refrigeration was common, it was well-known that salted foods would keep better than non-salted foods, an important fact when fresh foods were scarce. I experienced that when I lived in a remote area of the Philippines, where I regularly ate dried, salted fish. Not bad, actually, and sometimes I miss it! Maybe that helps to explain my weakness for bacon and ham.

Salt was even used as a disinfectant. I've also encountered people who would rub salt into wounds, thinking that it would help the wound to heal. If it stings, it must be good! Jump into the ocean to wash your wound. We now know that there are better ways.

Salt makes us thirsty, of course. Airlines and bars have been accused of giving out free peanuts and other salty snacks to cause people to buy more drinks! A possible point to be raised here is that the church, as salt, might stimulate thirst for the good things of God, for the satisfying things of the Spirit.

They say that in some places and in some times salt was mixed with dung and spread on the ground as fertilizer. As late as World War II British farmers compensated for the lack of nitrate fertilizers by using salt. I have serious technical reservations about this idea (in other words, I don't believe it), but that's what I have read!

Can salt lose its taste? Our text infers that it can. I've never run into sodium chloride that has lost its taste, but the idea of salt without savor is an important part of the lesson here, and we can get the point. All of these uses (or alleged uses and qualities!) of salt might serve as spiritual metaphors for a faith community, especially a community finding itself in a minority status. Such as we.

The images of both salt and of light, which go together in Matthew, demonstrate their value in relation to a context—to preserve and bring taste and to illuminate. The salt does it in the midst of the food or the soil, and the lamp in the midst of the dark. Verse 16 reminds us that salt and light do not exist simply for their own sake, but that their greater goal is to lift up "good works" and to give glory to God.

Like a pinch of leaven in the dough; like a sprinkle of salt in our food; or a shovelful of manure in the flower bed; or like a village carpenter's son wandering within a tiny country, God has a remarkable way of making a little bit go a long way, of taking something humble, and with it doing things of epic proportions!

We're warned about being neutralized believers, which I would take to mean claiming a faith but without having the "flavor" or savor; or having a decaying faith without the deep staying power; or one without the underlying nourishment that Jesus may have associated with the use of salt in his friends' gardens. The element in question is not required in great quantity, but it's crucial that we have it!

The expectation is that *we* become the epiphany, or the sign, just as the star of Bethlehem was the sign. Centers of light, and little bursts of taste: sources of encouragement and hope for those around us. As persons of faith we're not on salt-free diets. "You are the salt of the earth!" . . ."You are the light of the world!" Spice up someone's life! Brighten someone's day, and help light their way!

16

GETTING WELL

Epiphany 5, Year B
Mark 1:29-39

"Now Simon's mother-in-law was in bed with a fever,
and they told him about her at once. He came and took
her by the hand and lifted her up. Then the fever left
her, and she began to serve them . . . . in the morning,
while it was still very dark, he got up and went out to a
deserted place, and there he prayed. And Simon and
his companions hunted for him. When they found him
they said, "Everyone is searching for you."

Mark 1:30-31, 35-37

I find it difficult to take up the issue of healing because
I've been so turned off by the T.V. evangelists and their dubious
"entertainment" involving healing.

I've had close-up experience with it. While a missionary in
the Philippines in the early 1970's, assigned to a large
agricultural resettlement project, I had an office in Manila,
and our family lived there. I chose to be a part of a newly
organized church on the outskirts of Manila, and along with

some wonderful Filipino United Methodist families who lived in that neighborhood, helped to make it grow.

During that time, a Filipino faith healer by the name of "Dr. Rudy," from what was called the "Espiritista" group in Pangasinan, was supposedly performing miracles. He claimed to be healing cancer, even removing tumors without using surgical instruments. He simply used his fingers to make an incision, and when he was finished would wipe the place where he was working, and the opening was miraculously closed, with no anesthesia, no pain, and no scar. When asked how much he charged, he would say, "It's up to you, whatever you want to pay." People would often feel better immediately, and being deeply grateful, of course, would give him a check for one or two thousand dollars.

He had gained quite a following, and people were flying to Manila from the U.S.A. to have him deal with their medical problems, particularly cancer. A member of my local church, Dr. Ricardo Fernando, a surgeon and Medical Director of the Mary Johnston Hospital in Manila, and I were talking about this faith healer one day, and decided that we wanted to learn more about his activity. We didn't want to hinder anything that was helping people, but we also felt it important that the truth be known. So Rick and I went to a nice hotel in Ermita, where it had been noted by a local newspaper that Dr. Rudy would be performing surgery.

Interestingly, after interviewing us, they wouldn't let *me* come in and watch. They were suspicious of me, but they did let the right person in, Rick, who is small physically, quite friendly and unpretentious. So he witnessed Dr. Rudy's surgery while I waited in the hotel lobby. There was a smile on Rick's face when he appeared, and we went off for a cool drink and to talk. "It's a total sham, he said, purely sleight of hand." He explained that what he had seen involved some freshly harvested organs from a small pig, which as a surgeon he readily recognized, and the blood, which was plentifully spread around during the surgery, must also have been from a pig or a chicken.

We decided that it was important to share this information, because persons who could have been helped by timely medical procedures might have stopped going to a doctor when they urgently needed to do so. So Rick wrote an article for the Manila Times, and we began telling people about what we thought was happening. But, you know, people (the "crowd!") so desperately wanted healing that they continued to flock to Dr. Rudy. Subsequently, in the U.S., while touring as a missionary speaker, I ran into a number of such persons, particularly in Oregon.

I tell this story because it helps to illustrate some important points. It contrasts sharply with what Jesus did, and a close look at today's text will show this.

Closer looks, second and third looks, often reveal things in the Bible that we may not have thought about on first reading.

In this passage for example, a local synagogue was mentioned twice, and we're seeing here in Mark's writing evidence that temple worship was beginning to give way to the synagogue, or the local church. This had very important implications for the religious practice of the ordinary Jewish people. Another thing is that Mark speaks about the mother-in-law of Simon Peter, and we're suddenly made to realize that Peter was married! We might miss that, because none of the other passages involving Peter say it. We never do learn the mother-in-law's name, nor about her daughter, Peter's wife!

Today's passage, which stops before the healing of the leper, is seemingly not all that dramatic, and Jesus clearly does *not* want it to be dramatic. He doesn't use mud, or saliva, and in this case doesn't even speak with her! The fact that she began to serve them must have meant that *she simply got well*. A pure act of compassion on Jesus' part? It seems that Jesus and his friends were quite comfortable in being in that home. That she was brought after sundown was probably just a simple indication that the Sabbath was over. These folks were faithful Jews, and that would have been important to them.

According to Mark, crowds were beginning to form around Jesus, and the way in which he handled that fact is what hits me hardest about this passage: THE CROWDS! "The whole city was gathered around the door," it says, and he cured many. Word was beginning to get out about him. He cast out many demons, it says, and they knew who he was, and he would not permit them to speak.

Then in the space of a few verses we learn that *he got out of there*, going to a deserted place where his companions had to hunt for him. When they found him they told him that the *crowd* was searching for him, and then he said, "Let's go to other towns."

Crowds were a problem for Jesus then, and they're a problem now. The crowd wants to get well, right now! As evidenced in Jesus' last hours, the crowd is usually very narrow in what it wants, and can turn angry and dangerous.

We want to get well, and that's good. It's our expectations that are the problem, false expectations. People want physical healing and want to avoid death. This is O.K. But there's more to abundant living than that!

Sometimes there are deep-down things that have to be cleansed before healing can take place, like with a splinter that festers, or an abscess that simply will not get well unless it is lanced and drained and cleansed.

We wish for a miracle to avoid or postpone death. A respected friend told our study group, "I prayed to God, and held out for a miracle, but my husband died, and I thought I had lost everything. Soon I discovered that the miracle WAS there!" Christians should know that the avoidance of physical death is NOT the only alternative, and the restoration of total physical well-being is not the only goal. There is more to life than death! This is one of Jesus' most fundamental teachings, and this is the meaning of the cross!

We don't want to be sick any more, and that's good. But when we don't know what it means to get well, that's not good. I like it when I get well physically, and I don't like it when I'm sick physically. I like it when I feel young. It keeps getting harder and harder to feel that way. But by God's grace, and not the crowd's, I am learning that that I can get well and be well in the ways that really matter. Staying well physically takes a bit of attention, and attending to spiritual wholeness does too. It is God who makes us "well," and it is when we *choose LIFE* that we get well.

Fortunately, we have occasional instances where friends and loved ones who are "dying," or who are aging, or who suddenly have permanent, severe limitations, have come to understand this, have come to terms with it, have become at peace with it, and in a profound sense, "get well." Then WE are taught, and we are helped to get well.

17

BEHOLD THE NEWNESS

Epiphany 7, Year B
Isaiah 43:18-25; Mark 2:1-12

"Do not remember the former things, or consider
the things of old. I am about to do a new thing; now it
springs forth, do you not perceive it? I will make a way
in the wilderness and rivers in the desert."

Isaiah 43:18-19

Curious, how in our culture we love new things. Our
advertising cries out, "All New!" "See my new car, my new house,
my new computer, my new camera, my new guru!" In a
throwaway culture, with planned obsolescence, the voracious
appetite for things new sweeps us along, into all sorts of new
experiences, new challenges, new debt!

Is our attraction to new things reflective of a deep
dissatisfaction? Always wanting something new? Something that
we feel we're missing? No wonder I have a good feeling when
I read the passage from Isaiah 43, which says that God is about
to do a "new thing!"

Today's readings anticipate the joy of Easter, which will
contrast with the solemnity of Holy Thursday and Good Friday,

the days of apparent failure and loss. Our preparation for Easter reminds us that there *will be* a newness!

As spring draws near it's less difficult to believe that God continues to do new things. We see creation unfolding, literally, new life being born. Spring is bursting with healing and renewal; second chances, new opportunities.

Yes, there are accidents, earthquakes, wind, and fire, but there is coherence. Despite our anxieties and fears, the hope and possibility of fulfillment overpower futility. Sometimes we even find that things make sense, and it is good!

Though the cycle of the seasons goes round and round, the dynamic, ever-changing character of life within the cycle seems to suggest that we're *not* prisoners of a wheel of fortune, ever repeating, never new, so we celebrate Isaiah's words, "Behold the new thing!"

The Isaiah material spans a period of 200 to 300 years, so obviously it was not all written by one person. Some of it was surely written by disciples of Isaiah. Regardless, it was considered of sacramental importance to the Hebrew community. The more you study it, the more you can see why!

Today's reading is in what scholars consider Isaiah, part II, or "Deutero-Isaiah." It reflects the experience of catastrophic failure and the struggle of the people to re-establish their lives. The theme of a new exodus is here linked with the overthrow of Babylon, the oppressor.

Ironically, the people had thought that Babylon would become the instrument of God in putting down their former enemy, Assyria, but it didn't happen. It was gradually becoming clear that Israel could not put its trust in human-controlled, self-interest-motivated political entities, as much as these did affect Israel's life.

Likewise, *we* should not put our trust in the many "new things" that beckon us. *WE* may be called to a "new exodus." It is God who delivers, and it is right relationships that must be at the center of our search for fullness of life, personally, and as a nation.

Just as God led the people of Israel out of Egypt and through the wilderness, Isaiah proclaims that again God is able to deliver God's people from exile. In our here and now, in situations of profound failure, are the moments of divine promise and action. For Isaiah, it is through the "broken" people, the people of Israel, who have apparently failed again, that we have the new opportunity—the new promise!

So even before Lent begins we recognize that Easter comes in the context of failure, judgment, and grace. This, essentially, is the recurring Isaiah connection with the message of the New Testament: Behold the newness! The *New* Testament tells the story of how God enters into the human condition and provides an opportunity for a way out. This was a newness of understanding.

The Mark lesson is a story about healing, and there are two elements in it that have to do with *our* participation in the healing process. This passage was one of my favorites when working with church leaders regarding rural community development.

The first has to do with resourcefulness. Jesus was becoming famous, and a large crowd had blocked the entrance of the home where Jesus was staying. The friends of the paralyzed man couldn't get their loved one in to see him. Try to imagine these folks walking across the flat roofs of the houses, finding precisely the right spot, and then clawing and scratching an opening through a section of roof between the beams.

Try to imagine the bits of mud plaster and the dust falling upon the people inside. Visualize the calloused hands roughened by a life of hard work, bruised and bleeding from this labor of love, hands lowering the man down into the room to be with Jesus. And Jesus heals him. The paralyzed man's friends had to get their hands dirty and bruised to make this happen.

Another interesting element is that as an integral part of the healing event Jesus told the man, "Stand up and walk." He did say, "Your sins are forgiven," which caused quite a stir (and that's another interesting issue), but no other hocus pocus, just "Take up your mat, and go to your home!" In other words, no one can get up for you. *This* is your part! Get unstuck! You have to do that for yourself.

I can't help but think of the contrast between this challenge and Jesus' encounter with the rich young man, who, when hearing what was needed to enter the Kingdom of God, walked sadly away! He was not able to take up his part.

This early Easter message is about deliverance: from our failures, crippling conditions, and defeats. Perhaps even deliverance from success! Deliverance from ourselves. Deliverance from a war that would have terrible consequences, even for so-called "winners." There is some kind of deliverance for each one of us here, if we will claim it.

Newness is about second chances! I've had second chances, and I'm so thankful for these. It's about healing. It is in the context of this newness that we make life-determining choices.

God has not given up on us, because it gives God joy to be in relationship with us. It involves risk on God's part, because any truly authentic relationship is "lose-able." Loving involves risk. God-in-Christ involved risk.

There is newness, and we may behold it! But for the transformation to happen we may have to get our hands dirty, and we will have to stand up and walk.

18

THE EYEWITNESS

The Transfiguration of the Lord, Year B
Matthew 17:1-9
II Peter 1:16-21

"For we did not follow cleverly devised myths when
we made known to you the power and coming of our
Lord Jesus Christ, but we had been eyewitnesses of his
majesty. We ourselves heard this voice come from
heaven, while we were with him on the holy mountain.
2 Peter 1:16, 18

A little boy went to Sunday school for the first time, and
when he got home his mother asked, "Who was your teacher?"
The boy answered, "I don't remember her name, but she must
have been Jesus' grandmother, because she didn't talk about
anyone else!" Now there was a witness!

On a more serious note, do you remember the film "The
Witness," with Harrison Ford? The little Amish boy who saw a
murder became the focus of this exciting story, which pictured
the fear that some powerful police officials had of a boy who
knew the truth.

Many in the early church eagerly awaited Christ's return, expecting him to come in clouds with great power and glory *(Mark 13:26; Matt. 24:30; Luke 21:27)*. They would have seen the transfiguration story as an anticipation of this final appearance. And some of them, I suppose, would have been skeptical.

Six days after telling the disciples who he really was and how he was going to die, Jesus took Peter and the brothers, James and John, apart from the rest of the disciples to a high mountain. There he was "transfigured" before them. His face shone like the sun, the story says, and his garments became as white as light. And while they were there, Moses and Elijah appeared to them.

Peter later tells about seeing this. "We did not follow cleverly devised myths." This is how the Second Peter passage begins. Peter is saying, "I saw it with my own eyes!" This is interesting, because the Transfiguration is sometimes treated as myth.

How do we treat stories like this? How do we separate myth from reality? We have the age-old tension between weighing evidence and the need to make a faith response. Sometimes we see it with our own eyes! Other times, not having seen with our own eyes, we must measure new questions and issues against the mind and spirit of Christ as we can best know it: Love and caring for all people; openness to the new things which God is doing.

There are again significant differences between the accounts in the various gospels. Mark's account seems to be the most primitive. Luke has material unsubstantiated by Matthew and Mark. Matthew tends to omit material from Mark that is redundant or not so flattering to the disciples. Matthew very obviously repeats material found in Daniel 10:6-12. Matthew also moves the material in such a way that Jesus is seen to be minimizing the "hocus pocus", and is choosing to be fully human.

The author of Second Peter wanted first to bolster the faith of the church in the second coming of Jesus; and secondly, to warn against false prophecy and interpretation of Scripture. The transfiguration scene is surrounded by dark predictions of suffering and death (Matt 16:21; 17:9). The vision cannot even be told to others until "the Son of man is raised from the dead."

Why would Jesus want to keep this a secret? Why not tell everyone, so that they might believe? Yet we might ask: Do we know people around us who talk too much, too soon? People talking about what they're going to do, telling of their great plans, then not delivering? Most of us know persons who let their energy get dissipated in casual talk

Holding back energy, keeping a secret for a while, does in fact seem to have been a practice Jesus adopted on several occasions. When Peter confessed Jesus to be the Christ (Mark 8:30), when a healing had taken place (Luke 5:14, Mark 7:36, Luke 8:56), and at the Transfiguration, Jesus said to his followers, in effect, "Let's hold back the power, and use it when the right time comes!" These stories take their proper place in the context of the crucifixion. Then the character and purpose and timing of events in Jesus' life might be better understood.

Each one of us has probably, at one time or another, followed a cleverly devised myth, and I can't say that I blame people of today for being skeptical about their leaders and what they say. There's probably more skepticism about leaders, politicians, scientists, and about the church, than ever before. Too many times we *have* been disappointed with those who have made the big promises. What do we draw from this particular text? Are there are times when God "pulls aside the veil," and allows us to see God's truth with a special clarity and power? Do we have anything to fear from the truth, wherever it may be found?

What might be the mountain experiences for us? Things we've seen with our own eyes, experienced with our own lives? Most of us think back to moments of special grace and meaning, but it's different for each one of us: a summer church camp, or some other faith experience; a person who seems to be especially insightful, or good; a crisis; a near death experience; the death of a much respected or loved one; a moment when surrounded by rare natural beauty; "aha" moments of insight and understanding; the feeling of awe at the complexity of the human brain: its fragility, its toughness, its vulnerability, its capacity for healing.

I see another important lesson in this passage: we have nothing to fear from the truth, provided we try to stay connected with truth in its wholeness.

Interesting, vigorous discussions are going on about the brain and how it functions through bio-chemicals. Yes, our brains are like computers, and yes, it may be bio-chemicals that give rise to all of our capacity for thinking, remembering, and feeling, even feeling joy. But in the end, we make the faith statement that God made us, and we are not an accident. The world is organized around God's intelligent vision. God is great! Long live God's bio-chemicals!

I deeply appreciated the PBS special on Rachael Carson and her book, *Silent Spring*, about the use of chemicals to control insects. Yes, chemicals can control insects, but many times insects are good, and chemicals can be over-used! Truth in its wholeness. We have nothing to fear from the truth, and we should have no part in empty, cleverly designed myths.

So-called "special" knowledge can be destructive myth: messages designed to cause us to hate or exclude; appeals for easy answers; disinformation, misinformation, propaganda or sensational advertising; images projected about what is "The Good Life," or about who are the "evil ones." These are cleverly devised myths.

Now is a time for witness. We are to be signs of God's kingdom in this world. Not all church people want others to know that they're Christians, however.

There's an amusing story about a preacher who was at the door of the church shaking hands with the people after the service. He noticed one parishioner who seldom attended church, and as he grabbed his hand, he pulled him aside. "You need to join the Army of the Lord," he said. The man replied, "I'm already in the Army of the Lord, Pastor!" The Pastor said, "How come I don't see you except at Christmas and Easter?" He whispered back, "I'm in the secret service!"

God has given us a cloud of witnesses who have seen the vision with their own eyes and experienced first-hand the power of a life connected with God's love. It's no secret!

Cotabato War Zone

19

WEIGHING BREAD AND STONES

Lent 1, Year A
Matthew 4:1-11

"The tempter came, and said to him, 'If you are the
Son of God, command these stones to become loaves of
bread."

Matthew 4:3

The next time you go through the checkout counter at a
supermarket, Have a look at those grotesque tabloids and try
to identify some of the themes. Jesus spoke to most of these
themes, including issues raised by the very existence of the
tabloids themselves! Please note that I never buy, though I do
look! I cannot resist the temptation to look!

The Gospels show us that Jesus repeatedly dealt with the
basic *stuff* of our existence: money, possessions, status and power,
violence, anxiety, sexuality, the law, security, true and false
religion, deceit, the way we treat our neighbor, the way we
treat our enemy.

These are not just religious issues, but questions with which
every man and woman must come to terms, regardless of how
they feel about religion.

Our task as a people of faith during the Lenten season is not to make the Gospel easy, but to make it clear; not to create an experience for these 40 days only, but to deepen our commitment and evoke permanent change in our ways of living.

The temptation account in Matthew 4, or a similar one in Luke 4, is traditionally read on the First Sunday in Lent. Jesus' forty days in the wilderness, together with the "40 years" or "40 days" experiences of Israel, Moses, and Elijah become the format for our own time of preparation for Easter. We see how seriously Matthew took the problem of temptation and the power of evil. He presents Christ as confronted by three challenges. He shows them as powerful, but as resistible.

The first temptation came at "gut" level. Jesus knew full well about hungry people, and what hunger does to people. He himself was hungry, having been long in the desert. He was known to have prayed, "Give us this day our daily bread." The stones around him in that setting even looked like various sizes of loaves of bread. This temptation is intimately related to the other three. There's nothing that could have given Jesus a following more quickly than to have been able to produce bread from stones. Or from anything. Economic temptation. Bread. Money. Things.

The second temptation seems dramatic, but in some ways it may be the most subtle and difficult. "Throw yourself down . . . (the Tempter even quotes scripture!) Show how your God can save! Pastors, act out your fantasies! Watch out, danger lurks!

The third temptation is an offer of power. "Here, Jesus, take over. The kingdoms of the world in all their splendor can be yours! Here's your chance to put your wonderful agenda into place! If you'll just acknowledge that I am the 'most worthy one,' and that I am your Executive Director, it's all yours!" I can't help but think of the political process, and the lengths to which candidates will go in order to win. "Winning isn't everything—it's the only thing!" So they say. Jesus had a different answer.

One of the dimensions of this text has to do with our limited existence in the world of physical reality. Burt Reynolds said, "There are two things I've learned in my life: You should never race a guy named 'Rocky,' and never bring a girl named 'Bubbles' home to meet your mother (both of which I've done, by the way.)'" While Jesus' life was remarkable, even miraculous, he had a strong hold on reality.

The three inter-related temptations propose a violation of the fundamental relationship between Jesus-as-human, and God. They suggest that Jesus might challenge, or test, God. For the Hebrews, rebellion against God is called *Sin*. And we Christians call it Sin.

"Sin" is a word used by religious people. People who don't believe in God tend to use other words. Whatever you want to call it, it's a problem. It is the willful breaking of relationships. It is turning away from reality. It is the deliberate rejection of the right relationships involved in honoring God, pursuing righteousness and goodness, seeking justice and fairness, and practicing caring and peacefulness. Such a rejection of relationships is profoundly self-centered. It might be in the form of dramatic rebellion, or a simple careless drift into isolation and moral fuzziness. It is life-threatening. It can be "terminal," whatever you call it.

People have funny hang-ups about the meaning of "Sin," pouncing on all kinds of things that steer attention away from the really important questions. The supercharged subject of human sexuality is probably the favorite arena for this. Cigarettes and whiskey and wild, wild, women—or wild, wild, men—may indeed be fruits of Sin, but in the wide-screen panorama of the Bible, Sin is something deeper, more basic, more serious!

The deeper dimensions of a sexual escapade were well pictured in the film *"Fatal Attractions,"* with Glenn Close and Michael Douglas. A supposedly happily married man has a weekend fling with an attractive, aggressive woman who turns out to be psychotic. The situation turns life for him and his family into a living hell!

Scorsese's film, *The Last Temptation of Christ,* was controversial partly because in a dream Jesus was shown to have had a full range of human feelings, but it was not just that. One of the things that made the film distasteful for some Christians was the idea that Jesus was really tested, that Jesus was fully human in his experience of temptation and pain! Personally, I found the film rich and meaningful theologically, and one which raises important questions for our own spirituality. The night I went to see the film there were protestors from conservative Christian groups, and many security guards. We heard later that in some theaters Christian "crusaders" had slashed movie screens with knives and thrown red paint. Yes, Jesus *was* tempted, and yes, Jesus resisted. The temptations were real and not fake. He has been there ahead of us.

Some of us have some pretty impressive excuses as to why we are just how we are, and I'll be among the first to say that we must be compassionate and understanding about why people are the way they are. There comes a point, however, when we must take responsibility for our own lives. Blaming others and blaming the Devil, constantly calling ourselves victims, won't cut it. Temptation is a point where the rubber hits the road. We're all tempted. It's what we do with it that matters.

The image of turning stones into bread is vital for our reflection here, because there's a critical connection. Bread is vitally important. As a missionary I believed, and I still do believe, that Jesus calls us, in the spirit of Matthew's gospel, chapter 25, to address all of the needs of human beings, material as well as non-material, and to reaffirm that there is a seamless fabric of reality. We too easily divide life into little spiritual and physical parts!

We do live by bread, but we do not live by bread alone. Stones into wheat flour are not enough. George Buttrick, in his exposition on Matthew in the 1951 edition of *The Interpreter's Bible,* gives an example of a famished Bedouin finding treasure in the desert, crying, "alas, it is only diamonds!" Buttrick goes on to say that we in our deepest hunger also cry, "alas, it is only bread!"

We live by bread, but we also live by grace, forgiveness, and love, and we feed on the eternal hopes planted deep within us.

We live by bread, and as a people of faith we have been given bread and wine upon our sacramental table, and as we partake, we're led to remember some important things, among them our unity in the body and blood of Christ, our dependence upon God for the bread of life, the troubling reality that many are still hungry and not at the table, and that we are complicit in their hunger and their absence.

The problem of temptation is dead serious, but it can be overcome. Jesus *is* the answer, but not the soft and easy answer: not the answer of the neon lights, or those that our narrow selves and selfish otherworldly hopes crave; not the narrow and exclusive answer.

Jesus is the answer calling us into a new age now, right now, to be a new people, even now, and even and especially in the midst of a world of enchanting appeals and fatal attractions.

New Guinea Highlands

20

TAPPING THE ROCK:

A REFLECTION ABOUT WATER

Lent 3, Year A
Exodus 17:1-7

"The Lord said to Moses, 'Go on ahead of the
people, and take some of the elders of Israel with you;
take in your hand the staff with which you struck the
Nile, and go. I will be standing there in front of you on
the rock at Horeb. Strike the rock, and the water will
come out of it, so that the people may drink.' Moses did
so, in the sight of the elders of Israel."

Exodus 17:5-6

Water is a sign of God's care for us and God's commitment
to us: biblically, physiologically, geologically, spiritually. We see
this in the story of Noah and the flood, the rainbow as the sign
of the covenant, the great rain for which Elijah prayed to end
a terrible drought, and in John the Baptist and his water
baptisms in the River Jordan.

Today's passage is about water, but the message is *more* than
"The people were thirsty, and they found water!" The water
and the thirst have powerful symbolic meanings.

I like talking about water, because it's so central to our lives and can symbolize our most basic needs. We simply cannot go without it. All of life on earth which we know about, in fact, takes place within a watery medium. Even camels and lizards in the desert need water. Our bodies are mostly water. We belong to water, and water belongs to us!

In the larger picture there's nothing in the world more *common* than water. While living in the Pacific Islands we discovered that if you hold a globe of the world in just the right way, the only thing you can see is the Pacific Ocean with some dots of islands in it.

It's a bit difficult when you live in the Pacific Northwest to remember that some areas suffer great water shortages! While living in Northern Luzon in the Philippines I got a taste of what dry means, because the monsoon system extends down into that area. For part of the year there's a parchingly dry season where dust is everywhere and water becomes very precious. Visitors riding in our vehicles could not believe how the dust would penetrate the tightest suitcase! We would turn off all of our flush toilets, so that they wouldn't run by mistake, and we used a bucket, very sparingly!

If you've ever stayed more than a few days at the edge of the desert, you can understand why Moses' followers were murmuring and complaining! And let's remember, for the sake of our reflection, that this story is about OUR deserts and wildernesses, all of them, literally and figuratively. The personal and social areas where we have gone dry, dry, dry.

Most of us have seen water flowing from a rock. I've heard very plausible scientific explanations for this Exodus story (you know how it goes): the rock had many small cracks in it, and the surface tension within the layers held the water until the system of cracks and surfaces was utterly saturated—and then stayed that way. You know, a condition of homeostasis, or "balance," until a new factor such as an outside impact on the system would cause the surface tension to break, and then water would flow out. But when we reflect upon biblical stories, the question is not "How could that have happened?", or "How can we explain away the miracle?" Our question is, "What's the message?"

One thing I notice about this story is that the answer to their problem was not far away. Their need was water, and the water was available to them in a nearby rock. And so for us.

Stories about the flood and Noah's ark in Genesis, and the covenant of the rainbow in Genesis 9 provide us with meaningful connections between the practical and the symbolic dimensions of water. The rainbow tells us of God's love and commitment for us, despite our stubbornness.

The story of creation that we read in the first chapter of Genesis shows God joyfully weaving together the threads of God's imagination into the complex but beautiful fabric of a living, breathing planet!

The Bible shows us each phase of this creative process not as a science textbook, but as a hymn of celebration and praise, acknowledging the beauty and grace of God's handiwork. Water has become central in the celebration.

In the sacrament of baptism, which represents far more than repentance and new life, water speaks of our belonging: belonging to God, to each other as a faith community, and to our precious earth home. Let us open our thinking to encompass all of creation.

My experience with Pacific islanders has helped to teach me to love and appreciate and be concerned about the well-being of the ocean. I've met islanders who have never left their small island. They have been born and raised with the constant sound of the ocean on the coral reef. They have *never* experienced the *absence* of the heartbeat sound of the ocean!

But even the people of the desert, like the Hopi of our southwest, and the Kalahari desert people of southern Africa teach us the precious nature of water and how important it is to us. In their own way, they've learned how to tap the rock.

In water do we see the unique way in which human beings and nature belong together, in both salvation and healing, but even in tragedy! Let us confess the bad things we do to our water! The story of toxic wastes and how they leak into water is one part of our history as an uncaring, rebellious people. We read that toxic wastes are now being shipped like unwelcome relatives from site to site, state to state, country to country, nobody wanting them, and everyone trying to avoid the reality that they simply will not go away. There is no "away."

Some say that all of the major indicators concerning our water-based environment are headed in the *wrong* direction. Yet we know that healing is possible. Dead rivers *can* come back to life, as shown by experience, just as dead people—that is, people who have at points in their lives completely lost hope, can come to new life.

We are "Easter People." That means, among other things, that in the cycle of seasons, in the cycle of life and death, in the oases found in the desert, in the waters that flow from the cleft of the rock, we continually see the new stages of life springing forth. All creation illustrates the principle of renewal and the redemption of life, and we may participate in it!

Among Jesus' last words were, "I thirst." In a rather different sense, *we* are a thirsty people, personally and as a society. It is in a profound sense that we're thirsty, and our thirsts *drive* us. We also find ourselves in a wilderness, and we seem to be inclined to test God.

Our nation is certainly in a wilderness stage, and the answer is not to sit around arguing and blaming and complaining and waiting for others to solve the problems. We should try to be fair-minded, constructively critical, and willing to enter into serious forms of participation and cooperation. It's not enough to fly American flags on the 4th of July. If we really love our country, we'll participate in its change.

I think our church is in a wilderness stage. But there's water to be found, right here amongst the rocks! If we're motivated to find it, we'll discover that we're on the way to becoming a new people, and a new church, not like anything that we've been in the past.

We'll discover that we won't have to murmur and complain, "Is the Lord among us, or not?" We'll be tapping the rock!

21

QUENCHING THIRST: JESUS AT THE WELL

Lent 3, Year A
John 4:5-30

"Jesus said to her, 'Everyone who drinks of this water
will be thirsty again, but those who drink of the water
that I will give them will never be thirsty.'"

John 4:13b-14a

Our lectionary texts give us many opportunities to think
about water, and each one of us will have favorite images of
water: bubbling brooks, misting waterfalls, crystal clear lakes,
the ever-restless ocean, blackened skies with the coming of a
storm, dewdrops on a spider web, a cool, still spring; an ever-
flowing artesian well, flowing without a pump. Clean,
refreshing, life-giving water.

Quiet water like a mirror. Bubbling water in a hot mineral
spring. Waters that heal. A raging storm that puts the lights
out.

Jesus was passing through Samaria on the way to Sycchar.
He stopped at Jacob's well, which is still there. It's about an
hour's drive north of Jerusalem, which may seem a short
distance, but it's a long hike. Actually, he was taking a short-

cut—a pious Jew going to Galilee would probably have looped around to the east, to avoid contact with Samaritans.

Jesus and his disciples were TIRED. We know TIRED. When we're bone tired and think no one understands, remember that *Jesus knew tired.* They had been walking for hours.

Have you ever been thirsty? I mean really thirsty!? When in your entire life were you the most thirsty? Was there a time when you were so thirsty that you can still remember? I can.

One of the problems in the tropics is that even though there may be water all around you, often you can't drink it! Ocean, too salty. Rivers, not safe to drink. Or the dry season when there was little rain. When we hiked in the rain forest and were thirsty, sometimes we cut segments of rataan and let the water strizzle into our mouths. I remember being so thirsty once on a long trek in Mindanao that I resorted to drinking untreated water from a river. It looked clear and clean, but it was badly contaminated with invisible organisms, and within hours I was so sick that I thought I was going to die, and I wanted to die! THIRSTY. Jesus knew thirsty.

I remember fondly the wells in the remote villages, especially early in the morning and late in the afternoon, with women and children there mainly, sometimes discreetly bathing inside what we called "malongs", the piece of cloth sewed in a loop. Lynn and Denise always had "malongs." Sometimes the people would wash their clothes at the well, and sometimes they just stood in line to fill their containers to take home. Very often they would carry the water gracefully on their heads, which always impressed me, and helped to explain why they could walk so gracefully with or without a load on their heads. The well was an important place. Jesus, in going to the well, was going to "where it's at." *(Are we where it's at?)*

I remember participating in the digging of several wells, including some deep pit wells where we took turns going down deep into the ground. The well was almost always at the center of the life of a village. It occurs to me now that the *digging* of a well was a strong community act, and that descending into the narrow shaft dug into the earth involved risk, the taking of turns, and a high level of trust. To village people wells mean community, trust, sharing.

By the way, one of the most important uses of our gifts for the One Great Hour of Sharing is for the development of water resources. I remember the sharing involved in the development of a well, with the people doing the work, and our gifts of money providing a good hand pump and cement for a cap, to keep the well clean. Sharing.

Part of the spiritual challenge related to water concerns our stewardship of the water of the earth. Of all life forms on the watery surface of the earth, we human beings have been the least willing to preserve and protect the supplies of water upon which we depend. If spirituality is "connectedness," then this stewardship is a part of our spiritual life.

So water is marvelous, in and of itself. But Jesus was speaking of something even more profound and marvelous! His actions at the well clue us in to that. The woman at the well was someone considered to be unacceptable, someone to be avoided. Yet Jesus extended love and acceptance, taking her so seriously that he reveals clearly for the first time that he is the Messiah. Jesus turns her into the first missionary!

We note how Jesus again tries to take our spirituality to a deeper level, and to shake us out of our spiritual "dryness." A "faith-stretcher" for Lent!

This story took place in the middle of the day—why did the Samaritan woman come then? Was she behind in her work? Was she trying to avoid the crowd? If so, why?

Jesus repeatedly broke through custom, reaching out in simple practical situations to the sick and outcast persons of his day; breaking ritualistic barriers between clean and unclean; disregarding barriers of race and religion, and, here, doing the unthinkable for a pious rabbi: he engaged in public conversation with a woman stranger, who it turns out was from a group that the Jews looked down upon. Not only that, she had a questionable reputation! Imagine: Woman. Stranger. Samaritan. Reputation. Four big "no-no's" right there!

If Jesus had been worried about gossip, and possible charges of ministerial misconduct, he was going about this all wrong! So Jesus models an attitude of compassion and fairness toward excluded persons.

The woman at the well was a woman of the earth, an ordinary person, caught up in the daily life cycles of carrying water, washing clothes, loving, grieving, marrying, divorcing. She is US. Jesus took her seriously, and treated her as a real person.

He immediately took the conversation to a more serious level. At first she tries to avoid this serious talk—we note that she shifts the conversations by taking up a common traditional religious question, that of differences between the Jews and the Samaritans: "You're a Jew—and we're Samaritans. You say this—and we say that." She is *we*, skirting the real issue. But Jesus doesn't take the bait, and he steers the conversation back to real life.

She was taken aback by his reference to "living water." Apparently she seems to think that Jesus knows about what some people call a "sweet spot" in the well, or a place where the water seems better, perhaps closer to the underground spring. A special place to direct her bucket. But that's not what Jesus meant.

How did Jesus know about her five previous husbands, and about her current live-in male companion? We don't know from this story how he knew, but we're reminded that Jesus was special. Was he in tune with the gossip? Was he a "psychic?" Or was he just extra sensitive? How he knew is never made clear in this passage by our "story-teller," John, and it was not an issue.

John shows Jesus as revealing himself to her as The Messiah, the one the Jews had been waiting for. Apparently this is one of the first times that he had ever been so clear about it. And John's story shows the Samaritan woman first skeptical, but then moving toward belief. Was she the first missionary, without even knowing it? She went back into the city, and told many people, many of whom went back to see Jesus with their own eyes! And the Bible says, "Many Samaritans from that city believed in Jesus because of the woman's testimony."

We never hear about what happened to her, but we do hear the results of what she did! This is one of the interesting passages that tell us how women were the first at the critical moments in the life of Jesus: the first to know of Jesus' birth; the first to know he was the Messiah; the first to know of his resurrection.

Through this story Jesus takes us to deeper levels of understanding. He tries to shake us out of our spiritual dryness. In the Bible, consistently, thirst symbolizes *need*, and the living water symbolizes God's answer.

This is for us. This is for Lent. Are there thirsty ones among us?

In the words of John: Come to him all ye who thirst, and you will be satisfied.

22

FLEEING JERUSALEM

Lent 3, Year C
I Corinthians 10:1-13; Luke 13:1-9

"No testing has overtaken you that is not common to everyone. God is faithful, and he will not let you be tested beyond your strength, but with the testing he will also provide the way out so that you may be able to endure it."

I Corinthians 10:13

Preachers are given the unpopular task of pointing out the "underside" of the Good News. Lent is the season when we are required to recognize that Jesus moves faithfully, relentlessly, toward the dark hours of Jerusalem. The Good News of Easter awaits us, but it awaits us on the other side of the cross.

The message of Jesus facing Jerusalem is not narrow and otherworldly. It *is* about both the Jesus of history and of eternity, and it's meant for us. "Face reality." "Bite the bullet." Admit to your problems, and accept life's irrefutable physical and moral laws as you can best understand them. Face up to your responsibilities—for your own life, for the special people in your life, for your community. Strengthen your loyalty. Commit! Face the facts, and dance with the music! Daughter Denise recently shared with me the line: "Women are from Venus. Men are from Mars. Deal with it!"

A strong thread of discomfort and judgment will haunt us during Lent. Luke reminds us of Jesus' announcement that though the gardener is very patient, unless the tree bears fruit, he will cut it down. The story of the fig tree is dramatic, but we notice, gratefully, how the tree is given another year. The grace part and the judgment part are kept together in balance. Both texts assert that God is not simply God of our ancestors, but God of our here-and-now. Not just "God-Smiley-Face," but "All-Powerful-God-of-Justice-and-Truth."

We're told that even though we continually receive God's grace, we're still in danger of falling. The journey goes on. Those who enjoy special privilege are warned. Those who write checks on that wonderful current account in the sky thinking that they can bounce them with God right on through eternity, are setting themselves up for serious disappointment!

Our passage for today says that God's judgment is loving and fair, but it is sure. We are forewarned, warned that we must not get so comfortable and lazy in our trust of God's goodness that we think that our responsibility has ended and we can just relax. The empty tomb is on the other side of Jerusalem.

Paul admonishes us to take heed lest we stumble and fall in the arrogant notion that we no longer need God, no longer need to take responsibility. When we take God for granted, we do so at our own risk, for God is the One who will not be manipulated. And if we will not listen, God has excellent ways of getting our attention! God disciplines us, like a good parent, and the texts remind us that God is truly caring and faithful. "God will not let you be tested beyond your strength." *(I Cor. 10:13)*

Lent means much more than giving up meat for a few weeks. It's the traditional season of penance and discipline for committed, loyal people living under a covenant. The word discipline makes some of us shiver, as we recall a stern principal or the solemn words of father or mother. Paul presents another image of discipline: spiritual discipline as a way to well-being, wholeness, health, and freedom. He says in Hebrews 12:11-13:

> "Discipline always seems painful rather than pleasant at the time, but later it yields the peaceful fruit of righteousness to those who have been trained by it. Therefore lift your drooping hands and strengthen your weak knees, and make straight paths for your feet, so that what is lame may not be put out of joint, but rather be healed."

This journey-principle applies to a whole range of personal and societal desires and goals—the "if/then"s:

> "You want friends?" Then be a good friend! But it will cost you.
> "You want to feel comfortable and good, and to avoid sickness?" Then take care of your body! Watch your diet! Get your exercise! Everyone can exercise, in some way.
> "You want your children to fit your fond hopes and dreams for them?" Then take care of them. But it will cost you.
> "You want to enjoy the earth, and avail of its bounty?" Then take care of the environment.
> "You want your water to be clean and safe?" Then don't foul it. But it will cost you.
> "You want clean air?" Then take heed about the problems that our oil-thirsty driving machines cause!
> "You want job security?" Then make your work valued and viable for those for whom you work. You want your employees to respect you? Then treat them with respect. Value them with fair working conditions.

"You want your democracy to work?" Then get out
and vote, even if it rains on election day. You say, "What
can I do—I'm only one small person?" (It has been
said: "If you think you're too small to do anything
effective, you've never been in bed with a mosquito!")

"You want your local church to survive and grow?"
Then don't walk away from its problems and
opportunities just because you disagree with some of
the other church members."

I recently leafed through a book entitled *The Divorce Culture*,
by Barbara Dafoe Whitehead (Knopf, 1997). The book is more
about our culture and facing the challenges of relationships
than it is about divorce. It points out that divorce in our country
tells us a great deal about ourselves. As a divorced person I say
that divorce is always a sign of some kind of failure, even though
I'm deeply grateful that I've had a second chance at marriage.

Whitehead raises the question, "How has our divorce
culture affected our entire society's attitude toward
commitment? . . . Daddies disappear; mommies find new
boyfriends. Mommy's new boyfriends leave. Grandparents go
away . . . Pets must be left behind."

Whitehead sees a movement away from the family as the
domain of the obligated and committed self towards the family
as the domain of the free and unfettered self. When we don't
get what we want, we leave. We flee from Jerusalem!

A CNN poll reported that "11% of Americans surveyed say
that the best way to 'break up' a relationship is to just stop
calling." *(1-28-00)*

Henry Louis Gates, Jr. wrote an interesting article in *THE
NEW YORKER* entitled "The End of Loyalty" *(March 9, 1998)*.
Gates, like Whitehead, points to the clear trend in our society
away from commitment and loyalty toward the individual as
free agent, with the values of community and the ethic of public
service weakened in an alarming way: "Weak ties, casual and

fleeting associations have become central to our careers, displacing the deeper and longer-term relations of old."

But, says Gates: "Weak ties don't grow stronger with proliferation: hence the unedifying spectacle of a man who, it sometimes seems, has thousands of friends and none at all."

So we resume our journey toward Jerusalem, against the currents of our culture, against our desires for personal comfort, pushing against expectations of family and friends. Because what we're really after, reconciliation with God and neighbor and the transformation of our very own selves, is found in the context of this never-easy journey.

The way becomes more clear when we commit ourselves to face up to reality, and keep moving. All that we're after is partially though abundantly present on the journey, and it awaits us in full measure on the other side.

Morobe, Papua New Guinea

23

SIGHT AND INSIGHT

Lent 4, Year A
John 9:1-41, Ephesians 5:8-14

"One thing I do know, that though I was blind, now
I see."

John 9:25b

Just outside our kitchen door, in a tall Douglas Fir on the
edge of the Green Belt, is a newly built nest of a pair of Bald
Eagles. We were able to watch them through Susan's new scope
this nesting season as they went through the mating rituals,
the laying of eggs and incubation, the hatching, and then the
nearly three months of feeding and nurturing. I had the
privilege of seeing the one surviving eaglet in its awkward but
remarkable first flights. We couldn't see it all, of course, because
much happened down inside the nest. But often these
magnificent birds with wingspans of well over six feet would
be within easy view, and if reports about their eyesight are true,
they were eyeball to eyeball with us!

From time to time I found myself wondering what it would
be like to see as well as an eagle! Our *Audubon Society Encyclopedia
of North American Birds* says that the vision of hawks, and eagles,

which are in the hawk family, is probably the keenest of any living animals. The reason is that each eye of this bird, the central area of the retina, which provides the greatest sharpness of vision, has two fovea, small depressions that serve to magnify the images, each one having a specialized function. Furthermore, the fovea of the eagles and hawks have approximately one million visual cells per square millimeter. This contrasts with the 200,000 visual cells per square millimeter in the human fovea, of which we have only one per eye, and which are less pronounced. So the eagle has at least five times as many visual cells as we, and they are set in a remarkable physical arrangement that produces enlarged images that we can only begin to imagine!

But we humans keep trying for keener vision, with our expensive binoculars and image-enhancement night scopes! Surgeons now have a remarkable new technology called "microvision." In the end, though, we stand with St. Paul as he says, "and now we see in a mirror, dimly."

Few of us are blind. On the contrary, most of us have wonderful eyes well-suited to the lives that we live. Sometimes, though, we live as though we *are* blind. How are we to see, really see? For we live our lives in a world with many dark places, and sometimes we're like blind people in a dark world, as inferred in John 9:39, looking for a black something-or-other that isn't even there—never quite sure of what it is we're looking for, and when we get a tentative glimpse, we're still anxious and fearful that we're missing something.

Our story for today is about of Jesus' encounter with an unnamed man who started life on the opposite end of the seeing spectrum from the eagle: the man born blind.

His healing was the sixth of seven signs in the Gospel of John, a stunningly crafted "little book" for teaching about Jesus and sharing matters of the faith with new converts. A handbook for baptismal instruction. I wonder if some called it "The Seven Signs." Some scholars feel that today's chapter, the ninth chapter, has a completeness in and of itself. It seems to contain all of the essentials of the giving and receiving of the Gospel as writer John understood it.

A blind man is healed. Jesus takes some clay, mixes it with his spittle (yes, that's just what the text says!), puts it on the blind man's eyes, sends him to the Pool of Siloam in Jerusalem and tells him to wash. And as he does so, he begins to see. This one who was blind from birth, who had never seen color, form, motion, sky, earth, human faces, who had never seen the sun rise or set over his neighborhood, begins to appreciate the wonder of these things. According to John, he was given sight by Jesus. The name of the pool, Siloam, is cleverly used by John in a word form that surely refers to Jesus as the "one who was sent."

But surely this verse is not just about eyesight. It is also about *insight*, about perception, awareness, understanding, discernment, new life:

> —seeing just who this Jesus really is;
> —seeing ourselves more clearly as beloved children of God and being in touch with the deeper meanings and purposes of being alive;
> —seeing the burden of old life-baggage drop away;
> —seeing the truth: moving to a more correct understanding of reality;
> —seeing and appreciating the points of view of others;
> —being able to live an insightful life despite having limited physical eyesight!

In our work with rural communities in Asia and the Pacific Islands we would strive intentionally for what was then called critical awareness, or critical consciousness. Paulo Freire called the process "conscientization." It did *not* mean to criticize everything! It meant reaching a fresh understanding of the various forces working upon the life of the community to the extent that practical, transformational action resulted.

In Luke 4:18, in his "debut" in his home synagogue, Jesus read the passage from Isaiah 61: "The Spirit of the Lord is upon me, because God has anointed me to preach good news to the poor . . . etc., etc., . . . and recovery of sight to the blind." A message of liberation: from blindness to sight; from despair to hope!

What happens in the story of the man born blind is curious. We might expect the people in the story to rejoice as he who was blind sings and dances with ecstatic joy. We'd expect the family to join in, and neighbors, too, and we'd expect those who were the pastors to open the temple doors to celebrate, and praise God for the healing!

That's what we'd expect to happen, but that's *not* what happened! So we encounter a different kind of seeing problem!

The neighbors begin to doubt whether this man who is now able to see is the same one who was blind all those years. To these skeptical folk, the man says, "I *am* the man!"

The Pharisees, keepers of the Jewish faith, denounce what Jesus has done because Jesus healed the man on the Sabbath. They have a big argument among themselves and attack Jesus as an imposter.

The parents seem to be afraid to get involved: "Yes, he's our son," and "yes, he was blind, but you'll have to ask him about all the rest—we're not talking about it any more!"

It's the blind man who wins us over with his simple faith. The Pharisees don't like dealing with him, and have him put out of the temple. But he's found again by Jesus, and he indicates that he has become a disciple of Jesus.

The blind one gains his sight, and at the same time he learns about the blindness that still affects those who supposedly see. *Sight and insight.* Who, really, is blind, and who can see? We're reminded that blindness is not just a matter of sightless eyes—it is also a problem of skeptical minds and cold hearts.

Jesus quickly puts aside the question of "who sinned and caused this man to be blind." He would not accept this as an explanation of suffering. He refuses to play the "blame game." The meaning of the healing had to be seen in a very different "light." Jesus also puts down the preoccupation with the trivial issues such as working, or healing on the Sabbath. Or trying to deny that the blind man had really been blind. Or, "How did he do it?" "What did he do?" Or, "I can explain that!" The truth about God's gift of healing is greater than human beings can fully understand.

In a figurative sense, are we not *all* born blind? If only we *could* see. We see, but often we do not perceive. In the words of Sherlock Holmes: "My dear Mr. Watson, you see, but you do not observe." If only we could receive God's gift of healing, and the radical new insight that our total well-being is far more than physical wholeness or physical health, and that we can attain wholeness even without having perfect bodies or minds—or eyes!

"Amazing grace—how sweet the sound . . . I once was lost, but now am found—was blind, but now I see."

We're not talking about a new pair of eyeglasses, or even binoculars, or a night scope, and not having the eyes of an eagle, but new eyes of faith—not just sight, but insight, and healing, for our whole selves.

24

A SPRING THAT WAITS TO BE

Lent 5, Year B
John 12:20-33

"Unless a grain of wheat falls into the earth and
dies, it remains just a single grain; but if it dies, it bears
much fruit."

John 12:24

One of the things I missed while living in the tropics was
spring. We had other very good things, but I did miss the vivid
green colors and warm, life-giving rains that challenged and
finally overcame the stark gray winters of the Midwest. I can
remember looking out of the classroom window in April, just
dying for recess to come so that we could play baseball in the
sun, and I recall the adolescent "boy" feelings that were always
more alive and pulsating in the spring!

In Luzon we did have the welcome onset of the wet season
after the dusty months of drought, with the bright green rice
seedlings flourishing in the rain. New forms of life appeared,
and the hard-working people of the land prepared for the
new life-sustaining cycle. That was like spring.

Natalie Sleeth's hymn, "Hymn of Promise," has special

appeal for me as she celebrates the life of her dying husband by affirming the reality of transformation and new life, insisting that "in the cold and snow of winter there's a spring that waits to be!" That's one I want to have sung at my own memorial service!

In our lesson from John, the seed represents a dying to self in ways that are redemptive and life-giving, not only to others, but to ourselves as well. This text brings us closer to Palm Sunday and Easter, and the themes embody important key words for the community of faith: passion, pain, death, transformation, new life. Choices. Forgiveness and grace.

The "farm boy" within me finds the seed a powerful metaphor—it's actually the embryo, of course, within the seed, and it doesn't actually die, of course, but gives way to a new life form. So what? It's in sprouting seeds, lilies bursting from bulbs, and butterflies from cocoons that we get closer to the core-meanings of the Gospel and the message of Easter!

As Jesus moves toward Jerusalem the crowd wants to offer him a crown. He brings them back to reality. In this moment pictured by gospel writer John, Jesus saw no other way than the way of the cross, and perhaps we, too, might have a growing respect for that lurking feeling that in real life the things that really matter most almost always involve risk and pain.

To go around looking for suffering is sick. It doesn't please God that there is suffering and compulsive self-sacrifice. Jesus makes it clear that while we don't go out of our way to find suffering, we clearly make choices which open up the possibility of suffering. When we choose a cause as a free and controlled choice (and not as a compulsive or addictive choice) it can be redemptive. Yes, we can say, "I *choose* to stay with this, and even in struggle my life will become centered and fulfilled!"

As Holy Friday approaches, we ask, could Jesus have taken another route? Mightn't he have put on the biggest religious extravaganza that the world had ever seen? Couldn't he have done things even greater than some of our contemporary T.V. evangelists? Jesus said "no!" to that, and he pushed the crowd back to reality. Jesus had become aware that the final phase of his journey was beginning, and it couldn't be accomplished without going to Jerusalem.

Why did John write the gospel account in this way? Because John lived in a world where Christians were being harassed and killed. It was *tough* to be a Christian. This writing was read in local churches where the followers, particularly the new converts, could put their life as Christians into the perspective of the cross.

Love causes us to do unusual things. Have you ever wondered when doing something difficult or risky in a passionate way, "*Why* am I doing This?" I remember experiences in the Philippines when I was part of a human rights investigation team listening to the stories of families suffering military abuses. At times the stories were so painful to hear that I thought my heart would break. But these families needed so desperately to tell their stories, and the world needed to hear. I felt I *had* to do it, and I *wanted* to do it, and I *chose* to do it. There was a self-conscious awareness that my passion to do it involved intense feelings unto death, for in those dangerous days of my life I had crossed the threshold of not caring about my own physical survival.

I was then, and still am reminded that my own suffering is *so* minor compared with what many in our world are going through, and compared to what Jesus went through.

The amazing thing is that we can say this about pain and *still* say with conviction that God wants us to be happy and safe, and God wants us to take care of ourselves! The deeper truth here is that we find our highest forms of joy not when we are predominantly self-absorbed, but when we're reaching out to others. Joy sprouts from relationships where there's willingness to pay love's price.

Jeremiah wrote: "I will put my law in their minds and write it on their hearts," said the Lord." *(31:33)*. This is the New Covenant—the Law written on our hearts: hearts that feel, hearts that bleed. A radical new form for the covenant between people and God! Transformation. Conversion. New Covenant. Like a seed giving way to new life. Like spring!

Grace is a key word! Justice is a really good word, too. But the idea of justice might seem scary: justice, or getting what we deserve! I'm not sure that we really want to get what we deserve! But we don't get what we deserve—we get grace!

And it's for the whole world. John tells us in verse 20 that the Greeks had come looking for Jesus. This term, "the Greeks" might well be a kind of code word for the wider world. The Greeks had heard about Jesus, and they were interested. This is quite remarkable, really. Just try to imagine it! They must have looked like foreigners, dressed differently, must have spoken with a different accent, surely must have eaten food that was different *(Gyros and Souvlaki?)*. It's remarkable and wonderful that they were interested.

One wonders if Andrew and Philip were hesitant to take them to where Jesus was, perhaps worried that this would make things very different, and even cause the end of their seemingly secure ethnic-centered life together. And they would have been right— Jesus was to make it clear that what he represented, and what he was about to do, was for the whole world.

Are you still waiting for spring (I mean that season when we go out and stir the stuff up in the yard)? Are you waiting for your own personal spring? Give it a chance!

In the words of Natalie Sleeth's hymn *(Hymn of Promise, 1986, Hope Publishing Co.)*:

> "In the bulb there is a flower, in the seed, an apple tree;
>   in cocoons, a hidden promise, butterflies will soon
>   be free! . . .
> "In the cold and snow of winter, there's a spring that
>   waits to be . . . .
> "In our death, a resurrection, at the last, a victory;
>   unrevealed until its season, something God alone
>   can see!"

25

FROM CHEERS TO JEERS

A HERO'S WELCOME

Palm Sunday, Year B
Mark 11:1-11

"Many people spread their cloaks on the road, and
others spread leafy branches that they had cut in the
fields. Then those who went ahead and those who
followed were shouting, 'Hosanna! Blessed is the one
who comes in the name of the Lord!'"

Mark 11:8-9

Today we have a glimpse of Jesus as Hero. Oh, how we
hunger for heroes! Societies are known by their heroes: sports
heroes, pop music heroes, political heroes. These are often
people who don't always fit the classical idea of hero, which
supposedly meant someone (a man or woman) of exceptional
quality and strength who wins our admiration by doing noble
deeds, especially deeds of courage.

Sometimes when heroes are slow to appear, we create our
own, and they have to be larger than life! But then when our

heroes disappoint us we shoot them down. From Cheers to jeers!

Was Jesus trying to be a hero? That was probably the last thing on his mind. We know that the crowd wanted him to be that, and he refused. His refusal made him seem more "heroic!"

Jesus had to contend with the distorted ideas and expectations of the crowd as it welcomed him as hero. Some of the most important things we know about Jesus and his message we learn from situations where Jesus challenged the worldly expectations.

The triumphal entry was an ironic event. I say that because its meaning was very different than what it seemed! One part of the irony is that it brings us a new perspective on confronting real life. From Christ's willingness to face up to the powers that be, enduring suffering and pain, came new possibilities for redemption. There's a rich theological idea here: from his passion and resurrection we discover that from our own wounds and struggles may come some of our greatest strengths and possibilities!

Holy week and Easter represent God's offer of victory over the powers of darkness, the powers of sin and selfishness, and the power of death. But the victory comes only by taking on the powers, through the cross, not by hiding from them.

There were a lot of spectators on that first Palm Sunday, but it seems clear to me that God wants participants, not spectators! Every baseball team could use a hero who plays every position perfectly, never strikes out and never makes an error. The trouble is, there's no way to make him lay down his hot dog and come down out of the stands! As Mariners fans we are spectators. In life we are participants, not spectators!

Jesus came toward the city to be hailed as the Messiah. We remember that up to then he had made his principal journey the pilgrimage into his own inner being: in the desert for forty days, and before that as a child and a young man in Nazareth for almost thirty years, years which we know almost nothing about; the nights on a mountaintop, or hidden in the bush, alone, alone with his Creator, centering his life, seeking God's will, preparing to accomplish God's purposes for his life as he sensed them.

And now, with a raggedy crowd, he's coming through the towns, toward the big city. This was a busy time of year, lots of people, young and old, rich and poor, but mostly poor, lots of rumors, lots of expectations, nobody quite sure of what was going on. And the people wanted to get a good look.

Whatever else it was, it was entertainment! The story says that the people were pushing and pulling all around him, singing and dancing, shouting and singing praises. According to the Bible, they shouted things like "Glory to God, hail to the King, Son of God, Son of David!"

For some, the old prophecies may have been tumbling around in their heads. Hadn't Zechariah prophesied that the Messiah would enter the town sitting on the colt of a donkey, and hadn't Jesus acted like a king when he had literally "sequestered" the animal he needed?

"Shout aloud, O daughter of Jerusalem! Lo, your king comes to you; triumphant and victorious is he, humble and riding on a donkey, on a colt, the foal of a donkey." (Zechariah 9:9)

So there he was, sitting on a funny little beast, surrounded by the shouts and the colors and smells, the excitement and the enthusiasm of the people of old Jerusalem.

Were any of them thinking of the "New Jerusalem," and the great new day to come, when it is said that all people would come together to be with God at the great table, where everyone would find a place in the household of God?

Some of these people might have thought these things, but probably not *that* many. It's likely that what most of the people really wanted was some kind of justice and fairness. There was considerable anger and hostility towards the Romans, and they really did think they knew what they wanted, and they thought that Jesus might get it for them.

But this, too, blinded them to the truth of who Jesus really was, and even though Jesus cared deeply about their oppression, they couldn't see beyond their own expectations and ways of doing things. Unwittingly, in the confusion, they became instrumental in bringing about the death of this one whom they welcomed as King and hero of the Jews. So the crowd might have been doing the right thing to greet Jesus as a hero, but most of them probably did it for the wrong reasons: something to ponder! THE CROWD. That's us. I've become more aware this year, studying the lectionary texts, of what a problem the crowd was for Jesus. In his healing events, in his teaching, and now in the triumphal entry. And we know about THE CROWD and Holy Friday.

Like Jesus, heroes and heroines are people who have given their lives to something bigger than themselves, in physical or in spiritual deeds. And like Jesus, we normally associate heroes with journeys, adventures, and noble deeds. Things that involve great courage, risk, sacrifice. We honor them. They help inspire us to lift our own selves up, to reach beyond our selves, to see a greater vision.

But, like the crowd, we have our own strange ideas of heroes! Every time I go to hear a fine symphony orchestra, while watching and hearing those fine musicians, I think about how our nation casts its votes for heroes. It's striking that (the few) professional athletes, movie stars, and pop culture musicians are the ones who become the billionaires, while a classical musician who has spent large sums of money on training, years in disciplined practice, and who performs to the highest of standards most often lives on a subsistence budget! It is appropriate to point out that in both groups hundreds of thousands try for fame, and only a few make it!

The hero's journey is seen in many interesting ways. According to Joseph Campbell, the great contemporary thinker, the inward journey of every person to adulthood exhibits some of the characteristics of the journey of the hero: reaching out, going through uncharted territory, and returning as a different, and hopefully, a better, person.

Motherhood, says Campbell, is a journey of the heroine— a journey beyond the known, the safe, through a land of change and danger. And when the mother comes back with the child, she has brought back something very precious.

Kathleen Noble, who wrote the book, "*Sound of the Silver Horn*, Reclaiming the heroism of modern women's lives," (Fawcett Columbine, 1994) asks, "What is the female face of the hero?" She suggests that each woman ask herself, "Am I a heroine? Am I on a quest? The quest for a full, whole, and authentic life is lifted up as a worthy quest.

A hero we like to laugh about is Don Quixote, Cervantes' *Man of La Mancha*, the brave fool who went out to encounter giants, but instead found windmills. In a strange way, my favorite heroes in today's world tend to be somewhat like Don Quixote, in that they constantly run up against a world that is unresponsive to the spirituality of the unselfish hero. We're living in a world that is quite unimpressed with the spirituality of Palm Sunday with its king riding on an ass!

Parsifal's search for the Holy Grail has become the basis of many hero stories. The ones with which we're probably most familiar are those starring Harrison Ford as Indiana Jones!

Today, on Palm Sunday, we join the great procession, and we hail Jesus as a hero. He challenges us on that, and we're forced to re-examine our expectations. Jesus leads us, and gives us new clues! And, hopefully, Jesus awakens the hero or the heroine in us!

Dancers, Tonga

26

GETTING CLEAR OF THE TOMB

Easter Vigil, Year C
Luke 24:1-12

"But on the first day of the week, at early dawn, they came to the tomb, taking the spices that they had prepared. They found the stone rolled away from the tomb, but when they went in, they did not find the body. While they were perplexed about this, suddenly two men in dazzling clothes stood beside them. The women were terrified and bowed their faces to the ground, but the men said to them, 'why do you look for the living among the dead? He is not here, but has risen.'"

Luke 24:1-5

Tombs *do* have their attractive power. I recall how as kids in junior high some of us felt drawn to the nearby cemetery on Beach Road, a pleasant park, where we would go when we were feeling adventurous, and perhaps a little naughty. I remember sitting on a rock in a little glen, and with my friends trying my first cigarette (which I think was also my last cigarette). It was there that I first kissed someone of the opposite sex my own age. That was not to be the last kiss. Yes, cemeteries do have their pull!

What we learn from Holy Week is that we can walk into the darkness knowing that the darkness can teach us to see in a new way, for darkness does not have to be the bottomless pit or the "dark night of the soul." It can be a place of growth and nurture, a place of transformation. *Provided we are willing to move on.*

One Easter morning while scanning radio stations for some nice Easter music, I happened to land on a voice saying, "This weekend many will be celebrating Easter, the celebration of what some people believe was the resurrection of Jesus from the dead." Yes, the day when Jesus "allegedly" rose from the dead. It was a reminder that as a people of faith we live in a land of skepticism and doubt!

If there's anything portrayed in the New Testament *MOST CONFIDENTLY*, it is that Jesus was crucified, and that on the third day he rose from the dead. His tomb was empty, and he appeared to some of his followers in Galilee. And ever since, since his "alleged" death, that is, the world has found him more disturbing and influential than he ever was during his brief life on this earth!

Easter is not primarily about a happy ending. It's about the marvelous mystery of new life. It's all about *life*, and it's about *all* of life! It's about forgiveness, second chances, about the possibility of healing, about the moments when hardened hearts are softened and broken hearts healed!

The butterflies we hang in our chancel area at Easter symbolize rebirth. Scientists call it metamorphosis, or changing from one state to another. Caterpillars leave their silky cocoons to become butterflies. Whatever you want to call it, it's a striking sign and example of the miracle of change and rebirth, another manifestation of the healing process embedded in creation.

Who needs it? Nearly every day we learn about hopes and cares that seem to be getting permanently buried. Marriages, careers, family ties, communities, local churches. As one guy said, "It's hard to decide whether to watch the 6:00 o'clock morning news and not be able to eat or the 11:00 o'clock evening news and not be able to sleep!"

Our hopes are assaulted when the doctor tells us that the ache or the pain is a tumor, or, suddenly, we wake up to the fact that we've been side-swiped or rear-ended. But hopes can also erode gradually, in the day-to-day pressures of surviving, paying our taxes, trying to look after ourselves. Yes, we need Easter, and not just once a year. For Christians, Sundays are "little Easters"—that's more like it—once a week!

God has chosen to work in and through the darkness to bring forth life. A seed planted in the dark soil springs forth into life. In the book of Genesis we read: "The earth was without form and void, and darkness was upon the face of the deep." And then there was light. And it was good.

We can get clear of the tombs of our anxieties and fears, and our loneliness. Easter can mean escape from the tombs of our own self-defeating behavior. Facing the facts, recognizing our denial, laying hold of the truth that makes us free!

Easter can mean getting clear of the tomb of dead-end lifestyles. Our over-reaching, over-consuming, over-borrowing, over-extending way of living is rapidly becoming a graveyard marked by crumbling monuments. Some things should be buried, now, so that we can move on. We do have this strange tendency of ours to cling to them!

Easter can mean getting clear of rigid attitudes that are empty of grace and mercy, particularly in the name of religion, or getting free of the "me, me, me," inward spiral of self-preoccupation, where we get so entangled within ourselves that we are, in effect, permanently imprisoned in a smothering, silky cocoon!

Easter calls us to get free of violent solutions—the "kick butt" mentality, where we project our hurts upon others, discounting and depreciating the very people with whom we must live. How many of our responses are anger-driven, like those that are presently tearing away at our public schools and community programs, actions which are ultimately self-defeating.

Easter is getting clear of hopelessness and uncertainty, because Easter is about hope. In an intriguing way that hope is in us, mixed with our very nature. We can see the part hope plays in the resurrection. In a fine Canadian film depicting the passion of Jesus, "Jesus of Montreal," I heard the phrase: "hope, the most mysterious and irrational of all emotions." Some say that there is no way in which we can hope alone. We do our best hoping together, with our friends, within the healing community.

Our Lord was not to be found among the dead on the morning of that first Easter, nor is he to be found there now. Easter is not just about Jesus coming back from the dead. It's also about every one of us becoming more fully alive!

Our Easters will become real when we decide to claim the promise of new life, believing that we *can* be saved from ourselves and our tombs. Easter is our name, and we'll be known not for who we have been, but for *whose* we are, and by God's grace, by what we are becoming!

27

PLAYING THE TRUMP CARD

Easter Day, Year B
John 20:1-18; I Corinthians 15:1-11

"For I handed on to you as of first importance what
I in turn had received: that Christ died for our sins in
accordance with the scriptures, and that he was buried,
and that he was raised on the third day in accordance
with the scriptures, and that he appeared to Cephas,
then to the twelve."

I Corinthians 15:3-5

GREEN THE GRASS, RIPE THE BUD,
BLUE THE SKY,
SOARS THE BUTTERFLY!
RISEN IS THE LORD!

(adapted from an ancient act of praise)

Among those things that Easter tells us is this most
important one: The final word belongs to God! That's the glory
of this day, and in that glory we find our hope.

"The Angel said to the women, 'Do not be afraid;
for I know that you seek Jesus who was crucified. He is
not here; for he has risen, as he said.'"

(*Matthew 28:5-6a, a Year B Easter vigil text*)

On Friday, he who had raised high hopes among the people had died by the most shameful means. A cross, two nails, a jeering mob and a quick thrust of a spear had ended it all. Until the third day, and the final word: "He is risen!"

Try to imagine a cool early morning scene in a garden near the desert, with a blazing sun about to burst over the horizon. If you know anything about the desert, you know how spectacular the early morning hours can be. Mary Magdalene and the other women had gone to the tomb to anoint Jesus' body. That was scary for them—there were many ancient horror stories about death and ghosts. They *were* in for a big surprise, one beyond belief!

Easter begins not with the satisfying of our curiosity as to how a dead body could begin to stir, and move, and stand up. It doesn't begin with a big rock being rolled away and a man walking out into the garden of Joseph of Arimathaea. It's not about the Shroud of Turin and whether or not those faint marks are from the "very" body of Jesus. It's not just a happy ending for the local passion play that left us puzzled and disappointed when Pilate allowed the will of the mob to send Jesus to a painful death.

Easter is "God playing the trump card," getting in the last word in the great cosmic plan! The trump card. You know, the card in card games designated to be card over all cards!

With warm, happy feelings I remember how Dad had this phenomenal ability in Contract Bridge to remember just about all of the cards that had been played in nearly every hand, and to predict where the other cards were. He quickly discerned which cards would trump if played right. I recall games when the action would go right to the wire, and how, when the decisive trump card would complete the game, we'd explode with laughter and goodwill!

By saying "last word" we're not talking about "gotcha!" Some people like to play "gotcha!" My favorite example concerns Sir Winston Churchill's long-running feud with Lady Astor. She reportedly said, "Sir, if you were my husband, I'd poison your tea!" Sir Winston replied, "Madam, if I were your husband, I'd drink it!" But we're not talking about "putdowns."

God's trump card doesn't put us down, but like the trumpets at the Grand Opera, it lifts us up! It doesn't crow, "gotcha!" It proclaims the unconditional love of the everlasting arms.

Just when the night seems the darkest, then hope breaks through. Just when it seems that death prevails, another word, a final word is proclaimed, the last card played.

In the stage drama, "The Trial of Jesus," written by John Masefield, the centurion Longinus reports to Pilate after the crucifixion of Jesus. Longinus had been the officer in charge of the execution, and after his official report, Procula, Pilate's wife, calls the centurion to come and tell her how the prisoner had died. When he had finished, she asked, "Do you think he is dead?" . . . "No, Lady, I don't." . . . "Then where is he?" asks Procula . . . . Longinus replies, "Let loose in the world, lady, where neither Roman nor Jew can stop his truth!"

It's hard for us to wrap our minds around this. We may have an inkling, but we're so limited in understanding of how God can take the worst that the world has to offer, the most brutal cruelties and most grievous acts of hatred and greed, and transform them into words and deeds of wonder and beauty!

The crucifixion is not just about Jesus, but also about real-life situations in our world of 2003 in which real persons suffer because of cruelty or ignorance or fear. The resurrection is about real-life triumph and transformation! The cross and the resurrection are the ultimate protest against things as they are, in the name of *what ought to be,* and the announcement of the ultimate and final word.

The Bible doesn't say that everyone believed and lived happily ever after. What the Bible does say is that God's plan is to be fulfilled in the fullness of God's time. An exciting part of this is that for us as persons and communities the ending is remarkably open, unresolved. Our own joy and fulfillment are very much an open question, and depend so very much upon us. Easter is a new beginning *within* a final plan.

Have you ever asked yourself, "Am I fully alive?" Easter should make us more aware that life is a precious gift from God. Every breath we take, every step we take, every beat of our heart, is a gift. We exist by a grace and providence beyond our understanding. The truth about life is that it *is* a gift, and at any given moment life may be removed from us. This is the truth about life.

Another profound truth about life is that we enjoy its fullest meaning when we receive it as a gift and then offer it back as a gift. The resurrection opens our understanding to this greater dimension of being fully alive!

Each of us during some moments sense our incompleteness, our need for growth, no matter how well we may have lived or think we may have lived. You know: that sneaking suspicion, which seems to increase with the passing of years, that we're always just beginning, just now learning for the first time, just now unlearning mistakes, just now being led to see things differently, making a fresh start, just now, wanting to play another card. And sometimes there's the temptation to feel that we've been dealt a bad hand, short in the trump suit, or that we haven't been given all our turns.

Easter is when we can stop feeling sorry for ourselves and know that we can be long in the suit of hearts, and that if we're willing to take it, we have the promise of the Easter trumpets and God's trump card!

28

LIGHTNING AND GENTLE RAIN

Easter 3, Year C
Acts 9:1-6 (7-20); John 21:15-19

Now as he was going along and approaching
Damascus, suddenly a light from heaven flashed
around him. He fell to the ground, and heard a voice
saying to him, "Saul, Saul, why do you persecute me?"
Acts 9:3-4

Have you ever wondered if you were "saved?" John Wesley
did. I have. When hearing of someone's dramatic conversion
experience, have you wondered, "What's wrong with me?" My
years of experience have brought me to the point where I'm
convinced that there are many ways in which we might
experience the process of transformation, and unlimited ways
in which God uses people in their infinite variety of gifts.

Saul of Tarsus experienced a dramatic conversion with all
of the bells and whistles. The whole thing worked because he
was surrounded by loving, accepting, healing relationships
involving persons who almost certainly did not have dramatic
conversion experiences!

During the years when I did so much traveling by plane, I

would often sit next to someone who wanted to talk. I guess I became a bit "jaded" about this. I was often dead-tired after attending to an assignment in a country where it was invariably difficult to travel, and tended not to nurture the conversations. Quite often, though, when someone would ask me, "What DO you do?," we'd get into a religious conversation. Most of these conversations were quite gratifying. A few times I encountered "Christians" who were very intentionally engaging persons in conversation to press for some sort of spiritual decision and was asked, "when was your spiritual birthday?" My answer would be that mine didn't work that way, that mine was a gradual unfolding process, and that it is still going on! I have had people comment, "Well, if you don't know when you were born again, you probably weren't!"

In fairness to these friends, I've known a number of individuals who were literally turned around in their tracks and given a whole new life. My Filipino friend and "compadre," Camilo Toledo, who passed away recently, was such a person. He always reminded me of the apostle Peter. Camilo was a great friend of my son, Jeff, as well, because of the many interesting "practical" interests that they shared in common.

He was a high-energy person who cared passionately, loved freely, but would occasionally "crash," and his story is one of ups and downs: in his life, his ministry, his marriage. As a young man fresh out of The Philippine School of Arts and Trades, he became the driver-mechanic for the Methodist Mobile Medical Clinic in northern Luzon. He was handsome, athletic, quite the ladies' man, and in his own words, "sometimes ready to pick a fight."

In the space of about a year, being with the remarkable doctor and nurses of the clinic, joining their Bible study, and then after being in a plane crash with "Spotty" Spottswood, the Methodist "flying padre," on the rugged eastern coast of northern Luzon, bonding with his new friends as they successfully made the five-day hike over the Sierra Madre mountains back to the main highway, Camilo had a dramatic conversion experience, felt called to the ministry, completed a theological degree at Union Theological Seminary of Manila, became a pastor, and later a District Superintendent. Eventually he went as a missionary to Papua New Guinea, where we were living. Always with his ups and downs. Always with passion!

My journey has been more gentle, perhaps more steady, though I've had my ups and downs, too. New birth may emerge from triumphant resurrection, and from slow, prolonged emergence as well. I confess that right through college I knew more about the Whiffenpoof song than about sheep in the Bible!

A few years ago there was a little multi-choice questionnaire going around for pastors to evaluate themselves. The choices were things like: leaps tall buildings with a single bound; leaps tall buildings with a running start; can leap short buildings if prodded; bumps into buildings; cannot recognize buildings. Another section has to do with adaptability. The choices are: walks on water; keeps head above water under stress; washes with water; drinks water; passes water. And then there's communication, in which you're to choose one of the following: talks with God; talks with angels; talks to his or/herself; argues with self; loses arguments with self!

I'm not going to try to put myself on any of these scales, and will simply have to accept that I've never been struck down by lightning, and when compared with the Good Shepherd I always come up short.

I love the book of Acts partly because of the stories of conversion, and not just that of Saul of Tarsus. Just think of Ananias and Judas, who took Paul in. That took courage! Paul had been identifying Christians and sending them off to be imprisoned and executed. Judas (not Judas Iscariot, of course!) allowed his house to be used, and Ananias helped Paul until he regained his sight. The story of Cornelius is wonderful, and the Story of Lydia. And Tabitha. And Paul's jailer, in Acts 16. Each one was different in how they responded, each one precious, playing a part of the story in which we're a part!

As we examine some of the conversion experiences in the Bible, we might ask, "saved for what?" Perhaps for a deeper awareness of life's greater dimensions; perhaps for higher purpose. For a life more concerned about what it lives *for*, rather than what it lives *on*, more concerned about what it can put in rather than take out.

There was a study done at Johns Hopkins University years ago about an inner city district of Baltimore. A professor sent his grad students into that depressed area with instructions to identify 200 adolescent youth and then, with a set of criteria, predict their success. The study was undertaken, and the disturbing prediction was that only about 5% of these youth would successfully meet the criteria.

25 years later there was a follow-up study, and, surprisingly, most of the 200 individuals were located. The astounding finding was that more than 80 percent were successful in relation to the criteria. In the conversations with these individuals, the name of a certain high school teacher kept coming up, so they interviewed her. When she was asked what she did that was special or different, she said, "Oh, nothing, really—I just loved them."

So don't be anxious if you doubt your own spiritual experience, or that you're not a "full-fledged" Christian. God has many ways of reaching us, of turning us around, or using us, of giving us fulfillment.

Simply because we raise the Easter shout does not mean we have in an instant shed all Lenten wounds. We may, in fact, feel our wounds more sharply. Only a few of us will experience lightning—most of us will have to settle for gentle rain.

The important thing is that we seek renewal day by day, week by week, helping each other, and placing ourselves firmly in a community of growth.

29

THE HOMESICK RESTAURANT

Easter 4, Year C
Acts 9:36-43; Psalm 23

"Surely goodness and mercy shall follow me all the
days of my life, and I shall dwell in the house of the
Lord forever."

Psalm 23:6, King James Version

Have you ever been homesick? Real Bad? I have. As a young
single agriculturist in the Philippines, just out of college, I had
left my family for three years, had no e-mail, and was not to
make a single phone call during that time, as it was too
expensive! My mother sent me cookies from home that took
two months by boat mail to reach me. When they arrived I had
the finest chocolate chip cookie crumbs you ever saw. During
my first year about ten of my young American friends and I
gathered on the 4th of July weekend in Baguio City in the
mountains of northern Luzon, had a Christmas tree, prepared
a Thanksgiving turkey for dinner, and shot off a few fireworks.

I'm sure that my experience of homesickness was nothing
compared to that of many servicemen from our country, from

many different countries, who were away from home a lot longer, some of them wounded and prisoners of war.

What *is* home? Is it a place where you're free to say and do anything you please, because no one will pay the slightest attention to you?

Is home just an abstract idea? There are many people in this world who literally have no home, and there are also people who want to get away from home and never go back. There are many people in this world that could not go back, even if they wanted to.

What is it that stirs us in this romantic idea called "home?" Sometimes that's hard to put our fingers on, like when we go back to our high school class reunion, excited with expectations, hoping to find something special and gratifying, only to find that it was frustrating, not what we expected. Things were no longer the same. What WERE we looking for?

Home is a very real place for us, but it's also a symbol. J.H. Payne wrote the almost too-sentimental lines,

> *"Mid pleasures and palaces though we may roam, be it ever so humble, there's no place like home . . ."*

We can read about the longing of Israel-in-exile, longing to go back home, in chapters 43 and 60 of Isaiah. The story of the "Prodigal Son" is about a "home run." We have the beloved last verse of the 23rd Psalm: "Surely goodness and mercy shall follow me all the days of my life, and I will dwell in the house of the Lord forever!"

What *is* it about this vision that we evokes yearnings? The familiar? Security? Pleasant experiences? A recipe? A simpler, "purer" time? Is it that place where people call us by our nick names? A welcome? Or, simply a familiar person? How many homes were, in fact, REALLY like that?

Probably the most important element in the idea of home, is belonging. Robert Frost said, "Home is the place where, when you have to go there, they have to take you in."

The reality about *HOME* in the year 2003 is that it's not so nice to look at, when we include in our picture the broken homes, the poverty homes, the violent homes, the homelessness, the nursing homes.

Homelessness is found right here in our midst. It involves the dearest members of our congregation, in a heartbreaking way, for reasons that we barely understand, refuse to accept, and as a nation handle exceedingly poorly. Some of our own United Methodist Congregations in this city host tent communities in their parking lots, and are being sued by their neighbors. I admire their courage and commitment.

Our text in Acts fits in well here. Dorcas *(Greek for "Gazelle")* was well known for her caring deeds. She was also known as "Tabitha." Tabitha has set a standard, a lifestyle, for the church. Her friends loved her so much, and were so distressed over her death, they sent for Peter, who it is said restored her to life through prayer. The widows who had received garments from her displayed these gifts to Peter. She has been the inspiration for countless groups of women and men in the churches engaged in social service. My mother was a member of the Dorcas society back in Waukegan, Illinois. It's inspiring to read about the faith community mentioned in Acts 2:46:

> *"Day by day, as they spent much time together in the temple, they broke bread at home and ate their food with glad and generous hearts, praising God and having the goodwill of all the people. And day by day the Lord added to their number those who were being saved."*

There's a novel by Anne Tyler, called *Dinner at the Homesick Restaurant*, (Random House, 1996) about a guy named Ezra who ran a restaurant who decided to try to fix the kind of food for which lonely people were homesick. A beautiful idea. What if this church were a "homesick restaurant," and this (our communion table) the table?

I read a review of Anne Tyler's book by Stephen Shoemaker.

It included these words:

> "What are you homesick for? Justice? Justice you can
> taste is here, not perfect, but more than ever before
> and more to come. Mercy? Mercy's here, too, like you've
> never imagined. And peace, well-being in community
> and with God and inside your own skin: It's here, too.
> All signs of the Kingdom to come, but here in part
> already . . . There's forgiveness here and welcome
> home."

Are we hungry for the food? The potluck dinners? Thank you Tongan Fellowship! Acts says that they partook of food with glad and generous hearts. Are we hungry for one another? For communion and community? Acts says that the followers were devoted to fellowship.

Recently I was talking with a young man who asked me what I think about heaven. He was wondering what heaven is like. I had to admit that I don't really know, even though I do believe in heaven. I'd like to think that we can see some of the signs of what it's like in some of the passages in the book of Acts, and right here in this church, where some real human beings who are not perfect are still able to love and trust and accept each other.

The funny thing about Anne Tyler's Homesick Restaurant is that when you look on the menu there are no prices. When I go to a restaurant and pick up the menu and the prices aren't even printed there, I get nervous!

But in The Homesick Restaurant it's on the house! Welcome home! Here is where you belong!

30

KEEPING THE LAW

Easter 5, YEAR C
Acts 11:1-18; John 13:31-35

"I give you a new commandment, that you love one
another. Just as I have loved you, you also should love
one another."

John 13:34

Laws permeate the life of human societies, and we need
them. Like which side of the road to drive on! I've had to drive
on both sides, and when starting my driving on the "other"
side of the road in the commonwealth countries where we
lived, I actually had scary dreams in which I forgot which side I
was supposed to be on!

We United Methodists have our plentiful rules. The rules
of John Wesley, which are found (for the purpose of historical
interest, I presume) in the front of our *Book of Discipline,* say,
among other things, that we are not to engage in unprofitable
conversation, nor are we to speak evil of magistrates or of
ministers! We are not to put on gold or costly apparel, and we
are to carefully avoid softness and needless self-indulgence!

Right! Fortunately, we participate in the evolution of our church rules through a basically democratic process, hopefully reflecting the mind and spirit of the Gospel and of our tradition. For some it's too slow, and for some it is too fast! In my opinion, we've slipped backwards in some areas!

An ever-changing world results in stress upon laws and traditions. All human communities must find underlying principles that make it possible to deal with the new contradictions constantly introduced in contexts of change, and missionaries are often privileged to experience law and change in unique ways. In Papua New Guinea many of the villages have taken a breathtaking leap from the Stone Age to transistors, trucks, and computers in just decades!

I saw this first-hand on one back-country trek there with my friend, Ulrich Bergmann, a Lutheran missionary from Germany. After flying into a remote patrol post by Cessna and a four-hour hike up a steep, rocky river bed with jungle on either side, we came upon Kandumin, a village. Like many traditional villages in Papua New Guinea, Kandumin was built on the crest of a hill, where it could more easily be defended. The roofs of the bamboo huts were thatched with grass. As we entered the village I could hear the mumble of people conversing, and remember the pervasive smoky smell from the cooking fires, and the happy, uninhibited children. There was a little village chapel in the center of a circle of houses. Chickens and pigs roamed freely, and I saw a little girl carrying a piglet. In this culture little girls are usually assigned a baby pig to take care of, a solemn responsibility. Most of the women were dressed scantily from the waist up. A crowd quickly formed to welcome us. The two white men were a curiosity to most of the people!

This was about as traditional as a New Guinea village could get in our time, but there were already important symbols of change: plastic containers, a transistor radio. Some of the men had wristwatches. I even saw a brassiere, worn without anything over it—ah, our alleged western modesty creeps in! We were received as brothers and friends, as Ulrich was well-known to them as "their missionary," and we were accommodated in separate small grass huts built on low platforms, huts reserved for visitors.

The next morning, while Ulrich, fluent in their language, led some study sessions for the local elders of the church, I was taken to the "bush" gardens to learn more about how they grow food, fiber, beverage and medicinal plants. While the gardens might appear scruffy and primitive to someone looking down from an airplane, they're a sophisticated, totally self-reliant farming system with some crop rotation cycles of up to 15 years. That evening, after the meal, with Ulrich's help they identified and I recorded approximately 75 economic plants that these people cultivate and sustain.

I mention the gardens because there are so many rules, including very strict divisions of work between men and women. There were clear practices that had to do with planting and harvesting. We might consider some of the rules trivial or superstitious, but they were very important to these people, and were surely rooted in ancient experience. With good humor, in Melanesian Pidgin, the men demonstrated the garden work, even the work of the women, explaining that men don't do *that*, only women!

Beyond the garden rules, I was told how every 15 years they would build a new village on a new site and burn the old one down. The reason? . . . TRADITION! This tradition was transmitted orally. It was a good tradition, gathering up the wisdom of the ages for that tribal group. They had learned over time that if they did *not* move every 15 years or so, sickness and disease increased. But their understanding of sickness was beginning to change, and so were their rules. Increasingly they were using corrugated iron sheets, and nails, so the houses were lasting longer. They were beginning to use sanitary latrines.

I'm a bit amused when looking at the book of Leviticus as to how rules covered everything for the ancient Hebrew society. It's interesting to see how many laws there are concerning the loaning and borrowing of money! Chapter 15 covers a wide range of concerns and rules related to bodily discharges! The New Guinea tribes have similar rules, and these are considered very important. Often, I'm told, these are kept secret from outsiders: rules about bowel movements, menstrual periods, giving birth, and so forth.

The traditions in the New Guinea village are changing. Sons and daughters are going away to high school and coming back with all sorts of new ideas. For good or for ill, they're eagerly becoming consumers of the amazing products from places like Japan, China and the U.S.A. Some villages closer to the main highways now have 4-wheel drive pickup trucks, many of them community-owned.

This sort of thing is happening all over the world. Susan and I visited the Yucatan peninsula a few years ago, to see some of the ruins of ancient Mayan communities. I found myself wondering if one among several major reasons for the decline of that civilization was that they had too many laws, rules, and regulations, and were unable to make critical changes and adjustments.

The early church reached a point where laws and rules put it in grave crisis. In Acts 11:1-18, we read how Peter was being criticized by some of the "apostles and brethren," particularly those of the "circumcision party," for violating Jewish ceremonial law. He effectively explained what he had done, interpreting his amazing vision of God cleansing the unclean things, opening the way for including Gentiles to be a part of the church.

Of all people, Peter, an uneducated fisherman who hadn't been beyond the hills of his own country, played a key part in emancipating the church to be a movement not just within Judaism, but for the whole world. This was rooted in an authentic experience of the mind and spirit of Jesus. Unfortunately, there are circumcision parties in the church today, whose higher loyalties are to certain rigid rules or laws rather than to the "new commandment: that you love one another *(John 13:34)*." Issues related to homosexuality bring this out very clearly.

John, in his gospel, pictures Jesus in serious engagement with the Jews, but he never denies that he himself is a Jew. The Gospel writers address the subtle problem of legalistic forms of Christianity that preach Christ but get entangled with legalisms, tradition and culture to the extent that the spirit of Christ is lost.

Jesus posed guidelines that could have been seen as more difficult than Jewish law. He said, for example, that it wasn't enough just to refrain from doing certain things—even *thinking* about them could be sinful! Against this kind of teaching, who can be righteous? We have *all* fallen short, and we are made to know by this impossibly high standard that we're fully dependent upon the grace and mercy of God! So we come to measure our actions more critically against a greater commandment, the rule of love. John helps us to see that we're called to go to deeper layers of understanding and practice.

The Ten Commandments? Yes, they are ours as well as the Jews'. They are *still* at the center of our faith tradition. Jesus said that he came not to abolish the Law, but to fulfill it. Leviticus and the detailed rules? Which ones do we follow, and which ones do we not? If we decide to bind ourselves to the fine details of Jewish Law, we've got a major task on our hands!

The Law stands. But there is a greater law. We are bound by love, which is even more demanding. Christ fulfills the Law, but the Law is no longer the means for our salvation—we are made right by God's forgiving love.

We are bound to the Law in a new way, and now have to use our minds and the guidance of God's spirit. This spirit is moving in many places and ways: through our community of friends, where we encourage and challenge one another; through our conscience, the stirring of God's spirit within us; through discernment and reflection upon the teachings of Jesus, which often "confound" the law. We have to work at it.

We'll make mistakes, and may have to back up every now and then. But there's no other way.

In John 13:34, Jesus says: "I give you a new commandment. Love one another. As I have loved you, so you also should love one another."

Keep the law. Keep it in its proper place!

31

DISCERNING THE ABIDING PRESENCE

Easter 6, Year A
John 14:15-24

"If you love me, you will keep my commandments.
And I will ask God, who will give you another Advocate,
to be with you forever. This is the spirit of truth, whom
the world cannot receive, because it neither sees nor
knows the spirit. You know the Spirit, because the Spirit
abides with you and will be in you."

John 14:15-17,
The N.T. and Psalms, An Inclusive Version,
Oxford U. Press, 1995

Have you ever heard of therapy dogs? I have a friend from
my Papua New Guinea days, Peter Hale, who has dogs of the
Keeshond breed, a breed with roots in Holland as a companion
for the people on barges. Peter's dogs have been evaluated
and certified as "therapy dogs." He has shared remarkable
stories about the healing that has taken place when his gentle,
perceptive dog, Otis, made friends with hospital patients, in
each case taking a fresh, invariably appropriate approach,
sometimes even jumping up on the bed and snuggling up close

to the patient. This has been done with the approval of hospital officials, of course, who have come to appreciate the effectiveness of these animals in sensing un-wellness and providing a form of therapeutic presence. This effectiveness has been measured scientifically through indicators like blood pressure, consciousness and ability to respond.

Otis is no longer alive, but his effectiveness was so well-recognized that a foundation was created in his name to receive gifts to be used in studies that might enhance the effectiveness of therapy animals. A related web site is found through the Cornell University College of Veterinary Medicine, on the grants and endowments link.

"Healing presence" is a fascinating concept. Today's lesson in John immediately follows last week's text about assurance: "Let not your hearts be troubled." Jesus continues his parting words of teaching and comfort to his disciples, who correctly realized that they were going to be left alone in a hostile situation. We have a number of sayings about the promise of the presence of God's spirit. In I Peter 3:13-22 (a passage listed on our calendar of readings) we read about the presence of "The Spirit" for Christians in a persecuted early church.

There's an interesting structure in this chapter of John, which some scholars call an "inclusio," or a structure with identical lines that bracket a theme. The brackets are: 14:1 and 14:27b: "Let not your hearts be troubled. And the key theme, between the brackets, is "I will not leave you alone.

Jesus says that we will be given a "counselor, or advocate." These terms are used in ways that are different from what we're used to. If we want to come closest to the Greek usage, it would be translated: "The one who comes and stands beside you." So we move from the theme of worry to one of abiding presence, a presence which displaces our anxieties and fears.

This was a welcome message then, and it is for us, too, because *we* don't have Jesus walking around with us. We have the Bible, and we have the church, and we have 2,000 years of history as a people of faith, but it's not the same. We sometimes seem to be alone, and seemingly, we're left alone to make the tough choices.

Jesus tells us that we do have God's presence as we make these choices. We are not alone. Basically, most of the time, we do not want to be alone. The words lonely and lone-some have negative connotations.

Ralph Sockman said, when speaking of courage, "The power of en*courage*ment, or the ability to cause persons to take courage, is a quality even greater than the power of courage." Surely such a power is a gift from God. We note the contrast with dis-couragement.

Other dimensions might be identified as God's abiding presence: Conscience—the spirit of truth within us. What is conscience? Through the eyes of a child: "that three-cornered thing in here that stands still when I am good; but when I am doing wrong, it spins around and the corners hurt. But if I keep on doing wrong, by and by the corners wear off, and it doesn't hurt anymore."

Just as conscience is surely a dimension of God's presence within the individual, true prophets are a presence sent by God to be the conscience of a community.

I also think of the power of insight here, that which results in those "Aha" experiences that guide us, almost like a "presence." Surely insight is also a gift from God. But even these wonderful gifts: conscience and insight, are not the whole story of God's presence.

The abiding presence is also God's way to keep us from falling into debilitating despair, or on the other hand, from becoming hopelessly self-righteous. We're not called to be like our Lord, but to be in our Lord, and our Lord in us! Without the presence of God in us, trying to follow the example of Jesus becomes a goal so unattainable that it only shames and oppresses us.

We can see that as this biblical material was being written the early church was already developing the concept of the Trinity (we can never describe God adequately, but we come closer by describing God's fundamental essences or characteristics): God as Creator, or as our Holy Parent, with a perfection of the best qualities of father and mother; God in Jesus Christ, God-with-us in the form of a human being, to live among us, to teach us, and to give God's self for us, even unto death; and God as Holy Spirit, ever-present with us, now, today.

People through the ages have spoken about "angels," and they drew pictures of them. We may laugh at this, but many of us still hang figures of angels on our Christmas trees! I've seen some wonderful collections of miniature angels! It's said that angels are always related to someone, as messengers, as "empowerers." There were times when there were terrible arguments in the church about angels. The most famous argument was when in medieval times the theologians disputed as to how many angels could dance on the head of a pin!

We still use the term, of course: Guardian Angels in New York City, the idealistic young people who go around in pairs to try to be a presence that prevents violence to people; and we still have the Hell's Angels motorcycle organization! That's something else!

A problem is brought up in this passage: "The world does not understand." Only those who believe will understand. The world insists on external proof, and has many shallow, cynical ideas about love. The world lacks "discerning sympathy." Since we're a part of this world, discernment becomes an important capacity.

The lesson returns to the connection between faith and action. Who are those who really love me? The ones who keep my commandments!

Recently when I was TV channel-flipping I came across an old film called "Havana," with Robert Redford. He played a sort of ne'er-do-well gambler with a decent streak. Late in the film he confided to a woman he'd come to love and respect, when she asked about the nasty scar on his arm, that it concealed a diamond. When asked why, he replied: "When all else is lost, I'll still have this last chance." He later gave up the diamond to save the husband of that woman, knowing full well that in so doing he would never be able to see her again. The scar remained, no longer the site of a hidden diamond, but as a symbol of a new respect for his own self.

The diamond beneath our scars is more than a last chance. It's the Abiding Presence, which makes it easier for us to make the tough choices, to be humble, and to respond to others. It motivates us for the keeping of vows and commandments, and produces in us endurance in the face of suffering.

32

HONORING HONEST SPIRITUALITY:

GENERATION X

Easter 7, Year C
Matthew 21:28-32

"What do you think? A man had two sons; he went
to the first and said, 'Son, go and work in the vineyard
today.' He answered, 'I will not'; but later he changed
his mind and went. The father went to the second and
said the same; and he answered, 'I go, sir'; but he did
not go. Which of the two did the will of his father?'"

Matthew 21:28-31a

As a young missionary I spent several days in a spiritual
retreat with Dr. E. Stanley Jones, the famous American
Methodist missionary to India. Because of his remarkable
intellect and character, E. Stanley Jones had become
acquainted with some of the most influential leaders of India.
He was sympathetic with the independence struggle of India,
and became close to Mahatma Gandhi.

Gandhi once told him that he respected, even loved, Jesus, and that he had almost become a Christian. When Dr. Jones asked him why he had not, he answered, "Because of the behavior of Christians!"

This issue is with us today. Oh, so you're a Christian? Pardon me, but your behavior is showing! The churches have experienced great losses of the sons and daughters of my (the "mature") generation. Perhaps theirs is an honest spirituality which should be honored.

The parable of the two sons is found only in Matthew. It was given in one of Jesus' encounters with the chief priests and elders. Instead of answering these critical religious authorities in a straightforward way, he finesses them by telling stories and then turning the questions back to them. Here Jesus was saying in no uncertain terms that actions speak louder than words. What people do is more important than what they say.

It was an important issue then and is especially important now. If we care about our own journey of growth, and if we want our children and grandchildren to share our faith, we'll respect the hesitancy of so many younger persons to have anything to do with the church.

Terms like "Boomers," "Slackers," "Yuppies," "Baby Busters," and "Millennial Kids" abound, and pop-sociology literature is rich in articles about a so-called "Generation X." The "church-growth" web sites devote a striking amount of attention to ministry "aimed" (an unfortunate word, but that's what is done) at the Millennial Kids.

Labels can be grossly over-simplifying, but maybe we can learn from them. Busters were generally born after 1965 and up to the early 1980's, and the youngest are just getting out of high school. The oldest are a bit over 35 years of age.

Until recent years I thought that "MK" meant "missionary kid!" We're told that the "Millennial Kids," or "MK's" are the ones born from 1983 onward. The first of the MK's are reaching legal age. M.K.'s are especially sensitive to hypocrisy. THEY SEE IT IN THE CHURCH.

I associate this generation with the coming of the so-called "post-modern" period, which is said to be characterized by a robust skepticism about science, business, government and religion, or any areas of our tradition having "grand narratives," or specializing in "absolute truths."

Defining memories include experiences like the tragic explosion of the space shuttle "Challenger." Try to tell millennial kids that our future is with science, and they will point to Bhopal, India; Chernobyl; the great Alaska oil spill; the Hanford cleanup problem; and the wonders wrought by the chain saw. They're not surprised at the proliferation of corporate scandals. Try to tell them that their future is with politicians and government, and they will laugh. For a number of good reasons, including a rash of sexual misconduct cases among priests and ministers, they have little respect for the church.

In a popular book entitled *Generations: The History of America's Future 1584 to 2069* (William Morrow & Co., 1991), Neil Howe and Williams Strauss analyze marketing approaches to this young adult age group. They noted a Generation X web site that said, "Say it—and repeat it again until the words are burned into your head: WE ARE NOT A TARGET MARKET!" (don't "aim" things at us?) One of the principal points of Howe and Strauss is that this generation is media-savvy to a fault, is cynical about marketing ploys, and will tend to reject even subtle attempts to gather them in. They predict that once marketers realize this, the American media will be barraged with messages stressing bluntness over subtlety, action over words, the physical over the cerebral. Church, take note!

A most positive thing that we might say about Generation X is that they're crying out for honest spirituality. Their music reflects this, and so do their publications, which, it is said, show a remarkable respect for Jesus. With people living longer, some of us will be challenged with the reality of living with four and even five generations, each having its own sub-culture!

Thank God that Jesus transcends generations and cultures! If he didn't, how could so many Afro-Americans be Christian—claiming the religion of their slave-owner-oppressors? How could so many social and cultural groups around the world come to love Jesus, when he was brought to them by those who came with a sword to take their land and gold, or brought a culture-bound gospel that rejected their own cultural identity? And how can a generation of children whose parents have confused them with opinionated but complacent, compartmentalized religion still look with interest at the Jesus of their parents?

Honest spirituality is not easy. One of the most powerful, humbling experiences of my missionary career was when I served as organizer and guide for a World Council of Churches team mandated to visit several atolls and islands in The Marshall Islands. We were to hear the tragic stories of the people, many of whom had been uprooted by the U.S. government from the atolls of Bikini, Rongelap, and Enewetok, the area where The United States did much of its infamous nuclear testing. In 1946 the people were told by the U.S. Military Governor of the Marshall Islands, after (by his own account) "drawing upon the Bible, comparing the Bikinians to the children of Israel whom the Lord had saved from their enemy, and told them about the bomb that men in America had made and the destruction that it had wrought upon the enemy." He told them that by "lending" their atolls they would . . . "make possible the testing of weapons that would be for the good of mankind, and to end all world wars." (Richard, Dorothy E., *US Naval administration of the Trust Territory of the Pacific Islands,* Vol. III, Washington D.C., Govt. Printing Office, 1957, p. 510)

Later (in a 1968 petition signed by a majority of the displaced islanders of Kwajalein asking to return, they said,

"We believe in peace and love, not in the display of
power to destroy mankind. If maintaining peace means
killing and destruction of the fruits of man's efforts to
build himself a better world, we desire no part of it."

They've never been able to move back to their island homes,
and according to scientific calculation based on half-lives of
the radioactive elements present, there are spots on their atolls
that will be unfit for human habitation for 100,000 years.
Dealing with this has been painful for me as an American,
because we so vigorously profess our democratic values and
our adherence to fundamental principles of human rights.

One weekend we were at Ebeye, a tiny, unbelievably
crowded island village (8,000 people at that time) in the
Kwajelein atoll, and were asked to designate a member of our
group to bring the message for the big Sunday church service
there (United Church of Christ in The Marshalls). As we met
privately, my five friends turned, practically as one, to the only
American in the group, to ME, saying, "It is *you*, Dave. The
Good News this Sunday must be heard from the mouth of a
representative of the 'oppressor'. This is how it comes with
the most clarity and integrity." Even if it's through a translator!
A very humbling experience. Honest spirituality. Not easy.

I still have the well-worn Bible that I used that day, and the
order of worship of the service, which I can't bear to remove.
It is written in Marshallese. The scripture readings listed were
from Job 28 (*"Where shall true wisdom be found?"*), and John 8:31
(*"If you continue in my word, you are truly my disciples, and you will
know the truth, and the truth will make you free."*). I wish I could
remember exactly what I said!

We minister to a generation that is doing its soul-searching
in so many ways and in so many places, exploring different
ideas and experiences that are laudable in and of themselves,
yet the question of ultimate meaning and purpose remains.

St. Francis once said, "Preach the Gospel at all times, and if
necessary, even with words!" Let us honor honest spirituality:

integrity of word and action. Love is not just a warm, cuddly feeling. Think of it as a verb! Let's be less patient with our own selves, and more patient with persons who have serious questions about the institutional churches. Ironically, they may be closer to Jesus than many of the church people who often say, "Jesus, oh Jesus!" Many of them are simply calling the church to become what it says it is.

33

GATHERING SCATTERED LEAVES IN THE WIND

Pentecost
Acts 2:1-21

"When the day of Pentecost had come, they were
all together in one place. And suddenly from heaven
there came a sound like the rush of a violent wind, and
it filled the entire house where they were sitting."
Acts 2:1-2

The astounding Pentecostal event described in Acts 2 marks
the primary moment of empowerment of a community of faith.
Building on the Jewish thanksgiving celebration of harvest and
the giving of the Old Testament, or Old Covenant, the powerful
presence of God's spirit was felt, the New Covenant confirmed,
and the Church was born! Pentecost is for us a joyous festival
of hope sponsored by a community of faith living in a very real
and resistant world.

In ancient times the Feast of Unleavened Bread opened
the grain harvest. Pentecost closed the grain harvest and
opened the fruit harvest. Some scholars say that it was an
extension of a Canaanite agricultural festival along the lines
of the beliefs in Yaweh. Pentecost became for Christians a

richly multidimensional celebration of the church. It was especially appreciated and understood by the early followers of Jesus who were Jews. The Hebrew observance had great symbolic detail. It not only celebrated the harvest, but later commemorated the anniversary of the giving of the Law on Mt. Sinai.

But Acts 2 also represents a bold attempt to explain and challenge the problem of the scatteredness of humanity and the brokenness of creation. The Pentecost experience reflects the persistent yearning of the people of faith for wholeness and unity. Acts 2 is an especially appropriate passage for observing the sacrament of Holy Communion, as people of faith gather at the Lord's Table and claim their place at the common table of creation. It's a logical extension of last week's theme of unity (Year C) and the line that we used from Jesus' prayer, "That they might all be one." *(John 17:20)*

Even in those early times people were wondering about humanity's strangely scattered state, with its enormous diversity and twisted roots. It bothered them. With their limited understandings they were trying to explain it. The story of the tower of Babel, often seen as a story about arrogance, also fits well with this theme. Like the dual stories about the creation found in Genesis 1 and 2, the stories in Genesis 10 and 11 give us two ideas to explain the bothersome reality of diversity in language, culture and race among humanity: the people of the earth—like scattered leaves.

It bothers us today, too, if we take seriously the reality of the brokenness and fragmentation of the human family. Racial and ethnic conflicts and our inability to deal with those among us who are different are still the greatest practical and spiritual challenges we face as human beings. We are like scattered leaves in the wind.

Trying to get organized in a storm can be tough work. Susan and I were in a gale-force wind once in my little Coronado 26 sailboat, and I don't want to do it again! I've also been in typhoons, which can be incredibly powerful. Some of our most important tasks take place out in the storm, and we must be willing to face the wind.

Lest we feel discouraged about wind, it's not just crazy. Wind holds up airplanes. In fulfilling the requirements for my private pilot's license I learned a lot about the wind and how you *must* have enough of it rushing around the surfaces of the wings of your plane, or you'll simply stall out and fall to the ground. No one has yet been able to "suspend" that natural law! We can be lifted to higher levels while living in the wind! We've all swept leaves *with* the wind, and the wind can help, under the right conditions.

Our tradition holds that there's a grain to the wind. We can't command it, but it is not irrational. The winds of creation are essentially friendly, and we can be in touch with them. In the book of Second Samuel, chapter 14, the wise woman of Tekoa, in speaking courageously to King David, said, "God does not take away life; instead, God devises ways so that a banished person may not remain estranged." We find life structured in such a way that there is the possibility of cleansing, healing, and renewal. Peter, Paul and Mary have made Bob Dyland's song, "Blowin' In The Wind," famous. *"The answer, my friend, is blowin' in the wind!"*

It's a constant in biblical stories and poetry that creation is good, and is meant to be "whole." The brokenness that we see around us is not the accepted, expected condition with which we are to become comfortable. Disunity, disharmony, and chaos, "chaos theory" notwithstanding, are fundamental frustrations of creation's goodness and wisdom. God's creation is filled with forgiveness, grace, and second chances.

I'll never forget standing in front of a huge pile of stones in a park in downtown Papeete, Tahiti. Though they look quite ordinary, these are very special stones, because they were gathered from all over the Pacific. After Christianity was introduced to French Polynesia, Tahitian preachers carried the Gospel to countless island communities near and far. And each time they would "sprout" a new Christian community, they'd pick up a stone, put it on their canoe, and eventually place it on the growing pile of stones in Papeete. Similar missionary efforts were mounted by Pacific islanders all over the Pacific, a great movement of outreach and ingathering.

I see other images of people gathering scattered leaves. The festive dinner after our daughter Denise's wedding was a remarkable celebration of unity in diversity. There were rich and poor, young and old, black and white, the blind and those who see. A homeless woman, Bea, was there, because of the legal work of Paul, her new husband, with homeless persons. Best of all was the joyous dance, with Denise's Afro-American college room-mates, her blind friend, Jeff and his dog, Ashby, dancing (both of them!). The Afro-American gardener was there with his wife and their little daughter, so young she could hardly walk, and she was dancing too! All dancing. A glimpse of the dance of life that was meant to be!

I see people trying to help save our children, and to protect the environment, and heal our communities, and to call our nation to account, acting as responsible participants in creation, gathering up the scales of justice and the leaves of the olive branches of peace. They are claiming and reclaiming their special gifts. You, too, have special gifts! Claim them, gather them and enjoy them! Share them.

Tony Hillerman, in his novel, *The Dark Wind*, speaks of the wind in describing the beauty of a dawn. He claims that the winds of dawn are especially life-giving, and he tells of Chee, the Navajo policeman, greeting the new day.

> *"There was no one in miles to hear him. He shouted it, greeting Dawn Boy, greeting the sun, blessing the new day . . . He opened his shirt, extracted his medicine pouch, took out a pinch of pollen and offered it to the moving air. 'In beauty it is finished,' Chee sang."*

Even as we live out our lives amidst the winds that carry the fragrance of death, even when our bodies are broken and the sun is setting, we hold forth the hope that the winds of dawn will come again soon. We'll continue gathering leaves, and will offer our pinch of pollen.

Rajshahi, Bangladesh

34

NO SINGLE NAME WILL DO

TRINITY SUNDAY, Year A
Matthew 28:16-20; II Corinthians 13:11-13

" . . . the God of love and peace will be with you.
Greet one another with a holy kiss. All the saints greet
you. The grace of the Lord Jesus Christ, the love of
God, and the communion of the Holy Spirit be with all
of you."

II Corinthians 11b-13

In Papua New Guinea names and naming are considered
to have such power that intricate customs have developed
around them. In some tribes it's thought that if you can
somehow obtain the "true" name of someone, you'll have a
certain amount of power over them. In some northern New
Guinea groups the mother gives the child a name, keeps it a
secret, and then shares it with the child at puberty. The public
name might simply be something generic, like "Second-born
Daughter," or "First-born Son."

As groups would become "Christian," children were often
given an additional name at baptism, a "Christian" name, often
one from the Bible, though not always. I remember with some

amusement how names would reflect colonial heritage. My late friend, Kingsley Gegeo, was from a village in Papua, and he took me there to meet his family and friends. I met his brothers Benson and Romney, and his cousin, McKenzie. Papua was of course, "missionized" by the British! Though these were considered "Christian names," I don't recall ever running across them in the Bible!

I was asked once to carry a message to a student at the University of Papua New Guinea when I was going for meetings in the nation's capital, Port Moresby. I was finally successful in finding him, but only after learning with the help of friends that the student had changed his name. Going off to the University had been such a big step that he decided to give himself a new name!

We share in this idea that names have power. We Christians pray in the name of Jesus Christ. Our ever-changing vocabularies incorporate all manner of new techno-speak terminology that helps us to feel that we have a measure of control! In recent years I've noticed that an increasing number of adults have been changing their names, for one reason or another

There's a deep truth in the idea that naming something gives us a certain amount of power over it. The ancient Hebrews were extremely nervous, and rightly so, about presuming to name God. Naming our "demons," however, or our "idols," can be very helpful. Name it, claim it, and tame it! In Alcoholics Anonymous participants are encouraged to say publicly, "yes, I am an alcoholic."

Walter Wink deals with naming extensively in his trilogy: *Naming the Powers* (1984), *Unmasking the Powers* (1986), and *Engaging the Powers* (1992) (all published by Fortress Press).

We can see in the way that the gospels were written, and then in St. Paul's letters, that the church was gradually enlarging its understanding of their God who had reached out to them and had never abandoned them. It has been a long time since then, and now the phrase "Father, Son, and

Holy Spirit" sounds complicated and churchy! It's important that our journey of naming goes on.

Lately, trying to use inclusive language, we say, "Creator, Christ, and Holy Spirit." A growing number of us do this because we believe that naming names *is* important, and that God our holy parent is far more than Father, but is also Mother of us all! The Bible, in both the Old and New Testaments, carries some wonderful feminine images of God. Our God, one God, so great, so complete, so complex, so capable and good, has a personhood that is impossible to encompass with just one name!

This is not an exercise in the "holy arithmetic" of the Trinity, and I don't want to make an issue about inclusive language, though I care about that, quite a lot. This is not a matter of a "God with many aliases!" It's not, God, an actor, playing many personas. It is One Holy Being, supreme, many dimensions, perfect integrity. Contrast this with our own imperfect human character: many personas, imperfectly integrated!

The early followers of Jesus found themselves describing God in terms that have resulted in what we now call the "Trinity." God, Giver of Life, who created all that is; God Who Reached Back To Us, coming into history in the person of Jesus of Nazareth to give the clearest possible message about God's intention that the whole world be rescued from its dangerous self; and God Still With Us, active in our midst, even while we sleep, stirring our consciences and perceptions and opening doors, empowering us, listening to us, giving us courage and hope from day to day, our personal God who cares! Three comprehensive natures, perfect integrity, ONE GOD!

One of the marvels of biblical faith is that new possibilities are constantly open and available to us, with new language being born. We claim this freshness through the Church. We have a God of new life, who continues to create, reveal. New wine, new wineskins, the mysterious energy of an awesome God! Dependable God, like a solid rock, ever secure, yet whose ever-caring and ever-open relationship with creation continues to unfold, as does our journey into new lands of spirituality, and new depths of understanding!

By using many names in describing God we acknowledge that we have a God who *can not be put into easy categories* and can not be out-guessed or predicted! *Dependable,* but not "capture-able."

Giving God these major names showed how the church acknowledged a *dynamic* God and its own changing understanding of God. The church needs to continue changing its understandings! It finally accepted that slavery is wrong, and that ordaining women to the priesthood is right. There are a number of growing edges in our tradition where we're actively seeking God's guidance, and where we trust that through the active, enlivening, correcting spirit of God our faith community will stay close to the will of God.

There's always more to say when it comes to describing the reality of God in our lives and in the life of the world. It helps us to know and revere God when we give God descriptive names. This the ancient Hebrews did, again and again! We do it in our hymns. "God of the sparrow, God of the whale!" A mighty fortress; a bulwark never failing; our helper amidst the flood. In his hymn, "Source and Sovereign, Rock and Cloud," Thomas Troeger uses 38 different names, and for his refrain says: "May the church at prayer recall that no single holy name but the truth behind them all is the God who we proclaim!"

Caring-and-Suffering-God, who cares about the homeless, about victims of bombing and hate crimes, and war refugees, and unemployed timber workers, and spoiled environments, and people with no health care who most need it, and schools that are broke financially, and victims of drugs and crime and AIDS. God cares and God suffers. Willingness to suffer in this sense is not a sign of weakness, but of strength.

God-of-Awesome-Intelligence! As scientists and mathematicians try to define and understand the ways of creation we find that our awe of God's intelligence is deepened.

As each new window and door is opened, ever-more remarkable vistas appear!

God-of-Relationships: even as we speak of the many names we can give God, we confess a God who knows us each one by *our* own name! A God who knows our nick names! Our God is known in relationships, and so are *we*. We are known for whom we love, and for who loves us.

Poetry helps:

> "O burning Mountain, O chosen Sun, O perfect Moon, O fathomless Well, O unattainable Height, O Clearness beyond measure, O Wisdom without end, O Mercy without limit, O Strength beyond resistance, O Crown beyond all Majesty: The humblest thing you created sings your praise"
>
> *Mechtild of Germany*

No single name will do! So we name the names, putting ourselves at peace with "The Great I Am" behind the names, claiming the promise of life in the unending birthing of names!

35

TEARS AND PERFUME

Pentecost 2, Year C
Luke 7:36-50

"She stood behind him at his feet, weeping, and
began to bathe his feet with her tears and to dry them
with her hair. Then she continued kissing his feet and
anointing them with the ointment.

Luke 7:38

It was a sensual moment, really, and we have to assume that
most of those present were embarrassed, even shocked.

According to Luke, Jesus had been invited into the home
of a pious Jew for a special dinner. The NIV translation says
"they reclined" at the table, which suggests that it was the kind
of formal occasion where the guests of honor would recline,
half laying, half sitting, on couches, where they would not only
be served food and drink, but also discuss philosophical and
theological issues.

I assume that these were the "cool," politically correct
personalities with a high degree of verbal skill (polite
description)! Luke's few words about the setting suggests
material well-being, if not affluence. It sounds like Jesus did

not have a close, friendly relationship with Simon, but that didn't prevent him from being invited. While there were invited guests, the meal was most likely a "public meal," which was apparently a common custom in that culture in those days. The house was open, and it was accepted that people would wander in and out.

Then *she* wandered in! Into this refined and proper gathering of people of prominence. It was quite a stretch for her to presume to go into this setting, but she had heard that Jesus was to be there, and she wanted to see him.

The story seems to infer that the guests knew who she was. A woman with a bad reputation. What does *that* mean? If it meant that she sold sexual favors, I wonder if she recognized any of the men there! She was probably not destitute financially, as she was carrying some perfumed oil, which was not cheap.

She didn't speak. At least Luke doesn't have her say anything. What she did, however, was louder than words. Not simply "inappropriate"—it was outrageous! She went to Jesus, this woman who was called a sinner, and Luke uses the term in such a way that many commentators seem to assume that she was a prostitute.

She touched Jesus. She wept, and with her own hair wiped the tears that had fallen on his feet. She then anointed his feet with perfumed oil, an emotional, extravagant expression of gratitude and respect. Let's not forget that in the eyes of a pious Jew this woman has ritually defiled Jesus simply by touching him.

She has gone where she should not be. She has uncovered her hair in public. She has acted on her own apart from connections of family or other male authority. Just about everything that Luke says about her daring action is presented as shameful, impure, scandalous behavior for a first-century Jewish woman. He seems to be elaborating on his reference in verse 34 to the Son of Man as "a glutton and a drunkard, a friend of tax collectors and sinners."

With this story Luke vividly illustrates the feelings of a new faith community effusively grateful for God's extravagant love in Jesus. In a similar story in Mark (14:5) it was asked, "Why was the ointment wasted in this way? . . . For it could have been sold, and the money given to the poor!" Hard to argue with that—I might have asked something like that myself, and in other contexts I can imagine Jesus asking it. I suppose that this might be asked about the extravagance of soaring cathedrals, mighty pipe organs, air conditioning, and cushions in the pews! But Jesus said, "She has shown great love." In the Matthew version Jesus says, "She has performed a good service for me," and, raising the stakes, "She has anointed my body beforehand, for its burial."

The host, Simon, responds with a kind of party line judgment, which he directs not only against the woman, but against Jesus as well. "How could she?", and "Jesus, How could you? And since you did, how could you make this crazy claim that you're a prophet? And who do you think you are to forgive sins?" The power to forgive sins is considered big league stuff, a prerogative reserved for God alone!

Luke says little more about the woman, devoting the space to Jesus' response. He tells a parable about canceled debts, and asks who will be the more grateful—the one who is forgiven much, or the one who is forgiven little?

We have to wonder: Is it harder for comfortable, "nice" people to be Jesus-people? Are those who are forgiven little (or who *think* that their sins are "little" sins) so comfortable that they can't appreciate the liberating power of the Gospel?

The experience of forgiveness is at the core of the Christian faith journey. It's the underpinning of our relationship with God through Jesus. We *are* forgiven, that we may hold fast to the relationship, that we may also forgive and love our neighbor. Knowing forgiveness with conviction becomes a grateful, freeing, energizing force.

We might hope that Simon, a man who may have felt that he'd done the right things, said the right prayers, and followed the rules, must have been shocked into a new kind of awareness when Jesus shows his accepting attitude to this emotional woman who had been breaking the rules. Is there a Simon among us?

Yes, that emotional woman. It's the passion in this story which magnifies the meaning. Over the years I've known a number of friends whose unusual passion has given them a special grace and power.

Simon had a low opinion of the woman. He probably had a low opinion of Jesus. It's possible that he even had a low opinion of himself. What Jesus did in this story added value.

Books and more books have been written about forgiveness. Why is it so hard to forgive? Why is it sometimes so hard to receive forgiveness? Can forgiveness be real when it is not received? Does forgiving require forgetting? How is forgiveness best communicated? How do we handle the real-life baggage that we carry into our experiences of forgiveness?

Our focus here must be on how we might identify with this mysterious woman, trying to understand what made her do what she did; to feel that we ourselves need forgiveness and that it *is* available; and then, to discover that we, too, have our alabaster jars filled with a priceless, aromatic essence known as gracious love.

Jesus said, "Your faith has saved you. Go in peace." But according to Luke, she never said a word. Tears and perfume have communicated what words could never say.

36

THE SOUND OF SHEER SILENCE

Pentecost 3, Year C
I Kings 19:9-14

"Now there was a great wind, so strong that it was splitting mountains and breaking rocks in pieces before the Lord, but the Lord was not in the wind; and after the wind an earthquake, but the Lord was not in the earthquake; and after the earthquake a fire, but the Lord was not in the fire; and after the fire a sound of sheer silence. When Elijah heard it, he wrapped his face in his mantle and went out and stood at the entrance of the cave. Then there came a voice to him that said, "What are you doing here, Elijah?"

I Kings 19:11b-13

The noise of our culture rises in sharp contrast with the sheer silence experienced by Elijah, a silence which turned out to be filled with meaning. We live in a society so fraught with noise that the helpful voices buried in the sounds of silence have little chance. Paul Simon expressed this concern in his well-known song, "The Sounds of Silence":

"Hello, Darkness, my old friend—I've come to talk with you again. Because a vision softly creeping—left its seeds while I was sleeping. And the vision that was planted in my brain still remains—within the sounds of silence."

"And in the naked light I saw 10,000 people, maybe more. People talking without speaking. People hearing without listening. People writing songs that voices never shared. No one dared—disturb the sounds of silence."

How *does* God speak? How does God make God's self, and God's will, known? How do we discern truth? The Psalmist anguishes with a feeling of abandonment: "O Lord, I cry to thee; in the morning my prayer comes before thee. O Lord, why do you cast me off: why do you hide your face from me?

So, how *does* God speak to us? How *do* we listen with the "ears of faith?" Or in the words of Gibran: "With the ear of our ear."

Mother Teresa of Calcutta is quoted as having said:

". . . God cannot be found in noise and restlessness. God is the friend of silence . . . . The more we receive in silent prayer, the more we can give in our active life. We need silence to be able to touch souls. The essential thing is not what we say, but what God says to us and through us."

(Quoted in James Roose-Evans, The Inner Stage, Cambridge, Mass.: Cowley Publications, 1990)

Does God speak in voices? Some feel they have heard such. In "leadings"? I felt led to become a minister. No voice, but a persistent awareness that I was being called.

Does God speak through "open doors?" New opportunities? New interests, enthusiasms? New energies that appear for some cause, or some new purpose? Or through a new perception or insight in the quietness of our inner space? Clearly, there are many ways, and sometimes we hear wrong.

Elijah's experience of God takes place in a cave. God was both outside and inside, all around, but the experience was in a cave. In classic psychoanalysis, caves or caverns typically symbolize the hidden depths of the unconscious mind. Elijah's flight to that dark crevice on Mt. Horeb and his unique encounter there with God is an image that might be more useful to us today than in any other historical time.

Never before have we as human beings been so constantly bombarded by the insatiable demands of a noisy world. The concept of "privacy" is under constant assault and stress. The idea of an inner self shielded from public assault is rapidly disappearing, as any highly public figure might attest. Even when we retreat to our homes, the world comes along—by phone and modem, by T.V. cable and radio waves. What, now, is the last safe retreat of our personal private selves?

Is it the cavern of our private innermost thoughts, and beyond that, our unconscious mind? Perhaps even here we're attacked, as "Super-ego," our so-called moral watchdog, keeps "Id," source of our animal drives and our conscious self in line by cracking the whip of guilt feelings and sense of inadequacy. Usually resting, it sometimes flares up, shaming us into doing things we feel we ought to do, knowing our insecurities and fears. Deep within, most of us seem to have these voices which have haunted us since childhood, accusing us of being stupid, no-good, ugly, worthless, a bad parent, a bad child, a failure. Even when we're alone, we must struggle for silence and psychic space.

It's striking how many of these inner feelings are a lot like ancient portrayals of demons, and how they're so often presented in stories and pictures as powerful, large, shrewd and cunning. Angels, when we see them at all, are usually portrayed as happy and harmless, ineffectual, sometimes even bumbling. Our prevailing culture tends to see angels as amusing companions, but not very useful when it comes to getting the job done. I'd like to re-think this image!

The I Kings passage about Elijah doesn't say that God can *not* speak in earthquake, wind, and fire. It simply says that God *can* speak in the gentle stillness. Maybe we can say that God doesn't need to shout. We shout. The "demons" shout, and they tend to deafen us.

LISTENING is the form the Bible gives to our basic quest to be authentic human beings. This is the journey toward fullness of life, happiness, meaning. By listening deeply to the messages in special moments, we tap into the very Source of meaning, the mind of God.

One of the biggest mistakes that people make about prayer is assuming that it's simply talking to God, disregarding or discounting the idea of *listening* to God. The listening part is that which most needs to be developed in our culture, and it requires the most discipline. The Quakers know this, and there's a hunger being shown in our own time for the idea, as seen in the strong movement of people to various forms of spiritual discipline, such as transcendental meditation. In recent years, I personally have made it a point to have spiritual retreats at a Trappist abbey in Oregon. My goal has been to have experiences of active, responsive listening in a context of quietness.

The idea of spiritual retreat does not mean separation from the world, its needs, its issues. Jesus withdrew to the wilderness before squarely facing his journey to Jerusalem. When Mahatma Gandhi was wrestling with the question of how best to respond to the British tax on salt, and the law forbidding Indians from taking the free and plentiful salt lying on every beach, he went into "retreat" for weeks, and after many days of quiet reflection and prayer, the strategic answer finally came. He set off across India, walking toward the ocean to take some salt. News of his pilgrimage spread, and his journey was widely reported. After many days, he finally reached the shore, stooped down, picked up a single handful of salt. Millions followed him, and the British empire began to crumble!

Paul Simon continues:

> "And the people bowed and prayed to the neon god they'd made. And the sign flashed out its warning in the words that it was forming. And the sign said 'The words of the prophets are written on subway walls . . . and tenement halls . . . and whisper in the sounds of silence.'"

When Elijah cried, O, Lord, "I, only I, am left!", the interior word, wrapped in soothing silence, gave him the courage to creep back outside of his cave sanctuary and once again take up his journey with his people.

Our text affirms that silence does not mean the absence of God—God is present in and through the silence. But we have to learn to listen.

Slow down and put your spirit at rest.

"Be still before God, and wait patiently for God." (*Psalm 37:7, The N.T. and Psalms, Inclusive Version, Oxford U. Press, 1995*)

Cairo, Egypt

37

THE FIXIT PEOPLE

Pentecost 4, Year A
Matthew 9:35-10:8; Romans 5:6-11

"Therefore, since we are justified by faith, we have
peace with God through our Lord Jesus Christ."
(Romans 5:1)

I like fixing things and have come to think of myself as a
sort of "Mr. Fixit." When our children were little they would
watch me fix something, and they'd chant, "My daddy can fix
anything!" Later on they discovered that he could *not* fix
"anything." They still had a lot to learn about their father.

We Americans are a problem-solving people, and quite
proud of it! Give us a problem to chew on and we'll spend
hours locked in combat with it ! Fix, prescribe, advise. Back
seat drivers, armchair coaches, second-guessers. We missionaries
are famous for our pet projects and solutions, which we would
carry to each new place. An acquaintance, a Catholic priest in
Micronesia, started a marching band for high school kids in
every town that he served, appealing to friends and supporters
in the States for old musical instruments. Others would start
libraries with old books. An agricultural missionary who was

good with poultry seemed to think that everybody needed a poultry enterprise! My weakness, too, was "projects." I always had to have projects. In my ministry in rural community development I continually encountered this powerful propensity of leaders to prescribe and fix. I found it in myself, and in others.

Here's an interesting prescription: while evaluating church-supported projects in Bangladesh, I was told about an American tourist, a church person, who was deeply touched by the poverty and struggle of the people there.

He was in Dhaka, and had hired a rickshaw for the day so that he could go exploring. The rickshaw driver knew a little English, so they chatted, and as the day went on, the tourist was appalled to learn that at the end of the day the driver would have to give at least 75% of his meager earnings to the owner of the cart, sometimes more, because there was a minimum charge. Further questioning revealed that the carts were very inexpensive in relation to the U.S. dollar, only about US$35., so the tourist insisted that they go to the neighborhood where the carts were made. They went, and the tourist paid for a cart to be fabricated for the driver. He left Bangladesh feeling great satisfaction in the idea that he had "liberated" one human being from an oppressive relationship.

What he didn't know was that the very next day the driver hired another man, who then returned to *him* 75% of *his* earnings! Our tourist friend had not taken into account the universal "quality" of human nature: fierce self-interest! A workers' cooperative in Dhaka which owned an increasing number of carts had already proven to be a much more realistic and effective approach for sharing profits, mainly because of a practical system of accountability. This was crucial, because of what we are like as human beings, and I'm talking about *Sin*!

Today's readings are a look at different ways of dealing with challenges. Jesus chooses and equips his disciples in Matthew, and St. Paul, in Romans 5 explains to those around him just how God has made it possible for our relationship with God to be made right. It should be easy enough for us to appreciate God's project: that God has made a way to fix something that is broken—that is, our relationship with God, and our relationship with our neighbor.

We're smart at solving problems, but there's a problem: we're not "good" enough. The good news is that we have the most clever, creative, economically dynamic, energy-driven society in the world. People are literally dying to come here. The bad news is our self-centered individualism and enormous dividedness and alienation. We have one of the lowest voter turnouts of any democratic nation and the most persons in prison per capita. Of the so-called "developed nations" we have the one of the largest, (and growing, they tell us) gaps between rich and poor.

Hospitals and courts tell us how many families are attempting (and failing) to fix problems at home through violence. And the physical side of this is only one part. We must also recognize the shaming and psychological hurt being inflicted on children, and how it exacerbates problems. In many institutions beyond the family circle we see leaders acting with rigid authority. "You'll do it my way, because I have the power."

Increasingly, our people are trying to fix problems by taking them to court. It's good we have that recourse, but how many of the cases could be solved through mediation rather than litigation? Or we try to solve our problems through hardware— forgetting the software of reconciliation. So we use bombs and bullets. Sledge hammers for swatting flies. Or drugs. Gimme a "fix!"

I recall the years in the Philippines right after Ferdinand Marcos declared martial law, and how he ordered that the curbs be whitewashed and big fences put up along the highway from the Manila International Airport into the city so that visitors would not see some of the Philippines' worst slums. It did seem to fool some, but it didn't change the reality of the deep-seated social problems. We know what finally happened to Marcos.

Of all the things we're most clever at, denial seems to head the list, and as we approach our problems we often deceive our own selves about what the problems really are. We are fixers, so we seem to cling to the idea that we can fix *ourselves*. One of the sad things in this world is the spiritual beachcombing by those who have the vague idea that they can fix themselves. We watch them getting tossed about by every fad, caught in the inward, downward spiral of self-help, self-absorption.

While we're quite smart enough to make our gadgets work, and work well, we haven't shown our capacity to make our relationships work! No matter how hard we try, we have this deep self-centeredness that continues to do us in. If it were just a matter of smarts, we *know* enough to make this a rather wonderful world. But we're not *good* enough to overcome the deepest anxieties, fears, and self-centeredness without help. We know enough to be good parents. But we're not usually *good* enough, unless we ask for help. We *know* enough to overcome our addictions, our addictions of all kinds, but we've also discovered that it's not a just a matter of smarts, or intelligence.

Despite our flaws, and despite our past, God loves us and accepts us. The key is in our attitude—the willingness to admit to our predicament, and to receive the help. We are to confess our "problem," our weakness, our Sin, and our need for God. We are to attempt to lead a new life, and with God's help we can.

God put forward the solution by sending us Jesus, our model, our teacher, our example and friend, God in a person, who cared so much for us that even a cost of suffering and death on a cross was paid. The solution came at the right time, and was the right fix: reconciliation. For the whole world, the whole of creation.

Jesus remains our model for problem-solving: He healed the sick; comforted those who mourn; treated with compassion those who were outcasts; taught through interesting and empowering stories and parables; denounced unfairness and cast out demons; challenged abusive authority; announced the good news of God's forgiving love; and proclaimed hope for the poor in a seemingly hopeless world.

Such a simple set of answers, yet it cannot be proven to the skeptic. The solution has been distorted and manipulated by many, but it has also been grasped through faith by hundreds of millions over the course of two millennia.

How wonderful are our God-given gifts for creating tools, for analyzing, for perception, for discernment. And for responding! And yet, we depend upon God's ultimate fix.

38

REGARDING BARNS

Pentecost 5, Year C
Luke 12:13-21

"The land of a rich man produced abundantly. And
he thought to himself, 'what should I do, for I have no
place to store my crops?' Then he said, 'I will do this: I
will pull down my barns and build larger ones, and
there I will store all my grain and my goods.'"

Luke 12:16b-18

I love barns. I grew up in a dairy farming area in northern
Illinois where there are lots of them, some of them very
interesting. Little barns and big barns. Big barns with big hay
lofts, with milking systems and manure disposal systems. About
50 years ago the University of Illinois College of Agriculture
promoted a plan for round barns, with a big ramp to drive up
into the hay storage area for unloading, and then out the other
side. Below, the dairy cows faced the center, and the farmer
could throw the hay down from the loft into the center, within
easy reach for feeding the cows. And, of course, the "waste
product" was taken away through the carefully spaced doors
around the outside.

Our neighbors, the Durkin brothers, had a beautiful big barn with a soaring roof held up by huge curved, laminated trusses, and often in the spring, when most of the hay was gone, there would be a festive community barn dance in the loft sponsored by the Bonnie Brook Volunteer Fire Department. It was like dancing in a cathedral! Quite a wonder for the little boy that I was!

In that community barns were an essential part of maintaining a livelihood: a base for farming activities, and a place for storing the necessary resources. And now and then, a place to play! Not really for the purpose of storing up possessions!

I'm told that one of the fastest growing segments of the "gross national product" today is the storage business. Investors can't build these mini-storage, self-storage units fast enough! They provide safe, temperature-controlled environments in which to store the stuff for which we have run out of room at home. We Americans are building bigger barns, the storage units!

There may be nothing wrong with that, unless we develop the barn-building syndrome that afflicted the landowner described in today's text. His possessions had come to possess HIM.

The rich man needed bigger and better barns to store his riches. But let's be clear: the bounty that he had accumulated was not the result of wrongdoing. The story does not say that he had cheated anyone—in fact there is a comment that his land produced abundantly. The abundance is not the issue.

His problem was, ironically, that he had made his barns his cathedral, his ultimate source of security. The reality was that he was a mere mortal, in constant danger of losing the integrity of his own self. In Jesus' words: "What good is it for a man to gain the whole world and yet lose or forfeit his very self?" So today's lesson is about the danger of greed, the toxic deterioration caused by anxiety, as compared with the potential abundance in simple living.

Time after time in his gospel, Luke addresses the difficult subject of the burden of possessions, and we're told, basically, that to be truly rich, or "rich toward God", demands appropriate use of possessions, and a certain attitude about possessions. The rich fool apparently chose to store up the wrong valuables in the wrong place!

In this lesson someone from the crowd spoke out, asking Jesus to tell his brother to divide the inheritance with him. Why ask a rabbi? In those days, rabbis did in fact help to arbitrate issues that were matters of law. Today, in our place, pastors don't do that kind of thing, thank goodness! Beyond that, we might wonder: why ask a rabbi who had become well known by that time for condemnation of riches, for blessing the poor?

As we can see, Jesus' answer is very strong, and he even characterizes this guy as being called a "fool" by God. My mother didn't like it if I called anyone a fool. She occasionally quoted that verse in Matthew 5 that says, "He who calleth his brother a fool is in danger of hellfire!"

While thinking about this theme I realized that I know some interesting case studies about "Rich Fools."

I know families who have had big family problems over an inheritance. Family breakup over "small peanuts."

I know a man who was a bright young lawyer who seemed to have everything going for himself. He had a major job in a big organization. Then he blew it, because of his drinking problem.

I know people who seem to have every toy that you can imagine. A family with two snowmobiles, a boat with a big outboard motor, an RV, and dirt bike motorcycles. They had lots of tools. They traded in their cars often—and were deeply in debt. Both husband and wife had to work long hours and didn't have time to play with their toys!

Am I suggesting that we should not have nice things? No, of course not. I have to confess that this story is for me, above all people, because I have some very nice toys, too. We mustn't pull back from passages that make us feel uncomfortable, and my preaching is for me as well as for you!

Is planning for retirement wrong? I don't believe so, and I'm still doing it, even though I'm supposedly retired. I cannot help but remember the passage, however, that says, "where your treasure is, there will your heart be also."

It's curious what happens with so many movie stars and famous athletes. Not all, but many of them. What goes wrong? Why do people who have riches, fame, power, and beautiful children so often fall into suicidal depression? Why are they so commonly overtaken by drugs? What kinds of things happen in the brains of such people? Are *they* rich fools?

What does it take to make us happy? MORE? This is a "problem word!" More! And a related word: "Mine, mine, mine!" How much is enough? And this question is not only for us as individuals—it is aimed at any society which consumes such a large share of the earth's resources. We are judged.

If God's richness toward us never produces peace of mind in ourselves and does not result in graciousness toward others, but simply leaves us with self-reliant hoarding in ever-larger barns, then we have not yet truly connected with God.

When the gods of endless material prosperity fail, and they *do* ultimately fail, for every single one of us, we as a people of faith have the opportunity to avoid the final foolishness of this endless acquiring of things, things, things. We're called to learn to live with less while sharing more generously. We're given the opportunity to live lives of creative simplicity. The challenge is not to give away everything and to become poor. The challenge is not to hoard, but to share.

We must be cautious when trying to draw lines between wealth and happiness. It's no fun to be poor. I've never been poor, but I've lived up close to poor people. When I've asked myself, "Would the poor change places with me?" I've always come up with the same answer: "You're darn right they would!" But we mustn't infer that there's a direct link between wealth and happiness. There are both happy and troubled people amongst both rich and poor. It's a sign of spiritual maturity when we can wish people well when they are successful and sympathize with them when they fail. There would be no thrill in having everyone poor. What is it, really, that makes us happy? What is it that gives us fulfillment? Jesus tells us today that it is *not* bigger barns! It is in becoming whole persons, whole and connected and at peace. It is in putting aside the funny little mind games that we play with ourselves to justify our accumulation of things.

Actually, maybe instead of wanting too much, we're settling for too little! In the spiritual sense, are we setting our sights too low?

The good news of the Gospel is that we're free, if we'll only claim that freedom. Free from the bondage of these restless minds of ours, which seem so determined to generate anxieties and fears. Free from building more and more barns!

Shivalaya Dev't Prog., Bangladesh

39

STRANGE SACRIFICES

Pentecost 6, Year A
Genesis 22:1-14

"After these things God tested Abraham. He said
to him, Abraham! And he said, "Here I am." He said,
"Take your son, your only son Isaac, whom you love, and
go to the land of Moriah, and offer him there as a burnt
offering on one of the mountains that I shall show
you." . . . But an angel of the Lord called to him from
heaven, and said, "Abraham, Abraham!" And he said,
"Here I am." He said, "Do not lay your hand on the boy
or do anything to him; for now I know that you fear God,
since you have not withheld your son, your only son,
from me."

Genesis 22:1-2, 11-12

Today's reading from Genesis is the jolting story of
Abraham's near-sacrifice of Isaac. It's an inconceivable tale,
counter to our every understanding of the nature and
character of the God we see in Jesus. The testing of Abraham
seems extraordinarily cruel, and we rebel against it. The story

says more about the way the ancient Israelites understood God than it says about the true nature of God.

For important reasons the story is significant to Jews, but it's also important in the Islamic tradition, where it is not Isaac, but Ishmael (Abraham's other son, born of Hagar the slave), who is the potential victim. But important information about Ishmael is left out of the Hebrew story.

It's said that many synagogues have this scene of Abraham and Isaac depicted in their mosaic tile floors as symbolic of trusting in God. There's a connection between this story and the most holy of shrines in Jewish life, the Temple Mount. But this same rock is also central to Islam, sitting within the Dome of the Rock in Jerusalem and revered as the point from which Mohammad ascended into heaven. When we know the background of some of the biblical stories such as this one, it's easier for us to understand the passion involved in the struggle over who will control Jerusalem.

Beyond these few lines, the story has much more richness than we might ever think—in fact, some scholars think that this is one of the most rich and complex stories in the entire Bible.

It's clear from the beginning that the writer never meant the reader to think that God *would really* allow Isaac to be killed. We can note, for example, that Isaac carried the wood, but Abraham didn't let him carry the fire or the knife—he might have been hurt with these! And the Hebrew words used by Abraham indicate that he hoped against hope that he and Isaac would BOTH be going back home! There are other clues here that Abraham thought and hoped that God was really kidding about this sacrifice thing. But he pressed on, in "reluctant trust!"

One fascinating thing about the story is that there's another related tradition, a rather odd one, in which certain early Jewish commentators reasoned that Isaac actually was sacrificed by Abraham, but was later raised from the dead, and they base this idea on circumstances and information that are in lines found in the book of Genesis.

Christian writers developing the New Testament were quick to jump on the idea that Isaac carried the wood to the place of sacrifice, just as Jesus carried the wood cross to the place of the sacrifice.

Strange sacrifices? We're ALL against the sacrifice of children. We all abhor the abuse of children by unscrupulous people who work with children. Consensus!

But take another look! Look at the things we do to our children, compromising their future. We Christians, but also Jews and Muslims. All three peoples, the descendents of Abraham, sending their sons and daughters into war, holy war, if you will. Abraham and Isaac, Israel and Palestine; Abraham and Ishmael, Mohammad and Jihad. And for Christians, yes, the crusades, but later Ireland and Serbia, not to mention America's holy wars in the Middle East to protect its "interests." All three traditions offering their strange, vain sacrifice of their young.

But it goes beyond this. There are so many ways in which we compromise the present and the future well-being of our children. Look at how we hold out to them our destructive models of consumerism, our example in relation to alcohol and other drug consumption, how we condition them (through the modern tools for transmitting our culture, television and films and magazines) to live essentially dead-end lives. Look at how we are degrading the environment in which they, their children and grandchildren will live. Notice how we continue to cut our support for schools and important programs for children.

Conditions among many of the world's children and impoverished continue to worsen. More than 25 percent of U.S. children live in poverty, the highest rate among industrialized nations. The remarkable thing is that most of the severe problems facing the world's children are solvable.

Resources and solutions are available, but what is lacking is the moral will and political commitment to respond.

What did the Hebrew people REALLY see in this story about Abraham and Isaac? Probably the element of "reluctant trust."

We still have the "trust" problem. Helmut Thielicke (*How to believe again*) tells the story of a child who was raising a terrible cry—he had shoved his hand into an expensive Chinese vase and then couldn't pull it out again. The parents and friends tugged as hard as they could without harming the child's arm, with the poor kid howling loudly all the while. And finally, there was nothing to do except to break the beautiful, expensive vase. But then, as the broken pieces came to rest on the floor, it became only too clear why the child had been so hopelessly stuck. His little fist grasped a measly penny which he had inadvertently dropped into the vase, and which in his childish possessiveness would not let go!

Are we like that? There are some things we must be ready to let go. What are they? There are times when we must simply trust. A most important aspect of this: trusting in the "Jesus values" of forgiving love, grace and mercy, patience and kindness, truth and justice. There are times and situations when we're tempted to think that these won't work.

There are ways in which we're tested, though we don't have to assume that difficult challenges are God's will. I'm thoroughly convinced that God wills only that which is good for us. So does God test us? Why not? But tests that are not sought by God are still tests! Severe medical challenges. Professional difficulties. Economic stress. Bad accidents. None of us are free from these. In all of the testing circumstances of life we have the opportunity to maintain the integrity of our trust in the values we have grasped in the Community of Faith. And through this, trust becomes redemptive.

I'm thankful that we can say with conviction that God is not calling us to sacrifice our children, and never has. Protection of our children is a sacramental responsibility. So much for strange sacrifices!

But we *will* be tested, and can fully expect that for every test there will be a corresponding gift which will help to see us through.

40

LEARNING FROM THE SAMARITANS

Pentecost 6, Year C
Luke 10:25-37

" . . . But a Samaritan while traveling came near
him; and when he saw him, he was moved with pity. He
went to him and bandaged his wounds, having poured
oil and wine on them. Then he put him on his own
animal, brought him to an inn, and took care of him."

Luke 10:33-34

There's a 19th century "wild west" story about an old cattle
rancher who discovered that a young cowhand had been
caught in the act of rustling a cow. When the thief was dragged
before the rancher, he looked down at the frightened youth
and said, "Hang him. Nothing personal, son, I like you a lot,
you understand, but we have rules here in the West. Besides,
it will teach you a lesson."

Then one day, the old rancher died and appeared at the
Pearly gates before the divine judgment seat. As he stood there
he remembered all the mean, horrible things he had done on
Earth. He particularly recalled hanging that likeable young
cowboy, and he trembled in his boots. The Lord God of Heaven

looked down upon him in mercy and tenderness, and said, "Forgive him. It will teach him a lesson!"

Love of neighbor is a constant note in Jesus' ethical teaching, and probably the most characteristic element of his teachings. We hear it again and again in the Sermon on the Mount, where we're told to do "extreme" things like love our enemies, go the second mile, or if someone takes our coat, give our cloak, too.

There are some interesting ways of coming at the story of the Good Samaritan. A usual way of looking at it stresses the importance of our actions. Actions speak louder than words and titles and roles.

The story also illustrates that love knows no limits of race and it asks no explanations. It asks nothing in return. The one who at the given time and place I can help with my active love, that one is my neighbor, and I am his or her neighbor. Our neighbor is a very practical idea here—Our neighbor is that next person we meet, or anyone within our circle of active love, especially those who might happen to need us.

Good Samaritan stories come in all flavors. Here's one, a true story that I've heard from two different sources shared by Juan Feliciano Valera, a United Methodist pastor in Puerto Rico: A Policeman from a neighboring town was substituting for another officer on his day off. A 911 call was received. It was about a boy, two years old, who was suffocating from a button he had swallowed. The officer thought that the best way to get to the boy's home was to take the new expressway. What he didn't realize was that the exit he needed to use wasn't yet finished, and when he arrived at that point, he found that he had no way of going down to the street. He stopped at the unfinished exit ramp and paused in disbelief. Then, seemingly from nowhere a construction worker driving a bulldozer appeared. He asked the officer if he wanted to get to the street below and the officer explained his predicament. Immediately the dozer operator moved some earth, quickly preparing an emergency exit. The police officer sped away, arriving at the hospital just in time to resuscitate the dying boy. So the boy lived.

But there's more to the story. The police officer decided to return to the expressway the next day to thank the construction worker who had cleared the way for him. When he got there, the exit was closed again, but in a few moments, the operator again arrived at the scene. When the police officer started to thank the worker for his help, the worker stopped the officer and said: "It is I who want to give you thanks, because the boy you saved is my son."

Truly, creation is a seamless garment, and our neighbors truly have familiar faces! But I want to consider an additional angle this morning: *we very often learn the truth from those we depreciate or despise!*

A fascinating element in today's lesson is that Jesus explicitly calls the hero of the story "a Samaritan." But when asked who proved to be a neighbor, the disciples apparently could not bring themselves to say "the Samaritan." Instead, they said "the one who."

My reading indicates that Luke seems to have a special interest in Samaritans, and he represents Jesus' attitude to them in a more favorable light than does the tradition in Matthew. Last Sunday we saw Jesus' impatience and frustration when he was not received into a Samaritan village.

Remember why the Samaritans become important in this story: thousands of peasant-class Jews were left behind in the deportation of the Jews around 700 B.C.E. These people ended up mixing with foreigners, which resulted in what Orthodox Jews considered racial impurity. A serious socio-religious split developed, so great that the Samaritans were even rejected when they offered help to rebuild the temple in Jerusalem. Eventually the Samaritans put up their own, so they were also considered guilty of religious impurity! There were strict taboos against dealing with Samaritans.

When the disciples were asked by Jesus to name the one who proved to be the true "neighbor," they seemed to be unable to utter the word "Samaritan." They could only say, "the one who . . ."

We might ask, who in our day are the ones we cannot name because, in effect, we despise them? Is it possible that the poor, the homeless, or those who have HIV-AIDS know more about caring and sharing than we do, and that we would be most uncomfortable standing in the shadow of their kindness?

Our own attempts at funny stories tell us much about ourselves and who we think the Samaritans are! The people about whom we tell our hopeless racial or class jokes, like the "Polacks, or the so-called dumb blonds, or gay people. Our jokes often reveal just where we are!

A line from a beautiful Spanish hymn, "Cuando El Pobre," says:

> *"When the poor ones who have nothing share with strangers, when the thirsty give water unto us all, when the crippled in their weakness strengthen others, then we know that God still goes that road with us."*

I've been humbled while traveling in remote areas in the Philippines at the unreserved hospitality of the poor. It gives me a strange feeling, rich as I am, to be taking food, good food, from those who are so poor. It's a sobering learning experience. But we must be prepared to receive from as well as to give to those we think have less.

While children are not generally among those whom we despise, we may well be treating them as though they are if we think that they're to be seen and not heard.

I need to ask, "Who are *my* Samaritans? Who are the people that *I* have the most difficulty with, and how can I learn from them? Would this be Fundamentalist Christians? Right wing politicians? Atheistic humanists? I am challenged by this passage from Luke to stop and be more patient, to think through the messages, and to be more fair about my analysis.

Does this means that Democrats should be willing to learn from Republicans, and Republicans from Democrats? Now there's a radical idea! No one group has a corner on righteousness, or on immorality. We learn from one another, and we can all touch lives of others.

We need the truth, even when it comes from the so-called Samaritans. We need each other, and we need forgiveness, all of us, because there are so many Samaritans in our lives, people we look down upon in one way or another.

We're not being asked to respond to this by nursing our guilt, thinking that it's enough just to feel really "good-and-guilty." We're being asked to let our repentance take the form of getting on with our lives, being good neighbors in our actions and deeds, like the "good Samaritan," and being willing to learn from those who seem to be unlikely sources of goodness and truth!

Mindanao Musician

41

REVEALED TO CHILDREN

Pentecost 7, Year A
Matthew 11:25-30

"At that time Jesus said, 'I thank you, Father-Mother,
Lord of heaven and earth, because you have hidden
these things from the wise and the intelligent and have
revealed them to infants; yes, O God, for such was your
gracious will.'"

Matthew 11:25-26
The NT and Psalms, an Inclusive Version
Oxford U. Press, 1995

Serious seekers spend most of their lives trying to answer
the deep questions of life. For example, if the number two
pencil is the most popular pencil, then why's it still # 2? Should
vegetarians eat animal crackers? If pro is the opposite of con, is
progress the opposite of congress?

I have a dear friend whose son majored in philosophy. It
was a trying experience for the family, because for a few years
this young man questioned everything. "How do I know that I
even exist?" he would say, or "If a trees falls in the forest and
no one is there to hear it happen, is there any sound?" I suppose

you've all heard that one. And there was, of course, the usual questioning of religion. He got through this phase in fine fashion, and is a caring, mature, even wise, friend.

Today's scripture lesson is called by some scholars, "Matthew's pearl of great price." It has a ring of deep knowledge and conviction, and is like a burst of praise. It contrasts greatly with the sayings of Jesus that are pronouncements of doom on indifferent people and cities.

Philosophers can philosophize, and theologians can theologize, but we have a faith that is not hard to understand for those who are interested. Even little children can understand the truth and the way of Jesus.

"These little ones" mentioned in today's scripture passage, to whom the important things are revealed, are probably the ordinary people of the earth, the workers, the farmers, the fisherfolk, the village people, the "common" people. Jesus appreciated and respected them, and we can give thanks that it is they who seem to have such a clear access to the Christian faith. You don't have to be a great theologian to be a follower of Jesus!

Karl Barth, the German theologian who wrote wheelbarrow loads of thick books, was once asked what was the most profound theological idea with which he had ever dealt. His answer: "Jesus loves me, this I know, for the Bible tells me so!"

As I study the lectionary selections each week, I ask myself, "Where is the Gospel in this?" Today that question is very easily answered. The Good News is that every one of us has access to our loving parent God!

So, what *is* it that is hidden from the wise, and revealed to little children? I can remember when our children were small, hearing the "why" question over and over again! Why did you do that? "How come?"

Why do certain things happen? Why do bad things happen to good people? Why do the rich get richer and the poor get poorer? Why poverty? Why injustice? Are there really miracles? Are the remarkable things that happen to people of faith simply coincidence? Why are there so many different churches? Why do I have to die?

Why the earthquake in Iran? Why the mid-air collision between the two aircraft over southern Germany, resulting in many deaths?

The Old Testament has epic stories that tell about the exile of the Jewish nation to Egypt, or to Babylon—yearning to return to their home, with the plaintive questions, "why?" and "How long?"

Can we even begin to imagine the pain and confusion of the religious Jew during the days of the holocaust, with their suffering and death at the hands of people who called themselves Christians? "Why, O God?"

One of the fascinating things about us humans is this "need to know." When we "demand" to know, we find ourselves on a slippery path.

How do we deal with issues that seem to pose contradictions to our rational western, so-called "post-modern minds?" Are we really that rational? Why is it that people do not seem to learn from history?

At the core of this reflection is the problem of evil. Why did God make the world in such a way that there is wickedness, or pain?

Books that deal with the problem of evil would fill a great library, and many of them are helpful. They point to important ideas that help us to make sense of the questions.

The answer to life's most important question, "How may I find Eternal Life" (or life in all its fullness, or life truly abundant, or whatever we want to call it), is strange in its simplicity. Jesus is saying in this passage that it's so simple that even a child can understand; so amazingly simple as to confound the wise!

Life will continue to hold mystery for us. Even so, we may be sure that it makes sense to God, Ultimate-Wisdom-and-Truth.

Thinking more broadly, but still with simplicity, my sense of what our New Testament tradition tells us as a whole might be expressed in points like these:

> God does not will for us to suffer, and does not like to see us suffer.
>
> God does not seem to make it a habit to violate what we call natural laws. God, according to biblical tradition, does seem at times to intervene.
>
> We live in a world with limits.
>
> God does not turn away from suffering, and we are *not* to accept pain and injustice as inevitable.
>
> We are not to assume that our suffering means God's disapproval, or that our plenty means God's approval.

My reading of the Bible tells me that we can *not* divide our lives into compartments—religious and secular, for example, or of separate areas of science and faith. These all belong to a seamless creation. Those who try to run away from the world in order to find themselves will lose themselves in a dark, deep, self-centered cave. Those who turn away from faith will miss out on the goodness and beauty, the "intimate vastness" of mystery.

That we live in a world of powers is an idea both biblical and pragmatic. Whatever we might call them, there are dynamic forces at work in the world, and whether we call them the powers of good and evil, or the devil and his henchmen, or the principalities or powers, we must deal with them. Walter Wink tells us that we see them in the form of economics, militarism, propaganda, education, language, ideologies, rules, roles, values, the legal system, politics, sports, religion, families (*Unmasking the Powers*, Fortress Press, 1986). Perhaps all of our social reality falls under the category of the powers, these pieces of our lives, many of which seem to have their own inner energy.

Jesus is telling us that they need not have ultimate power over us! Even when bad things happen to good people, they need not be separated from God's love, and *may* turn misfortune into blessing.

God's secrets are hidden from the wise. But the truly important truths are made clear to babes.

Perhaps we should ask *what is God's "why" to us?* Many of these "whys" are questions we should be leveling at ourselves as human beings!

42

SEEDS, STONES AND THISTLES

Pentecost 8, Year A
Matthew 13:1-9

"Listen! A sower went out to sow. And as he sowed,
some seeds fell on the path, and the birds came and
ate them up. Other seeds fell on rocky ground, where
they did not have much soil . . . , Other seeds fell among
thorns, ... , other seeds fell on good soil and brought
forth grain, some a hundred fold . . . ."
Matthew 13:3b-5a, 7a, 8a

Parables were among Jesus' favorite ways of teaching a truth.
Someone has said that parables are "metaphors that enable us
to see what we don't yet have eyes to see." A lot is being made
these days about computer-generated models called "virtual
reality." Perhaps parables are also a form of "virtual reality."

This parable apparently addresses questions like, "Why does
the gospel apparently fail in our time, despite its joy and its
power?" Or, as we asked last week, "Why do bad things happen
to good people?"

The parable really does seem to be about us, the "hearers."
Think about it! It is we, the self-hardened, like the hard soil;

or even when we are like good soil, but lack depth. The message is for those of us who live divided lives, the soil of our lives cluttered with stones and thistles, thorns and dandelions. We mean well, but things get so complicated! Maintaining a commitment to the right things seems so difficult. This lesson is for a church, like this one, that is struggling to survive and grow in difficult soil.

In the end, it's a hopeful parable. It speaks of the seeds falling on the good ground and bearing fruit 30, 40, even 100 fold (actually that's not uncommon for some species of plants, so we shouldn't think of this as a miraculous number)!

Matthew's 13th chapter is particularly rich in meanings! It contains 8 parables and two parable interpretations! There are different kinds of parables, of course, including stories drawn from life, true stories or fictitious stories to illustrate a point (usually one point), or "example" stories, brief similes, or an occasional allegory. This one is called a "true parable" because it's told to illustrate one point, and is drawn from observations of everyday life. "You see, it's like this. It's like . . . : (a sower, or a woman baking bread, a torn garment, a lost sheep, a shepherd, a woman searching for a lost coin, or a fisherman hauling in his nets.)

I suppose Jesus taught this way because he wanted the truth to be made clear. We all love stories; we all build on what we already know. In verses 14 through 17, which were not a part of our reading this morning, Jesus quotes from Isaiah, noting that: "This people's heart has grown dull, and their ears are hard of hearing, and they have shut their eyes"

And then Jesus says,—"if only they would look with their eyes and listen with their ears, and understand with their heart, and turn"—"I would heal them". The parables are presented to make truth known, not to hide it, despite what we might think of verse 11 in chapter 13. From the very beginning, the church has insisted that being a follower of Jesus does not require knowledge of secrets or special knowledge.

Trying to translate metaphors into other languages, however, can be difficult, inadequate, and even inappropriate. One time in Mindanao, I was present for a sermon delivered by a guest pastor from the States, done through a translator. He preached on The "ships in God's Navy: Discipleship, stewardship, fellowship, friendship (he didn't mention "receivership?")!!

Direct translations don't work well in most cases. Try Hotdog, or 7-up! (in Ilocano these two drew a great laugh from our Filipino friends!)

I love the use of garden imagery, partly because you can't take the farm out of the boy, and because I love my garden, but also because I believe that garden images most accurately describe the earth as is was intended to be, and because they are quite universal.

I have some special images of the sowing of seeds in the so-called "less-developed world," where people work very hard to try to ensure a little more security for their families by planting seeds—on any little available spot, even if they don't own it. Often they don't know if they'll be pushed from their land, or find it impossible to get to their gardens or fields because of war or other violence. I can see in my mind the little children helping to plant, many times with nothing but a pointed stick to make a hole, and then pressing the seed in with their calloused little bare feet. And when the seed bears fruit they are thankful.

There's a hymn in our old hymnal called "We Plow the Fields and Scatter" that's an obvious reference to this passage, and many of you have heard the Godspell version, entitled "God's Good Gifts": "We plow the fields and scatter the good seed on the land, but it is fed and watered by God's almighty hand."

I think of sayings like "sowing his wild oats," for someone living a fast life when they're young, or, "sowing the seeds of our discontent". And there's something meaningful about a plant growing under very difficult conditions! Do you remember the famous book and movie: "A Tree grows in Brooklyn?" Remember how appealing was that tree growing through a hole in the sidewalk?!

In verses 18-23 of this chapter we see an interpretation which was probably added later, a sort of repetition of the parable, with the focus on the hearers of the word, or whether or not we are good soil for the word of truth. This is one of the few places where the gospel-writer has Jesus saying, "Now here's what I meant:"

We're reminded that life is filled with examples of sowing and nurturing seeds: sowing, dealing with the rocky soils, the bare spots, the sour areas, thin soils, the stones, the thistles.

I can't help but think of how various kinds of social and political conditions become the "soil" for religious experience. Notice how economic insecurity and other kinds of fears can result in a powerful feeling of need on the part of some to have authoritarian leaders, dogmatic pronouncements, black and white answers, and often, to have a clearly defined enemy!

This can be such a powerful phenomenon that even the seeds of a gospel of gracious love can come out looking very much like other forms of rigid, dogmatic religion. All that I know about Jesus tells me that he wouldn't like that. We might wonder what were the stones and the thistles that have caused the tragic conflicts in the Middle East.

We also might wonder how needy, self-centered leaders can come to have a frightening and destructive control over followers. What stones, what thistles would cause persons to grow up in this way?

In the garden beautiful things also happen: seeds and bulbs changing into succulent green shoots; cross-pollination; and through composting we see the conversion of useless, ugly, waste materials into the very lifeblood of a garden.

Let's recognize the primary meaning of this parable in terms of spirituality—for us personally, and as a community of spirituality. Above all, this means holding fast to the central values that mark us as an authentic church, the "Jesus values." That's the genetic material, our DNA, you might say. If we want to survive and grow as a church, then above all, we must BE what we were meant to be, and not think that we can flourish just by using various "cutesy" gimmicks as fertilizer. Spirituality means connectedness, which must include the concrete realities and issues of our daily lives.

We are stewards of soil, and of many different kinds of seeds. Decisions confront us whether we like it or not. God has made us co-participants in the creative process. We do have to make life-determining decisions, and we must give each other space for doing so. Usually we should do it together with friends and loved ones. This ongoing process of decision making is a reality that we must be willing to live with, caringly, for our entire lives. It's a struggle born of hope.

"Some of the seeds fell on the path, and the birds came and ate them up. Other seeds fell on the rocky ground, where they did not have much soil . . . . Other seeds fell on good soil and brought forth grain, some a hundred fold."

Matthew pictures Jesus ending his parables in the same way he begins them: "Listen," he says! Listen. "You are sowers of seed, stewards of soil!"

Pangasinan, Philippines

43

WORLD CLASS WRESTLING

Pentecost 11, Year A
Genesis 32:22-32

"Jacob was left alone; and a man wrestled with him
until daybreak . . . Then he said, 'Let me go, for the day
is breaking.' But Jacob said, 'I will not let you go, unless
you bless me.' So he said to him, 'What is your name?'
And he said, 'Jacob.' Then the man said, 'You shall no
longer be called Jacob, but Israel, for you have striven
with God and with humans, and have prevailed.'"

Genesis 32:24, 26-28

This story about Jacob wrestling with the "stranger in the
night" brings back memories of high school and college
wrestling. I don't know what kind of images you get when you
hear the term wrestling, but I get some really vivid ones. Not
the hokey, blatant, violent pictures of entertainment wrestling
on T.V., but the inter-collegiate wrestling. I think of the stress
and strain, the sweat and the pain! I went out for wrestling for
a while when I was in high school, and then again as a Junior at
the U. of Illinois, when a close friend who had been an all-state
high school wrestling champion told me that I had a chance to

make the team. As it turned out they didn't need me, and the coach, instead of telling me, "Dave," you're in over your head," assigned me to a partner about 10 pounds heavier than I, and much more skilled, which really made life miserable for awhile! The coach achieved his aim, and I stopped wrestling, which was probably wise!

The Bible story says that "Jacob was left alone; and a man wrestled with him until daybreak. When the man saw that he did not prevail against Jacob, he struck him on the hip socket; and Jacob's hip was put out of joint as he wrestled with him . . . . And then the man said, "You shall no longer be called Jacob, but Israel, for you have striven with God and with humans, and have prevailed."

This is a very old story, dating back to the earliest of pre-Israelite times. Let's refresh our memory:

Jacob was the son of Isaac and Rebekah. Isaac was the son of Abraham. Isaac was about 20 years older than Rebekah, and they had two sons, Jacob and Esau. The joys and the sorrows of this story are quite captivating, because Jacob turns out to be such a tricky guy. (Or, might we way, "resourceful!")

The time comes after many years for Jacob to go back home, where Esau lives. He dreads this, because he has cheated Esau so many times, and he doesn't want to face him. He does clever things to reduce the risk of trouble, and twice he sends his family ahead to Esau so that if there is any trouble, *they* will be the ones to bear the brunt of it!

Our scene for this morning shows Jacob taking his two wives and two maids and eleven children and all of his possessions as far as the stream where Jacob will send them on ahead to be with Esau. Jacob then stays behind to spend the night.

Obviously, the next part of the story has to do with a dream, which becomes a marvelous metaphor. The Bible says that a man wrestles with Jacob presumably through the night, until daybreak. Jacob accepts this struggle, and Jacob goes through it alone, without any help. There's obvious awe and admiration on the part of Israel at the courage and great strength of their ancestor, even though this is expressed in the form of a dream.

It's only while he is into this struggle, the story goes, that Jacob begins to realize that he is wrestling with God!

Even though this is in the early part of the Old Testament, this is a deeply Christian theme in the sense that looking at it backwards we see that it's the same God, with the same qualities revealed in Jesus, who contends with us—or persists in dealing with us—"wrestling with us"—forgiving, blessing, and transforming us through gracious love.

The theme of struggle and hope is fundamental to the Christian faith. We remember Christ's struggles—with the authorities, with temptation, with death.

As we look through history we notice the great figures in the church and how many of them struggled as well: Wycliff, Luther, Wesley, for example. Or Martin Luther King Jr, Desmond Tutu, Oscar Romero.

And each of us here has his or her own kind of struggles, just as Jacob did. Some of them involve guilt and fear! The reality is that if we're to take our faith seriously, we must face up to these struggles, and a certain amount of wounding will take place. But out of that comes the blessing. There is no getting to the Promised Land without going through the wilderness!

Are we willing to wrestle with our personal problems: A habit that is undercutting our well-being? An anxiety or fear that is making our life miserable? An old grudge that is spilling its poison into our relationships? A family member who needs to be told the truth, and we can't quite gather the strength to say it?

Jacob's story reminds us of our limitations. He came through the night intact, but limping. Even when we are victorious in our struggles, we'll still bear wounds. For it is only in surrendering our illusions of strength and self-sufficiency that we know the power of God.

As St. Paul Says in II Corinthians 12:9-10:

> "So I will boast all the more gladly of my weaknesses, so that the power of Christ may dwell in me. Therefore I am content with weaknesses, insults, hardships, persecutions, and calamities for the sake of Christ; for whenever I am weak, then I am strong."

I'm interested in a pattern that we find in this story. The religion of Jacob seems to be an "If" religion. And God's answer is an "even though" answer.

Jacob says, in Gen. 28:20, a little ahead of today's passage: "*If* God be with me and will keep me in this way that I go and will give me bread to eat and clothing to wear—then the Lord shall be my God . . . and I will give a tenth to thee."

This is the "*if*" religion, done for the God who metes out favors, who accepts prayer as a tool of success, and religion as the key to prosperity. "As long as God gives me this or that, then I'll believe." IF God will answer my prayers, then I'll "play church" with God. I regularly run into people who call themselves Christians who seem to have an "if" religion.

The story of Jacob shows us how fiercely we humans desire to put God at our disposal. But God constantly, effectively, stays out of our grasp!

The religion of "even-though" is seen in how God uses Jacob: According to this story, EVEN-THOUGH Jacob is a wheeler-dealer, God uses him. We have an "even-though faith." The disciples did; St. Paul did; and Seaview does. Even though we have cracks in our ceiling, and wrinkles in our carpet, and only one set of restrooms, and little insulation, God is using this humble neighborhood church!

The religion of "even though" is beautifully typified in the Old Testament by Habakkuk, who said,

"Though the fig tree shall not blossom, neither shall fruit be on the vines; the fields shall yield no meat, the flock shall be cut off from the fold, and there shall be no herd in the stalls, yet will I rejoice in the Lord." (Habakkuk 3:17,18.)

And this is of course the way of Jesus and the way of the cross. It's an "even-though" way.

In Hosea 12:4-6 we have a kind of gathering up of this story, with the word of the prophet: "But as for you, return to your God, hold fast to love and justice, and wait continually for your God."

To be ready and willing to wrestle with the great issues of our time is a sign of promise, because God allows us to cling to God. Again and again we see that God will not let us capture God, but will always press the mystery and freedom of God. Yet God will not push us away, and will bless us at the break of day, if we have not given up.

Jacob emerges from the struggle a cripple, but with a new relationship with God.

Furthermore, there's a miraculous change in Esau's attitude. These new realities are apparently the new condition that God had intended. And we are not to see our scars and wounds as defects, but as honorable, visible signs that we have been touched by life.

44

AWESOME WONDER, MIRACLES OF FAITH

Pentecost 11, Year C
Hebrews 11:29-12:2

"And what more should I say? For time would fail
me to tell of Gideon, Barak, Samson, Jephthah, of David
and Samuel and the prophets—who through faith
conquered kingdoms, administered justice, obtained
promises, shut the mouths of lions, quenched raging
fire, escaped the edge of the sword, won strength out
of weakness, became mighty in war, put foreign armies
to flight. Women received their dead by resurrection.
Others suffered mocking and flogging, and even chains
and imprisonment.

Hebrews 11:32-36

Wonder and awe are at the heart of religious experience.
Our "wonder" energizes. In the 16th and 17th centuries,
wealthy families counted among their most prized pieces of
furniture shelves that were little more than "knick-knack"
shelves, but which they called their "wonder-cabinets. Our
ancestors used to go on what they called "marveling trips."
They'd put the triumphs of their expeditions in their "wonder

cabinets." Unique butterflies, four-leafed clovers, seashells. And while we frown upon taking exotic things from their natural environment, we can't help but relate to their awe of the beauty of nature.

We might entitle this section of Hebrews "The enduring practice of faith," and the list of faithful witnesses is no less than "awesome."

The author, most probably not Paul, but one of his close associates and followers, finally comes to realize that there are so many awesome examples of faithfulness in the Old Testament that he reverts to shorthand, naming names, even mentioning individuals who had obvious flaws. In verse 35 he mentions "women who received their dead by resurrection," apparently referring to certain miraculous events where the dead were brought back to life.

Wondrous miracles of faith, victories and triumphs that were achieved in hardship and martyrdom. The multitude of faithful remembered as a great cloud of witnesses. And these gathered faithful assemble to observe each new generation as they undertake the challenge to remain faithful. On a "lifelong journey, like a race to be run with perseverance."

The beloved hymn, "How Great Thou Art," carries the line, "O Lord my God, when I in awesome wonder consider all the worlds thy hands have made—."

Truly, a sense of wonder and awe *is* at the heart of our religious experience, and we might say that the author of Hebrews is placing the mighty works of God as shown through the faithfulness of this great cloud of witnesses, the endless line of splendor, in his "wonder-cabinet."

Do you allow your mind to be blown away by the beauty of God's creation, by the bounty of God's creation?

My mind was blown away this last Friday, as Susan and I were sailing away from Spencer Spit, on Lopez Island. The morning fog had finally lifted, though there was still some lingering mist along the Rosario Strait. As we approached the opening between Blakeley and Decatur Islands we saw about a dozen boats in a holding pattern. I thought that they were simply waiting until they could make a safe passage south through the Strait. But as we approached, I saw some fins of Orca whales which were lazily drifting around, not far from the boats. Then the Orcas started arching and splashing! "Sue! Get up here quick!" We ended up staying there about 45 minutes, watching 25 to 30 Orcas, some of them passing right under our boat. Such large, peaceful creatures, not at all aptly named as "killer whales!" Actually, they're part of the dolphin family. In awesome wonder we experienced something for which many people wait a lifetime!

One of the beauties of taking a vacation on the water is that you're constantly exposed to the rare beauty of the birdlife, the sunsets, the agate-strewn gravelly beaches, the vivid green on glistening rocks at low tide, an occasional lavender starfish in a tide pool.

Did you ever try to take a puppy for a walk? It takes forever. Not only does the puppy naturally resist the tug of the leash, but it must stop and pounce on every leaf on the sidewalk, investigate every stick in the path, track every bug that crawls along, and of course smell every inch of the earth. All is new; all is wonderful. In an age of skepticism and cynicism we all-too-often leave the matter of wonder and joy to children and puppies!

Geneticist/mathematician J.B.S. Haldane observed that "The world will not perish for want of wonders, but for want of wonder," and Albert Einstein once said, "The most beautiful experience we can have is the mysterious. It is the fundamental emotion which stands at the cradle of true art and true science. Whoever does not know it can no longer wonder, no longer marvel, is as good as dead, and his eyes are dimmed."

Did you know that in Europe in the 16th century Bibles were "chained books?" They were literally chained to the walls of churches and to posts so that over-zealous parishioners would not make off with them. The Bible was known as a book of the wonders of God!

At the other end of the wonder spectrum are the ridiculous things that happen to us: A woman by the name of Rachael Murray lost her small cell phone, and in an attempt to locate it, dialed its number. Sure enough, they heard it ringing, faintly, inside Charlie, a friend's bloodhound! A veterinarian advised Murray that the best way to recover the phone was to let nature take its course (*Newseek*, January 12, 1998,).

One of the early explorers with Cortes, remembers his first spellbound vision of the Aztec capitol: "Gazing on such wonderful sights, we did not know what to say, or whether what appeared before us was real" (Weschler, *Mr. Wilson's Cabinet of Wonder*, N.Y., Pantheon, 1995)

Our wonder is born when we cultivate an openness to all that cannot be understood, and scarcely believed. I would contend that this is essentially a religious experience, one upon which we may build.

Sure, there are lots of ugly things in this world, too, and that can be a part of the fabric of our wonder. The truly remarkable thing is the creative and redemptive power available to each one of us, despite the ugliness and pain.

And that is essentially what the book of Hebrews is about, with its solid appreciation of the awesome story of God working in history, and our connectedness with that story, through our faith.

45

GETTING OUT OF THE BOAT

Pentecost 12, Year A
Matthew 14:22-33

"Peter answered him, 'Lord, if it is you, command
me to come to you on the water.' He said, 'come.' So
Peter got out of the boat, started walking on the water,
and came toward Jesus. But when he noticed the strong
wind, he became frightened, and beginning to sink,
he cried out, 'Lord, save me!'"

Matthew 14:28-30

I wish I had a quarter for every fishing story I've heard about
someone walking on the water! When we lived in the
Philippines I heard stories about the famous war photo of
General Douglas MacArthur stepping off the landing barge at
Lingayen beach. It made him look like he was walking on the
water, an image not overlooked by his critics!

The walking on the water passage is found not only in
Matthew, but also in Mark 6:47-52, and in John 6:16-21. And
we might note the passage in Mark 4:35ff where Jesus calms
the storm.

We're not being advised to try to walk on water! This passage does not say that we can do it, too. Our lesson says, basically, that Jesus is different, unique, and Jesus can help us.

We have to remember that this was written in the years of the sixties and seventies, about 35 years after Jesus' death. Jesus' followers were only few, and they were experiencing great difficulty. Peter had been martyred. This was the time of Nero, who was killing Christians. Some were being burned on crosses, and some thrown to the lions in the Coliseum.

The incident described here was said to have occurred between 3 and 4 o'clock in the morning, which might have been a direct reference to the darkest days of Jesus' followers, when they really did fear that they would sink and drown. Some scholars see social and political dimensions to this. It's a masterful social caricature which is well within the biblical tradition: an arrogant king pitted against the truth-telling prophets (Matt, 14:1-12), and a carpenter-teacher from Nazareth who can walk on water! Quite stunning, and it was meant to be.

We also need to note that the series of events that we see in this portion of Matthew's gospel represent a summary report of Jesus' widespread contact with every social sphere of the region: the marketplaces of villages, cities, and rural areas: farmers, fisherfolk, soldiers and civilians, the rich and the poor, rural and urban, the lame, the halt and the blind! The young and the old, women and men, Jews and gentiles, Jews and Romans. Very inclusive, is this story, and it was meant to be.

In this text, just after the feeding of the 5,000, Jesus wants a "time out," but he's finding it hard to get privacy. So he sends the disciples ahead in the boat, and he remains alone until about 3 a.m. Matthew says that the crowd wished to make him king. Jesus knew what their agenda was—they wanted him to carry the flag of revolt against Rome, and let themselves go unchanged. Jesus kept hammering away at the message that each person needs change, some sort of personal transformation!

Scholar-preacher George Buttrick commented that these events seemed to draw a sharp line across his ministry—a certain amount of disillusionment with the crowds was setting in, and from this time onward he seems to devote himself less to the crowds and more to the disciples. He would also begin to break with the Jewish law. Perhaps he sensed a new moment in his life, and wanted to be alone for reflection and prayer.

So he made the disciples go ahead. And while they're on the lake in their boat, Matthew says that a fierce wind came up. Storms were not an unusual thing for lake Genesaret, which was known for its fierce squalls.

We read that Jesus came to them, walking on the water, which has evoked many different kinds of interpretations and comments. Some scholars call it a "pious legend." Others call it a "resurrection appearance." Some translate the phrase walking on the sea as "walking by the sea." But here again, as we saw last week with the feeding of the five thousand, the question should not focus on how this could have happened, but on the central question, just "who, really, is this Jesus, and what was he up to?"

Peter is the central figure in the account. Matthew repeatedly puts forward Peter as the "representative" disciple, the holder and guarantor of tradition. This story reinforces that view, which gradually moved Peter, the "rock," into the special place of authority in the Roman church.

Countless sermons have been preached on the line in Matthew which says that Peter begins to sink when he takes his eyes off of Jesus. We're told, in effect, that faith is strong when its motive is pure. Purity of motive, insofar as that is possible, is the beginning of faith's power. A divided mind, a divided, compromised life, rob us of our spiritual power.

Peter, as usual, was impulsive. He dared to try to walk. You've heard the expression, "If you want to walk on the water, you've got to get out of the boat!" Peter was both courageous and cowardly, and in the end he was helpless, afraid, in the face of the storm. BUT HE DID GET OUT OF THE BOAT!

And maybe that's what is being asked of US. To get out of the house, off the couch, away from the TV, the computer, and the telephone, to discover how gravity, through our legs and feet, can help us to put down roots and be effective! In a great Sesame Street musical piece: "You gotta put down the ducky, if you wanna play the saxophone!"

The purpose of Matthew's story is surely to let us know that Jesus comes to us in times of crisis, when the limits of our human resources have been reached. Jesus comes into the places which are beyond our hope, and when we no longer expect him. Today's lesson tells us that he does what human beings cannot do. This symbolism is not new. The Egyptians had already represented the impossible by a human figure walking on water!

Christians were not saved from death during that terrible time of Nero. It is said, however, that stories like this brought them comfort and strength, so you might say that they were saved *in* death. None of us is saved *from* death, but we are not hostages to death, and as Christians it's our conviction that in the broad sweep of human history, death and destruction are never the final word!

It was not easy to be an authentic Christian during Nero's time, when Matthew's gospel was written. In Nero's time Christians were labeled "cannibals" because they participated in the Lord's Supper, partaking of what was referred to as the "body and the blood of Christ." Even in recent years people of faith have been called "communists," simply because they've stood with the poor and participated in their struggles for justice. Such people are still called ugly names when they take sides with the outcasts of our society, just as Jesus did.

"Use me, Lord. But only in an advisory capacity, please." Harry Emerson Fosdick said "The saddest failure of the church is not hypocrisy. It is that there are so many who have never gone beneath the form of religion to find the power which is at its very heart." They've not made the commitment that energizes.

Here's a commitment story about two guys from the city. They were born in the city, and grew up in the city, but they decided that they'd had it with city living.

So they bought a farm down in Texas, and made up their mind that they would try to live off the land like their ancestors did!

They decided that the first thing they needed was a mule. So they went to a neighboring farmer and asked him if he had a mule he would sell. The farmer answered, "No, I'm afraid not."

They were disappointed, but as they visited with the rancher, one of them saw some honeydew melons stacked against the barn and asked, "What are those?"

The farmer immediately knew that these guys must be naive city slickers, and that he could have some fun. "Oh," he answered, "those are mule eggs. You take one of those eggs home and wait for it to hatch, and you'll have a mule."

The city slickers were pretty pleased at the thought of this, so they bought one of the melons and headed down the bumpy country road toward their own ranch. But suddenly they hit a bad bump, and the honeydew melon bounced out the back of the pickup truck, hit the road, and burst open. Now, seeing in the rear view mirror what had happened, the driver turned his truck around and started back to see if he could save his mule egg.

Meanwhile, a Texas jackrabbit came hopping by and saw this honeydew melon burst on the road. He hopped over to it, and standing in the middle of that honey-dew mess, began to eat. And here came the two city guys. They had seen their mule egg burst open, and now this long-eared creature was sitting right in the middle of it. One of the guys shouted, "Hey, our mule egg has hatched! Let's get our mule!"

But when they ran towards it, the jackrabbit took off, with the men in hot pursuit! They gave it everything they had, but they couldn't catch it. So they fell wearily onto the ground gasping for air, while the jackrabbit hopped off into the distance.

One of the men raised himself up on his elbow, and said to the other, "Well, there goes our mule. I guess we lost him."

"Yeah," said the other guy, "but you know—I'm not sure I wanted to plow that fast anyway!"

Commitment! Let's not be another sad Jesus-follower story: a person or a local church that doesn't want to get too serious, that doesn't want to plow too fast, that doesn't want to get out of the boat!

When storms come up on your sea, when you wonder how you're going to survive, when all of the forces in your life seem to be pulling you under, when the powers of darkness seem to be overcoming all that is good; when you're bone weary, anxious, at the end of your rope—listen for the still small voice in the storm, saying, "Come to me!" Get out of the boat, center your faith on what is sure and true.

46

GETTING EVEN

Pentecost 13, Year A
Genesis 45:3-11, 15

"Then Joseph said to his brothers, 'Come closer to
me.' And they came closer. He said, 'I am your brother
Joseph, whom you sold into Egypt. And now do not be
distressed or angry with yourselves, because you sold
me here; for God sent me before you to preserve life . . .'
And he kissed all his brothers and wept upon them;
and after that his brothers talked with him."

Genesis 45:4-5, 15

A newspaper ad read: "Lost—one dog. Brown hair with
several bald spots. Right front leg broken due to auto accident.
Left hip crooked. Right eye missing. Left ear bitten off in a
dog fight. Answers to the name 'Lucky.'"

Today we have the story of Joseph, a bright, handsome,
comfortable boy, a seemingly lucky boy, who encountered
terrible misfortune, experienced the depths of exile and
humiliation, but then rose to remarkable heights of power.
Here's a great story!

The story of Joseph is the last part of the book of Genesis. Many of us will remember the story very well from Sunday School days. But let's look through it again. It's a story about a man who has been terribly wronged, but who chooses not to get even. He chooses to work for the restoration of a precious relationship.

We've all heard the macho comment: "Don't get mad— get even!" Joseph chooses not to get even, but to get reconciled.

What more could you want in a story? Mystery, drama, power, sex. And plenty of humor. A seventeen year old boy, the apple of his dad's eye, arouses the bitter hatred of his older brothers. Joseph had snitched on them when they were bad, and he had obviously been receiving extreme preferential treatment from his father. The classic symbol of this favoritism was his beautiful coat of many colors, with long sleeves (Some scholars say the coat probably had long sleeves to show that Joseph was not to do manual labor).

To top it off, Joseph reported having dreams in which he had become quite the VIP—in one dream the people were all bowing to him. This was not guaranteed to win friends and influence people!

Well, the brothers had had it up to here with Joseph, and one day while out with the flocks they decide to get rid of the boy. "This kid is too much," they say, and they make plans to kill him and throw him into a pit. But brother Reuben convinces them to spare his life, and to put him in a pit only until they could sell him to some Ishmaelite passersby (who happen to be their second cousins!) Interesting that this should come up! Ishmael, as you know, is considered to be the ancestor of those of the Muslim faith. Ironically, they didn't get Joseph sold—he was kidnapped by another group, some Midianites, while the brothers were eating lunch.

And so, as we have read, Joseph ends up a slave in Egypt, but his ability and trustworthiness comes to be recognized, and he ends up having the Pharaoh of Egypt giving him awesome responsibility and power.

In the manner of a soap opera, we have crisis after crisis! Danger even appears in the form of sexual harassment of Joseph by the wife of the captain of the guard, a woman who likes Joseph way too much. She says, "Joseph, I want you, I'm going to have you! But Joseph rejects her advances. This makes her really mad! When she tries to grab Joseph, he flees, but alas, in getting away he leaves his coat in her grasping hands. "I'll get him," she says, and she uses the coat to try to prove that Joseph has tried to seduce *her*!

The spurned woman does convince the judge, so Joseph lands in jail. Very bad. For a while it seems that he'll be there for the rest of his life. But word of his gift for interpreting dreams eventually gets back to Pharaoh, and Joseph is summoned to help interpret the Pharaoh's dreams.

Joseph is very good indeed at interpreting the Pharaoh's dreams, and so the Pharaoh restores him to a position of confidence and power. In fact, he is put in charge of the grain, which makes him one of the most powerful figures in Egypt. He wears a special signet ring given by Pharaoh that is like a blank check of power. The ring has a seal on it, so he can write letters, imprint the wax seal with this ring, and people have to obey. He wears garments of fine linen, a gold chain of honor, rides in a chariot, and criers go out ahead of him wherever he goes, to announce his coming. Phew. All this, and he didn't even have to run for election!

And then the plot thickens! Joseph's long lost brothers take a trip to Egypt to try to get grain for their clan, because there was a terrible famine in their place. Joseph recognizes them, but they don't know who he is. Joseph plays tricks on them to test them. But Joseph isn't trying to get even—he simply wants to work toward the restoration of the lost relationship.

In the end we have a heartwarming story of reconciliation, described in our scripture for today. And Joseph, in a most humble attitude, gives God the credit for all his accomplishments.

Joseph's story is remarkably consistent with the recurring New Testament theme that God calls us to radical forms of forgiveness and love, and we can leave retribution to God. Let's not be too quick to claim that it is only with Jesus that we have the higher forms of forgiving love. We have some good examples in the Old Testament, including this one.

We should note that this is essentially wisdom literature. This kind of story was used to teach important lessons about morality and faith. Some say that stories like this interpret themselves. So maybe the preacher should just read this and then sit down. Sorry, no such luck!

There are lots of homecomings and family reunions in the Bible. Some of them have a unique "twist." The common denominator is that they show God active in some way, turning bad to good, or bringing liberation to captives, sight to the blind, food to the hungry.

A primary point of today's lesson is that overcoming alienation and separation between persons who have deeply wounded each other is possible, but never easy. The cross continually reminds us of the immense cost of reconciliation.

We might add the theme of divine providence. Was it "lucky" that all of this happened to Joseph? Was it God's will all the time? Was this the silver lining of Joseph's exile? Was this just meant to be, with Joseph merely acting out the role of a puppet?

Here we guard against on the one hand the idea of a manipulative god-with-puppet-children, and on the other hand the idea that God is remote, uninvolved, and uncaring. Both of these points of view exist in the church. I hold to the idea that while God may have been opening the way, Joseph was indeed making choices, and these choices made a redemptive difference.

The Church has consistently insisted that God knows, and does care; that God is still at work; but that God has given us freedom to act and freedom to rebel! We take God's providence very seriously, and we take our own responsibility seriously as well.

So Joseph was making choices. The story of Joseph shows how good choices can even reverse evil action and create opportunity for good. Providence involves more than God watching over sparrows. In every situation there is redemptive possibility. God does not will everything that happens, but God wills that something good come of everything that happens. At the moments of greatest despair there is still opportunity to look for and to nurture grace. When bad things happen, we respond as redemptively as we can, trusting that good things will flow. Our own free will is still operating in this.

A frustrating reality is that "payback" is the common human response. While living in Papua New Guinea we were constantly reminded of this because of the tribal fighting that continues to this day, where, if one group is harmed in some way by another, then, according to ancient custom, they have to pay the other group back. So the bitter chain of retribution continues, generation after generation, between tribes, between families. I was told when we first arrived in New Guinea that if I accidentally hit someone on the highway with my car while driving, I was not to stop, but to drive very fast to the next town, and go directly to the Police station. Because of the custom of "payback," my life would have been in grave danger. And a number of times we read in the newspapers about foreigners who were quickly sent out of the country after having been in serious accidents, because of the danger of payback.

We might think that this sounds primitive, but just think— we still have serous feuds in certain places in this country; we still see "instant retaliation" as official policy on the part of some nations, including our own. As conflicts deepen and become more complicated in the Middle East, experience shows that the policy of retaliation does not work very well at all.

Occasionally in New Guinea a group, usually a so-called "Christian" village, would depart from the payback system and offer forgiveness, without retribution. This was always such a breath of fresh air, and seemed so dramatic. But that's the Gospel: gracious, forgiving love.

What if Joseph had followed the custom of "an eye for an eye, a tooth for a tooth?" Joseph was different. It's quite wonderful that the first book of the Bible lifts this up, in the same way that Jesus lifts up the value of loving our enemies. Joseph did not turn to revenge, but turned to love.

Too often we fall into the retribution patterns of thinking— as individuals, and as a nation. God is calling us to break these patterns of getting back at people, of playing the "blame game," patterns that are all too common in our communities and in our world, even within our families.

Joseph was pointing us in the right direction. For him the important thing was not getting even, but restoration, grace, reconciliation.

47

HATE YOUR WHAT?

A STUDY OF PRIORITIES

Pentecost 14, Year C
Luke 14:25-33

"Whoever comes to me and does not hate father
and mother, wife and children, brothers and sisters,
yes, and even life itself, cannot be my disciple."

Luke 14:26

I come from a closely knit family. I remember that it was
very hard to go to the Philippines at the age of 22 as a young
single missionary knowing that I wasn't going to see my family
for three years. I remember that when I returned after that
three years, re-entering the States by ship through the port of
New York City, they drove all the way from Chicago to meet
me. Am I supposed to hate them? I left them, but HATE?
Gimme a break!

My brother, Dick, is a marvelous, friendly, fun-loving guy.
He took care of our son, Jeff, when Jeff was in college, when
we were half way around the world. I'm supposed to hate him?

I have three wonderful sisters who keep in touch with me through thick and thin, and I have three devoted, supportive, caring children.

Hate, no! That's not the point of this lesson. The point has to do with priorities, the cost of living out our values and holding fast to our integrity. For the Christian it's about the high cost of living—that is, of faith-living.

Concerning priorities: A cartoon in a newspaper depicts a jet liner that had made a crash landing on the ocean: As the life boats begin making their way away from the sinking plane, a woman turns to her husband to ask, "Alfred, are we still in first class?" Priorities.

But back to the lesson from Luke: I'm deeply grateful that my family never forced me to choose between them and my faith. They supported me! In fact, they help to make me accountable. Their responses have been honest and open, and they don't let me get away with any fancy "reverend" stuff!

The term "hate" used in the English translation is a staggering word, but it was meant to stagger. This passage is a good example of the importance of "biblical criticism." It doesn't mean criticizing the Bible, but means considering each passage carefully in light of everything we can learn about its background. According to some scholars, the term for hate used here actually goes back in its roots to an Aramaic word meaning "to love the less." And they say that in Greek, words for hate vary greatly in type, and in degree.

When reading this passage we might quickly remember that in the Ten Commandments we're to honor our mothers and fathers. In studying the Bible, the context is EVERYTHING! We should remember that Jesus was getting deeper and deeper into trouble. It seemed like he was quite uptight, and on this journey he was saying strong things in sharp ways! He was on his way to Jerusalem, on the way to the cross.

And here were the crowds of people following him. He knew where this road was leading, but the people did not seem to understand. He turned around, stopped them, and asked: "Do you really know what you are doing?

They were following him for a lot of different reasons, I suppose. Some may have simply wanted a change. Some were hungry and wanted to be fed. There were sick people who wanted to be healed, poor people who wanted to become rich. There was a dead person, carried by relatives who wanted him revived.

They followed, full of hope and eagerness to get what they thought they needed. Jesus turned around and said: "Are you sure that you really want to go my way? Do you know where I'm going?

Some scholars say that Jesus may have been trying to "thin the ranks" of the crowd following him. There were too many people. Did he simply want to narrow his conversations down to the really serious followers?

Jesus was after a primary and undivided allegiance. He was not despising natural ties. On the contrary, he blessed little children. He spoke of God as a parent. He preached again and again in the tradition of the prophets about right relationships.

Priorities! Putting some things first, and some things second, and putting some things way down the list. And letting some things go.

There are a number of verses that come to mind with this passage: Who is my mother, or my brother? Whoever does the will of God is my brother, and sister, and mother."

Seek ye first the kingdom of God, and the rest will be added unto you." What is this kingdom that we would seek?

The Lord's Prayer doesn't say, "Thy kingdom come in heaven!" It says. "Thy kingdom come on earth, even as it is in heaven." Life transformed, right here, in accordance with the will and purpose of a loving God.

Putting first things first can sometimes mean attending to our own personal needs and those of our families. And it can take us to levels beyond the personal! The priorities of our nation must surely be subject to the judgment of God, and we as conscientious citizens have accountability, *at least* to the extent of our votes, and our capability to use our influence over the things our government does. Getting our house in order as nation or town, and counting the cost! This would seem especially important in light of the glib political rhetoric about families, and family values!"

The priorities of God and country? Is it my country, right or wrong? No, our loyalty for country must reflect deeper values. We must be able to say that the greatest love for country is reflected in our willingness to participate in its change— that it may do justice, love mercy, and walk humbly.

Maybe Jesus was trying to get us to see that it really was a possibility, and still is, that people may be rejected by their families because of their faith.

My family right or wrong? My children right or wrong? No, says Jesus, there are values more important than those. Blessed is the family where those values are shared.

Our lesson today certainly eliminates the idea of "cheap grace." Be wary of religions or leaders that promise an easy way, where everything is sweetness, peace and light! Harold E. Kohn offers a brief verse on "Crookedness:"

> Brooks become crooked
> From taking the path
> Of least resistance.
> So do people.

The church is not a country club; not a social fraternity or sorority. We're a faith community centered around ultimate values, ultimate commitments. Worship is not a program to entertain, and the pastor's sermon is not a mere educational talk. Going to church IS important (even though I often tell people whose bodies are hurting to stay home this Sunday and take care of themselves!) Participating in church activities in ways appropriate to our individual reality IS important.

Consider that our rather troubling text for today is inviting us to a LETTING GO. Letting go of some of our deepest "attachments," and to see where our loyalty to them may be in conflict with our loyalty to God. Letting go of those things that seek to own us, so that we will be free to go where God's spirit is leading us. Putting into perspective those primary relationships that keep us at a distance from our truest and best selves.

We establish our priorities, count the cost, and pay the price. We do have help in getting our priorities straight: the still small voice within; the witness of our faith tradition; and we have each other.

There's a very positive message embedded here, particularly in the parables part: That is, we CAN be successful in our journey of faith. Whether building a tower, and counting the cost, or confronting a king, and being ready with our alternatives, there IS a way. Christians can know that they are following one who did count the cost, and who was capable of seeing the journey through.

School, Agusan

48

LOSTNESS: STORIES OF STRUGGLE AND HOPE

Pentecost 15, Year C
Luke 15:1-10

"Which one of you, having a hundred sheep and losing one of them, does not leave the ninety-nine in the wilderness and go after the one that is lost until he finds it? When he has found it, he lays it on his shoulders and rejoices. And when he comes home, he calls together his friends and neighbors, saying to them, 'Rejoice with me, for I have found my sheep that was lost . . .'"

"Or what woman having ten silver coins, if she loses one of them, does not light a lamp, sweep the house, and search carefully until she finds it? When she has found it, she calls together her friends and neighbors, saying, 'Rejoice with me, for I have found the coin that I had lost.'"

Luke 15:4-6; 8-9

LOSTNESS is a common human experience. We encounter it often. One day, while taking my three granddaughters to the Seattle Children's museum, I saw a child panic, thinking that he had lost his mother. Screaming uncontrollably—until reunited with Mom.

LOST is the story of human society. We struggle in the face of the most grave problems of the greater human community: poverty, injustice, war, the greenhouse effect, racism and bigotry, and, these years, terrorism, an ultimate manifestation of alienation and anger. There seems to be no end of the signs, locally and globally, that have to do with LOSTNESS.

LOSTNESS is the paradox of our age: we have more conveniences, but less time; we have more degrees, but less sense; more knowledge, but less judgment; more experts, fewer answers; more medicine, but less wellness, more technology, but less security! We've been all the way to the moon and back, but have trouble crossing the street to meet the new neighbor!

The stories of the lost sheep and the lost coin are stories of struggle and hope, and we can make them our own, because of the very fact that there is lostness all around us!

The passage about the lost sheep and the lost coin remind us of the importance of not giving up: not giving up on persons, including ourselves. Jesus is telling us in these teachings that it is love that motivates *the search that will not end*—until that which is lost is found.

We've heard people talking about their "search for God." This scripture lesson infers that God is already reaching out to us! Luke 15:1-10 is a wonderful, hopeful parable: "What one of you, having a hundred sheep, if one of them is lost, does not leave the ninety-nine in the wilderness, and go after the one which is lost, until it is found?

Note that the shepherd is a male image of God, the woman looking for her lost coin a feminine image of God.

Note also that the number 100 for the sheep and the number 10 for the coins are complete numbers, numbers that are VERY different if even one item is missing. I've also read that it was very common in that culture for a bride to wear a necklace made up of 10 coins on a string, and that if one of those coins were lost, the woman would feel terrible until that coin was found to make the necklace complete.

The story of the lost sheep is found in Matthew, too. It's one of Jesus' common examples as he tells us about how much God cares for each and every person.

The first three verses of this passage tell about the Pharisees and the scribes, who murmured as the tax collectors and sinners drew near to listen to Jesus.

My Interpreters' Bible says that something new was happening here. While the Jewish Rabbinical literature emphasizes over and over again the importance of repentance, the "good shepherd" is a new figure. It is something fresh— the good shepherd *searches* for the lost sheep, and reclaims it and rejoices over it. Jesus was very deliberately picturing himself not only as a shepherd like the one spoken of in the 23rd Psalm, but beyond that, a friend of the lost, and even beyond that, as we see in John 10, the shepherd who lays down his life for his sheep.

Luke seems to assume that Jesus spoke repeatedly to the Pharisees and scribes in defense of his ministry to those who were lost. His concern for sinners, outcasts, and downtrodden was so extreme that the Pharisees were having a hard time handling it! Ironically, they were just as lost as the so-called sinners!

In Luke's writings Jesus had many encounters with Pharisees—they were one of the common Jewish sects or denominations. They believed in a strict observance of Jewish law. They were "proper Jews." They were "the nice people." There were Pharisees among the Christians. It says in Acts 23 that St. Paul was a Pharisee. There were Pharisees who were not Christian who were regularly friendly to Christianity: Gamaliel is an example. At more than one point Pharisees warned Jesus to get out of town, so that he could save himself from angry adversaries. Jesus regularly sat down to dinner with Pharisees. Perhaps they were lost, too!

Just try to imagine that Jesus has sent us a holy messenger to inform us that he is coming to West Seattle at the end of the month. So we spread the word, and all of the churches start getting ready! We really clean house. We paint our church, fix the oak doors. We put up banners: "Welcome, Jesus!"

And Jesus comes. But where does he go? Not to the churches, but to the bars, to the hangouts, and he ends up talking with the most unsavory, unaccepted outcasts of this town.

I don't know exactly what I should do about this, because I'm not going to the bars and hangouts myself, and I'm not sure what you would think if I did, and it's a pretty complicated question in the year 2003, but that's what had happened, in effect, with Jesus, and that's why the Pharisees were generally upset. In the end they participated in getting rid of him. Jesus' love for the lost, his understanding of forgiveness, his total goodness were so great that they set standards utterly impossible to fulfill. Forgive seventy times seven times? If anyone slaps you on the right cheek, turn to them your left cheek?

The measures that Jesus used seemed humanly impossible— but they were an accurate expression of God's love, God's forgiving love, God's pursuing love—so great that it never rests.

We have modern stories of missing children, whose parents never give up; of veterans missing in action, whose loved ones struggle for years, decades, to find them. As I stood in line at a Post Office recently, my eye fell upon the bulletin board that has pages of photos of persons who are lost. Missing. Most of them children. "Endangered missing," "non-family abduction," "family abduction," "believed to be with someone dangerous— use caution." Lost. But loved, and *searched for*. From time to time our T.V. sets carry the images of workers searching for survivors in rubble, not giving up.

It occurs to me that struggle and hope are very FUTURE-oriented. They are positive energy not stuck with the past, not mired in any present condition of lostness. The parable of the lost sheep is geared for FUTURE.

In so many ways, and in the eyes of the world, the Africans in South Africa might have been justified in feeling futility and hopelessness, letting their rage burst out with total and final destructive force.

Yet look at what has happened—there was no giving up, and despite the violence and despair, hope and struggle, which are always bound up together, show forth in finding the lost forms of redemptive, healing possibility. Thank God that in such contexts struggle and hope have become a lifestyle lived out by more than one generation. We have so much to learn from them.

We might focus on the sad stories of other persons wandering far from the circle of God's love. But what important things are slipping through the cracks of our own lives? Are we willing to search for them? Is there anything lost within you? Qualities, talents, unfulfilled potential that you're failing to redeem? What's the character of our own lostness, each one of us? Are we willing to struggle with it, to get "unstuck?"

As the human family gets launched into a most challenging and difficult new century we must realize that struggle and hope simply have to become a part of our continuing lifestyle, a journey.

The JOURNEY, and not just arriving, will continue to be the mode of faithful Christian discipleship. If we accept that, we infinitely reduce the possibility of ever being lost again!

The journey IS part of the arriving, and part of our fulfillment is in the struggling; and even though that for which we yearn may always seem to be just beyond our grasp, we do taste it, and we know that if our struggles are within the circle of God's loving intention and will, the arriving will finally come to pass

49

POWER IN THE GATHERED COMMUNITY

Pentecost 16, Year A
Matthew 18:15-20; Romans 13:8-14

" . . . For where two or three are gathered in my
name, I am there among them."

Matthew 18:20

A story from the Midwest tells of a Methodist circuit rider who in the middle of winter went on a bleak Sunday morning to one of the tiny remote chapels of his parish, only to find that there was only one person present, a farmer who had braved the cold and the snow. The dedicated pastor held the service just as though there were a hundred in the congregation. He didn't leave out a thing! When the service was over, the lone parishioner thanked the pastor, saying that it was very generous of him to hold the service, even though there was only one person present. The pastor said, "My brother, if you were taking a load of hay out to the range for your herd of cows, wouldn't you feed the one, even if the others didn't show up?" "Well yes, pastor," said the farmer, "but I wouldn't dump the whole load!"

Surely the point of Matthew 18:20 is that God's help comes powerfully through the gathered community. This line is not for our consolation when we have a disappointing turnout for the worship service!

Jesus promises that as the community of faith gathers in God's name, God will be in the midst to empower and encourage. While God is with us when we're alone, and we're never forgotten, many of God's special gifts to human beings are mediated through the community and are not easily accessible through isolated individuals. This is a universal truth, not one limited to the church.

My experiences in the Pacific Islands reinforce my conviction about the power of community. In Fiji I heard about this in the stories of the great canoes, a large model of which is in the Fiji National Museum in Suva. Construction of the great double-hulled ocean canoes took about ten years, and before the community would begin, they would build a great barn in which the work would be done—otherwise the canoe would have begun to deteriorate even before it was finished! The crews of these canoes set out on voyages of a thousand miles or more, trading, exploring, migrating.

As described in the journals of early explorers, westerners who first saw these canoes remarked at their size, speed, and maneuverability. It was reported that one such canoe could contain a dozen cattle in its two holds, and tons of coconuts. That they could accomplish such projects was surely because of the interrelated factors of sharp focus on goals and values, the strong, accepted leadership of the chiefs, and the general social cohesiveness of the groups. It was a commentary on the efficiency of these communities that they could provide for the basic needs of the people and still devote major resources to building the huge canoes.

They no longer build such canoes in Polynesia, but you can still see the powerful bonds of community in most places in the Pacific Islands. At the risk of romanticizing the culture of Pacific Islanders (because they have serious problems, too), I would still lift up the image of groups talking their problems through, reaching decisions through lengthy deliberation, with a maximum of expression by people of varying points of view. Finally, when the time seems right, final decisions are made, and even those who disagree know that they've had their chance to express themselves. I contrast this with groups that are inclined to take a quick vote, that put dissenters down, but then learn the hard way that months, sometimes years, have to be spent dealing with dissatisfaction and alienation.

Community can go awry, of course—as with a mob, or under the control of a narrow, selfish leader. Groups can definitely use their power to exclude or distort or exploit. Human institutions that ignore democratic process of gathered community are likely to commit serious errors.

It has been interesting over the years to be a part of various local ministerial associations, where one can see how different denominations view the role of the pastor. Some churches put their pastors on top right at the center, giving them power that is easily abused. It's common to see periods of flashy, somewhat dramatic numerical growth, then conflict or scandal, then a split, then years of struggle and attempts at reconciliation and healing. And, of course, we, the so-called "ecumenical" churches, are not totally free from such patterns.

Though a study of church history reveals examples of bad decisions by church councils and conferences, and while it is certainly true that the "majority" is *not* always right, on the whole several (or many) Christians in prayerful dialogue are more likely to arrive at the truth than one authoritarian leader, even though the decision-making process takes longer.

We're in it together, whether we like it or not! As a Church. As a community. As a nation. The problems of New York City or Washington D.C., or even Timbuktu, may have seemed very remote a few years ago, but now we know how close they really are! For some years, many people have been moving from cities to suburbs, to escape the problems. This may be an appropriate action for some families, but in the final analysis we never really break free from the larger realities. The whole world is in it together, which we'll know and feel more acutely as matters such as the global warming effect or acid rain, or contamination of our underground water reservoirs continues.

A boy, when asked what is a net, said, "It's a bunch of holes tied together with a string!" The key here, is "tied together." A net is a good example of something that has functions and a power that string simply does not have on its own. We're tied together. There is power in the gathered community.

Our passage for today is one of the earliest references to the Church. The writer of Matthew obviously had an experience of the early church, and Jesus' followers were trying to answer the question, "What does it mean to be the church?" And I like to say, "Let the church BE the church!" I'm enjoying some of the new forms of ecumenism coming into being. As a missionary I found myself working more and more closely with priests and nuns of the Roman Catholic Church. In most local churches nowadays we have persons from a variety of church backgrounds, and we welcome them into full participation.

Our observance of the sacrament of Holy Communion is far more than food hooked to memories. It's at the table of the Lord that we gather, literally and symbolically. Sometimes our ego, our pride and resentments work against our coming to the table. Sometimes we don't even know we're hungry until we get here, and we find our appetite returning.

This is the power of the gathered community, with its memories, and hopes for the future, and the power of its prayers. But it's just as much for the *present reality* of being with one another, being fed with the bread of life. Here we feel that the things that God most fervently wants, for us and for the whole world, are the very things that *we* want. This gives us power. It renews us, and sends us back into our struggles with renewed vision and hope.

What if the local church could become an open, welcoming community of people who desire to grow together in love; a place of peace and encouragement where God's Good News in Jesus is announced—forgiveness and new life available to each one of us—tall or short, young or old, gay or straight, rich or poor.

A place where the truth is told, where promises are kept, and where hope is kept alive; an accepting environment where persons can struggle in helpful ways with life's important questions, feeling it safe to disagree.

A place where children find visible, positive, hopeful models and examples of all ages, and feel affirmed in the values of caring community.

A supportive fellowship for those interested in serving the wider community through loving deeds.

Not a perfect community, but a powerful community!

50

LISTENING TO OUR TEARS

Not in the Lectionary
Pentecost 22 or 23, Year C
Luke 19:41-44

"As he came near and saw the city, he wept over it,
saying, 'If you, even you, had only recognized on this
day the things that make for peace! But now they are
hidden from your eyes.'"

Luke 19:41-42

I have a little problem. Sometimes when I go to a movie I
cry. I was brought up in a time when "real men" were not
supposed to cry—it was a sign of weakness. So when it happens,
I do it as quietly as I can, and when my nose starts to drip, I just
let it drip, as long as I can stand it. I don't want the people
around me to know I'm crying, and then when I've reached
my limits I get my hankie out as quietly as possible and start
mopping up, trying not to let anyone know. I usually get found
out.

What makes you cry? What do our tears say about us?
Thinking about the good old days? They say that nostalgia just
ain't what it used to be!

Poet-theologian Frederick Buechner, in his little book, *Whistling in the Dark (N.Y., Harper & Row, 1993)*, writes,

"Whenever you find tears in your eyes, especially unexpected tears, it is well to pay the closest attention. They are not only telling you something about the secret of who you are, but more often than not, God is speaking to you through them of the mystery of where you have come from and is summoning you to where, if your soul is to be fulfilled, you should go next."

Tears are a great biological gift. In addition to their essential function of bathing our eyes, they're a physical manifestation of our emotional and spiritual experience. Sometimes it's hard to know what to do with them. If we indulge them, we might be prone to self-pity, which may not be helpful. If we suppress them we could lose touch with our deeper feelings and highest impulses.

I was close to tears recently when I received a letter from a 90-year-old British man, Geoffrey Baskett, whom I knew as a missionary in Papua New Guinea. He was a radio announcer for Kristen Redio, and is an author of books for children. He had written me a scathing letter just after my divorce, telling me in no uncertain terms how very wrong I was. I perceived his letter as a conversation-stopper, so rightly or wrongly, I let the matter be. I didn't answer, and I hadn't heard from him again.

Until recently. He told me that he had experienced being "shunned" by people whom he had thought were friends, and he said that it felt awful. He said that this made him realize that he had shunned a few people himself, and I was one of those people. He told me that he did value our friendship, and he very humbly asked my forgiveness. The simple sincerity of his letter was deeply moving.

To be honest, when I had received his critical letter, though I knew that he didn't understand my situation, I respected the fact that he felt very strongly about my divorce, and about divorce in general. I answered the second letter immediately, telling him that I accepted the fact of his strong feelings, that I certainly did forgive him, and I do want to be his friend. As I've said, his humility and courage to share his feelings were deeply moving, and my own tears told me how much I cared.

According to Luke, in chapter 19, Jesus wept over Jerusalem: "O Jerusalem, if you only knew the things that make for peace." Luke shows Jesus as knowing, even then, that Jerusalem was in deep trouble and was going to be crushed. He cared, and yet he could not, or would not, intervene. Historians tell us about Jerusalem's terrible fall.

Jesus was overcome with grief in the Garden of Gethsemane, feeling alone and betrayed by the people he most trusted. He wept.

Peter, moments after he had denied knowing Jesus, "went out and wept bitterly." *(Luke 22:62*

Theologian A.W. Tozer wrote that "The Bible was written in tears, and to tears it yields its best treasures."

There were times when Jesus got angry, with a rush of emotion surely related to tears. In Mark 9 Jesus gives his disciples a tongue-lashing for not being sympathetic to those who were not in their "in-group" who were casting out demons or giving a cup of water, using Jesus' name. In the same passage, Jesus was terribly upset with those who were misleading children. The Jesus of love and mercy used images of force and fury to show how deeply his emotions ran! We learn from these stories of passionate concern, and we learn when we listen to our tears.

Sometimes we cry when "it hurts," and sometimes it hurts a lot. Sometimes we cry simply because we care a lot. We can't have love without tears. It's a blessing to care a lot, even if we care so much that it leads to the shedding of tears and the experience of pain.

World scenes on our television screens in recent years have moved many to tears, and sometimes the tears lead to action.

Our tears join with the tears of others, forming a river of compassion. The church has a historic, sustained, intentional involvement in emergency relief and rehabilitation work throughout the world, much of it empowered by tears.

And there are times when I feel like weeping and shouting, "O America, if you only knew the things that make for peace!"

There are two particular moments in the life of the church where I find myself deeply touched and humbled, sometimes to the point of tears: ordination services for the young pastors, and the retirement celebrations for those in their golden years. It's inspiring to hear the stories of the retirees told by their friends, stories of sacrificial service, of integrity and strength of character and of faithfulness, the men and women who have been in ministry in difficult places and during difficult times. And virtually all of them, as they look back, speak of the joy and satisfaction that they've experienced. Then you wonder what lies ahead for the eager, expectant young leaders as they begin their own fresh, original journey.

Sometimes, when we're doubled over in laughter, we cry. A deeper chord is touched, sending forth an indescribable song of release and healing. One Saturday night in the mid 1980's, in Mindanao, Philippines, after a grueling, stressful week of visiting remote villages where there had been terrible atrocities perpetrated by renegade military units, I went with other members of an international human rights observation team to a karaoke club in Davao City. Pastors, priests, lawyers, journalists, we gave thanks for each other, reaffirmed that our risky venture was a righteous cause, God's project, and that we would move ahead, whatever might happen. How we laughed at each other trying to sing! Laughter, tears, and sighs too deep for words.

Our Loving Creator must shed tears, must feel the pain, and would prefer to have us shed tears too, rather than give in to easy painless answers that would violate the very essence of our freedom and responsibility! Our journey often leaves a trail of tears, but the trail leads to a good place, where we will be fulfilled.

51

LEARNING TO LIVE WITH GRACE

Pentecost 17, Year A
Matt 20:1-16

"Take what belongs to you and go; I choose to give
to this last the same as I give to you. Am I not allowed to
do what I choose with what belongs to me? Or are you
envious because I am generous? So the last will be first,
and the first will be last."

Matthew 20:14-16

Needing some stamps, I went to the post office in the sleepy
provincial town in Isabela and fell in line, about the tenth person
from the window, and immediately found myself in friendly
conversation with those around me. Before I knew it, there I
was in front of the window, at the head of the line, which had
evaporated and re-materialized behind me. Quickly realizing
that I was the beneficiary of the legendary Filipino hospitality,
I argued, feebly, but there was little I could do except to express
my thanks and buy the stamps. Compounding my frustration
in the numerous experiences of such special treatment was
the fact that for centuries Filipinos have experienced so much
unfairness.

It's not that hard to understand and finally live with justice. Most human beings seem to have a sense of what is fair, even though they might not live it. What seems harder is living with experiences of grace (especially when we think someone else is getting more grace than we!).

In our text, those who want God's outcomes to be predictable and human-like are warned. We can not restrict God, and If *we* try to play God, we're in for some big shocks. God will not be pulled toward smallness, to our human-sized aspirations, our narrow human experience. To the contrary, God pushes us toward greater stature!

Again we're reminded that God's ways are different! Christians live in a sort of upside down world, one where the first will be last and the last first, where the least will be the greatest, and the greatest will serve. And even if you've been the greatest of sinners, you have another chance if you're truly sorry and seek forgiveness.

In our story from Matthew we see that a landowner pays everyone the same, even though some have worked all day, and some only a little. What in the world could this mean? Here there's no seniority, no merit pay? Do they have a weak labor union?! This passage would not go over well as the scripture lesson for Labor Day weekend!

It could be that this was directed to certain Jewish converts in the young church who resented that Gentiles could come into the church as "latecomers" and still experience the full measure of God's grace! We note that the landowner, who symbolizes God, vs. 15, says: "Do you begrudge me my generosity?" This is a passage about *grace*, not about justice. There are many stories about justice as well. This is a story about the freedom of God, and the fact that things are not always the way we think they ought to be. It's about the generosity of God in bestowing gifts, even on those who may not deserve them.

The landowner happens to symbolize God. This is not the usual example, because landowners on this earth are *not* God, and it is not uncommon for them to do bad things. In Jesus' day landowners could do just about anything they wanted to, and that's still true in many parts of the world.

One reason why Jesus may have told this story is because of what happened a few verses earlier in the "Rich Young Man story." After that Peter said, "We have left everything and followed you. What shall *our* reward be? Was Jesus thinking that his followers were trying to bargain with him? Did he then answer with this story? Are *we* sometimes too busy thinking about what *our* reward will be?

The amounts of money that Jesus uses here are quite large. If we made the denarius our base figure, or the minimum income that a family could live on without being considered caught in poverty, what would be the value of a denarius today? One minimum wage? Two? In my experience with shelters for the homeless, some families having two minimum wage jobs are losing their homes—they just can't keep up with the rent.

When I think about the "ordinary" people, the "little" people, I have to think of low pay, limited job options, welfare, its dilemmas, its abuses. We could talk about the question of who *really* works for their living.

I've met people, and I imagine you have, too, who really do believe that their prosperity is purely because of their own cleverness and hard work, and that most of those who are poor must be lazy. Perhaps they've not learned to live with grace, and they think that it's only their own smarts and goodness that put them where they are. Rather than thinking, "how fortunate I am! How many fine opportunities I've had." Of course, hard work, patience, and faithfulness are good—But there's an attitude that Jesus is trying to deal with here. Economic success does bring temptations and spiritual dangers!

As I've said, it appears that Gospel writer Matthew had aimed today's story at certain Christian religious types with a Jewish background, those who seemed to think that they were the "level-one" righteous, and who often resented that Gentiles could come into the church as latecomers and still be full-fledged church members, experiencing the full measure of God's grace!

If we're inclined to ask more from God than grace and the simple joys of our faith, or if we desire that others have less because *we* think that they're less deserving, are *we* really ready to enter that strange new place called "Eternity," where it is said that God's will is done, and where there is perfect caring and harmony?

Isn't it fascinating how jealousies and resentments dominate our thinking when we think that someone else is getting more than we are, for the same work—although there really *are* classes of people who consistently get paid much less for the same work. Many of them live in other countries, but many of them live nearby. There are companies in our own land where there are differences of up to ten times, and occasionally 100 times between the pay of the lowest and the highest workers! In this case it is not a matter of grace, but of injustice, pure and simple!

Most of us are more comfortable with the idea that people should get what they deserve! Or, I deserve whatever I can get my hands on; or, I deserve whatever I can get away with! Living with grace means recognizing that we do not get what we deserve, and that's good news, because often that which we deserve is a kick in the pants!

Living with grace does not mean that I am more special than other people, and that I may bend the rules. The rules still apply! Living with grace does not mean that I may sin all the more, so that grace may abound!

Living with grace leads us to look at a related idea. Sometimes we're too hard on *ourselves,* refusing to believe or accept that God loves me, even me! Why would we find it so difficult to live as loved, forgiven people? Why is it that we work so hard to be approved, accepted? How proud we are of our works! How loveless we can be towards those who do not work as we work, particularly those who are different.

In the words of St. Paul: "For by grace you have been saved

through faith; and this is not your own doing, it is the gift of God."

The Old Testament has some wonderful lines which speak of God's grace: "Let the wicked forsake their way, and the unrighteous their thoughts; let them return to the Lord, that he may have mercy on them, and to our God, for he will abundantly pardon" (Isaiah 55:7). I am still learning to live with that—maybe you are, too!

Learning to live with grace means learning to receive life as a gift, and to live that gift with love; and to learn to receive forgiveness as a gift, and to offer it back as a gift, which also means learning to rejoice when others receive it too!

52

LAZARUS AND THE RICH MAN:

A STUDY IN SEPARATION

Pentecost 17, Year C
Luke 16:19-31

"There was a rich man who was dressed in purple
and fine linen and who feasted sumptuously every day.
And at his gate lay a poor man named Lazarus."

Luke 16:19-20a

Do you remember the film, "Trading Places?" Dan Aykroyd
plays the part of a rich young man who offers to trade places
with a clever street beggar, played by Eddie Murphy. Some
very unexpected things happen, and we begin to see that riches
are not simply the reward for smarts and hard work. Poverty
and riches are complicated!

In Deuteronomy 8:11-12, Moses warns the people of Israel
on the eve of entering the Promised Land of the danger that,
when they have entered the land and attained prosperity, they
may become proud and forget Yahweh—a warning also
obviously applicable to individuals. In 31:20 He warns more

specifically that when they acquire wealth, they might turn from Yahweh to other gods.

The story about Lazarus and the rich man may be among the most vivid pieces of writing in the Bible. This one is so strong that I even hesitate to read it in church! That bit about the dogs licking his sores, and the description of the agonies of hell is powerful stuff!

It's a study in separation, of chasms in relationships. It's a commentary on materialism. We have to believe that Luke has Jesus telling this story not just to talk about concepts of heaven and hell. He's telling it in order to address the perplexing dilemma of appalling wealth and near absolute poverty that exist on earth, often side by side.

We must deal with this as individuals, yet we're also challenged to deal with it structurally, as a society. This particular story is not about how to administer social welfare—that is, the actual practice of dealing in a fundamental, long-term way with the poor among us. We may look to the larger witness of Jesus for guidance about that, or to Deuteronomy, or draw it from the biblical vision of Shalom. This story simply points us to the issue of separation and its importance as an ultimate and final matter.

Our society has a serious, over-arching problem: materialism. Each one of us here is faced with the problem, because we live and breathe the "air" of our society.

The rich man was not really that bad. He was probably a pretty cool guy, with his nice house, and his fine clothes and all! It doesn't seem that he was intentionally cruel. At least he didn't drive Lazarus away from his gate. Would I have allowed someone like that to camp outside my gate? Or would I have called the police to have him driven away? It would seem that he even allowed the scraps from his table to be given to Lazarus. He probably gave a typical amount of his wealth to charity. What, then, really, was the nature of his sin, that Luke, our writer, put him in hell?

We're not told that the rich man had been particularly evil, and we're not told that Lazarus had been particularly good. *Not particularly bad. Simply rich.* That seems to present a certain set of problems. And that describes us.

It's said that Lazarus is the only person in the parables who gets a proper name. That name is the Greek form of Eleazar, which means "one whom God has helped." It's a rather common name, and this is probably not the same Lazarus as the one mentioned in John 11. The rich man isn't named right here, though some say that he is Dives, named elsewhere, and the word Dives simply meant rich, so it was probably a generic name.

The story is stronger than at first glance. When the dogs licked Lazarus' sores, it made him *ritually* unclean forever, and a proper Jew would go to great lengths to avoid such a person. Yet in the end the rich man asked to be allowed to lick water from the finger of Lazarus.

According to my *Interpreters' Bible*, the famous missionary Albert Schweitzer was deeply touched and influenced by this story, and after studying it came to feel that Africa was the beggar lying at Europe's doorstep. He later founded Lambarene Hospital.

There appear to be two distinct themes here. First, the Kingdom of God represents a reversal of values (this is reflected in many passages: 6:20,24 "Blessed are you poor, for yours is the kingdom of God, and "Woe to you that are rich, for you have received your consolation") And, secondly, in Luke 16, verses 27-31, we find the assertion that the impenitent rich have already had ample warning of their fate in the Law and the Prophets. Further warnings, or even miracles, will not help them.

The poor man Lazarus had apparently become as transparent as a window glass, separated, unseen by the rich man, even though he was right there at the gate. Lack of caring created a great distance, one that grew from day to day, though they lived in the same little world. And when they had both died, the distance remained. But then it was FINAL.

There's a difference between "boundaries" and separation. We all have our private "space" as individuals. God made us, each one, to be unique, special. It's inappropriate for us to invade the private space of another person, and it's up to us to try to protect our own. Even God does not seem to invade that space, but allows us to open the door from inside. When someone crosses into our space in inappropriate ways, we're not obliged to respond.

But separation is different. It speaks of loss of connectedness, loss of relationships, absence of love. Assuming that we've been created to be in relationships, separation is a tragic condition.

Even the excuse that Lazarus was ritually unclean and must be avoided could not hold up under the ethical standards of the Law of Moses.

Separation, transparency, disconnection. We might also call this a study in indifference, or lack of passion. It is all-too-often a permanent condition where we keep our problems at arms' length. Our text speaks of someone desperately in need, reaching out for help, but treated with indifference.

Perhaps the rich man was too absorbed in himself to be able to see. Here was someone who felt his affairs were very important. Maintaining the estate; maintaining the elements of privilege. Very serious business. Locked into a position of wealth and privilege. Was he actually separated from life?

With the rich man, we might say, "I wasn't indifferent . . . I just didn't know! If I had only known!" But we *do* know. Some years ago I did a photo essay on rural people and places in The Philippines. Some of the photos showed extreme poverty, and I was moved to use an anonymous quote: "Lord, I stand before you as one who can never say, 'But God, I did not know . . .' For that which I have seen and heard has left me innocent no more."

We can readily see that selfishness and indifference can make for hell on earth—why should we doubt that it would bring us hell in God's great cosmic plan? If we live without compassion, are we not digging the chasm deeper? Each time the rich man walked past Lazarus, and each time he listened to the self-serving, comforting speeches designed to justify his condition of privilege, was he not digging the chasm of separation deeper, further building his own hell?

And by the same measure, each time Lazarus experienced the separation and rejection anew without becoming embittered, he was creating an appealing spiritual identity. Lazarus, despite his pitiful condition, was on a journey of growth.

I find it interesting that Jesus refused to have this story end with a miracle or sign. This would seem consistent, as Jesus again and again insisted that peoples' hearts are not changed by signs and miracles. Signs do not redeem—they may jolt us, they may scare us, but in the end it is our own will, our commitment that must be transformed.

The rich man had not been mean. He had not been "bad." But it appeared that he had been alone, even with others present. He had not shared his life. He had not wanted to dirty his hands, and now, when he asked for the tip of an unclean finger, he was refused. The distance had become too great.

Jesus told this story to save. Our future is still open, and our story does not have to be the story of this rich man.

Lanao, Philippines

53

WHEN THE HONEYMOON IS OVER

Pentecost 18, Year C
II Timothy 1:1-14

*"Hold to the standard of sound teaching that you
have heard from me, in the faith and love that are in
Christ Jesus. Guard the good treasure entrusted to you,
with the help of the Holy Spirit living in us."*
II Timothy 1:13-14

One of the joys of having a computer these days and being
on the Internet is receiving the various bits and pieces of humor
and "useful" information. Much of it is of dubious validity. For
instance, Polar bears are left-handed; there are more collect
calls on Father's Day than any other day of the year; and the
average life-span of a major league baseball is 7 pitches. One
that interested me is that Hallmark produces greeting cards
for 105 different kinds of relationships and occasions. I mention
this one because we may well have the most over-gifted and
over-recognized society that the world has ever known, with
the certificates and plaques of appreciation, the trophies and
awards of every large and small achievement (mostly small),
that you might imagine.

I'm not against showing appreciation. In fact I'm all for it, and think that we might do more of it in the life of the church, as many richly deserve it. What I'm doing here is lifting up one of the themes in today's passage from Second Timothy, that of *endurance*. Second Timothy is the most personal of the pastoral letters. It's an earnest note of encouragement from a veteran missionary to a younger colleague. Paul's words are a testimony of assurance and hope in the face of his own certain martyrdom.

At a meeting of the pastors of our district we were invited to share recollections of our baptism. I was baptized as an infant, so have absolutely no memory of mine. One of the pastors shared recollections of hers: she was eight years old, so she remembers it well. She remembers that it was a deeply moving experience, and that the days after her baptism were like a "honeymoon" with Jesus. For days, even weeks afterward she would go home from school and sit with her Bible on a rocking chair near the oil stove, reading, hungry to learn of God; eager to grow in a relationship with Jesus. And then, gradually, the excitement cooled; she studied less and less, and her attention became more and more preoccupied with the stuff of school and friends, and "life." The honeymoon was over. She settled into a longer-term pattern where she fluctuated between a maturing of faith, forgetfulness, renewal, doubt, and then back again to inspiration and faith.

She mentioned a verse in the book of Revelation (2:4) where John writes his vision of the words of the Lord: "You have persevered and have endured hardships for my name, and have not grown weary. Yet I hold this against you: You have forsaken your first love."

Jesus' followers in the early church had this problem. They wavered between faith and doubt, hope and fear, conviction and apathy; between a determination to follow Jesus without counting the cost, and an anxious need for recognition and praise. *We* have this problem.

II Timothy 1:6 says: "For this reason I remind you to rekindle the gift of God which is within you . . ." or in the New

International Version, it says "I remind you to fan into flame the gift of God which is in you."

In Luke 17 we see Jesus' words to his disciples in relation to the tough times ahead. We feel the impending destiny of Jerusalem and the cross. Luke writes from a desire to encourage and challenge the early followers of Jesus during trying times.

We can almost hear the plaintive cry: "Please give us more faith! We're only beginners! Please help us!" But the passage says in no uncertain terms that we should not expect a great big thank you for doing things that are simply expected of us.

Our "rescue" is truly by grace, through faith. But there is still duty, which calls for endurance. What we expect from God for doing our duty is not big "thank yous," not reward, but rather grace and goodness. Does it bother you to be called away from your favorite television show to listen to a discouraged friend? That's what friends do. Does it bother you to be the last one to leave the soccer field where your children have been playing because no one else has picked up the cones and the goals? That's what moms and dads do. That's what servants do. Big surprise! That's what servants do!

And often anonymously. One wonders how much time would be spent in community service if nobody knew what we did? How hard would we work on the new project if someone else got the credit for it? Yet, biblically, we're promised that the One to whom we answer finally, God, our Heavenly Parent, "sees us in secret, and will someday reward us openly." (Matt. 6:4)

Along another vein, one thing I learned in my work in rural community development was that while you appreciate it if and when people are grateful, and fortunately, many are, you mustn't get into the trap of working for "thank you." First of all, when we participate in the growth of others, some of the most important things we do may make them feel uncomfortable, and they're not likely to think that feeling uncomfortable is all that great. Secondly, some of the most important things we should be doing have to do with empowerment, an experience which leaves people thinking, not, "Wow, look at how great our helper is," but "Wow, look at what we've been able to do for ourselves!" And then they don't think of *you*. Some of the most significant, helpful relationships do not involve "thank yous."

Unfortunately, in the long haul, often working without thanks and assurance, we *can* lose that glow of our new-found faith. This passage is about faith and endurance. So you can't pray, because you don't have enough grace? You can't be charitable, because you're too weak and too poor yourself? You can't organize yourself to so something good for people around you, because you don't know where to start? You can't break that habit, because you don't have enough inner strength? You can't deal with that relationship problem, because you're not strong enough to make the first move?

Our "lesson" seems to be saying, "Don't kid yourself! This is not a moment for self-pity! Don't let yourself off the hook! You must start with what you have, seek to be faithful, and let it unfold. If we want to keep our spiritual lives vital and fresh, we must pay the price. This means being open to God's spirit; opening our lives to others in love, thanks or no thanks; and assuming some kind of self-discipline, in our reflecting, in our reading, in our sharing with others.

Jean Bolen writes in her book *Crossing to Avalon*: "When new life stirs within the womb and a mother has the sensation of her baby moving within her for the first time, it's called "quickening." The same word is associated with Christian pilgrims who went to sacred places to "quicken" the divinity within themselves, to experience spiritual awakening or receive a blessing or become healed. The seeker embarks on a journey with a receptive soul and hopes to find divinity there.

When our spiritual honeymoon is over, we must address the continual need for renewal. When we settle in for the long haul on our faith journey, we must go for growth in maturity and endurance, nurturing a relationship with God that rests upon the assurance that pleasing God is far more important that the signs, the accolades and the recognition given by the world.

54

BANDAIDS, ASPIRIN, AND WHITE CHICKENS:

WHEN HEALING GOES DEEP

Pentecost 19, Year C
Luke 17:11-19

"Then one of them, when he saw that he was healed,
turned back, praising God with a loud voice."

Luke 17:15

The two men had come to see me because the hilot (a
native healer) had asked them to find a white chicken, and
they knew that the Rural Center was a good place to start. As a
matter of fact, a couple of months earlier I had brought a
shipping crate of fifty White Leghorn chicks down from Manila
to use for breeding purposes on our demonstration farm,
hoping to improve the laying performance of our native hens.

The hilot had claimed that the blood of a white chicken
was needed to work a cure for Antonia. I knew her, as she had
often attended worship with her small children at the Rural
Center. It was harvest time, and Antonia had worked too hard.
She became so tired that she couldn't sleep, and had slipped
into a deeply disturbed state.

Something made me resist this request, though I did want to help. The men were polite when I told them that I needed the chickens, and I didn't believe that the blood of a white chicken would help. They seemed to appreciate my offer to contact a local doctor, to see if he might have some advice. I was soon to learn that they found their white chicken elsewhere!

At least 50 people were gathered around Antonia's thatched hut later that day when I approached, and I saw the blank gaze on her sun-worn face as she stood at one of her windows, sometimes shouting, not making sense. She was outrageously tired, and not in the least responsive to those trying to calm her.

The hilot was about ready for a "treatment," and I was invited inside, to be with the family. Antonia was literally captured and carried to the floor of the main room, where she was held down by several strong people, and the hilot rubbed a specially prepared paste over her body. I cringed as he chanted and pounded her with his fists, all over, a physical assault that may well have exacerbated her condition. I wanted to run away, but didn't. After the so-called "treatment," Antonia went back to her window, and still didn't sleep.

I had brought some sleeping tablets that the doctor had recommended, and the family was to encourage her to take some. If she wouldn't cooperate, they were to pulverize the tablets and put the powder in her food. We had prayer together, and after a few hours I left.

I learned that after several days Antonia did eventually sleep, but she was never again the same. Her attendance at Sunday morning services was less frequent, and she hardly ever spoke. I don't know that I ever saw her smile again. It was as though a light had gone out.

It troubled me later that I had refused the request for the white chicken. One less White Leghorn wouldn't have made any difference to me. What harm would that have done? Giving it, or not giving it, either way, the terrible pounding on her body would have taken place. I'm glad that I did do more than pray. But there's still something unresolved for me about that experience, as Antonia's so-called "healing" seemed empty.

I wonder: How much of our healing *is indeed* somewhat empty? Granted, all healing in its multitude of forms are a gift of God—whether it involves bandaids, aspirin, cat-scans, quadruple bypasses, or white chickens.

Our passage in Luke 17 is especially interesting because it shows a case of healing that goes deep. Ten lepers were healed. Nine went away immediately, probably very excited about getting on with their lives. They may have been thankful. The Samaritan, the one from a group of people usually considered unacceptable, came back! He did not get on with his old life— he began a new life. His healing went deep. This is a story about healing, and gratitude, and then a changed life.

At first glance the story would seem mainly to be about gratitude. Ten were healed, and only one returned to give thanks—a Samaritan. The outsider among the outcasts was the only one to return and express his thanks. What started as a story about healing ends up being a story about faithfulness and gratitude. An outcast—a rejected one—bows down, giving thanks to God!

Gratitude is obviously a great virtue, and is considered a "Christian" virtue. Paul gives emphasis to this in Colossians 3: "Be thankful. Let the word of Christ dwell in you richly, teach and admonish one another in all wisdom, and sing psalms and hymns and spiritual songs with thankfulness in your hearts to God." (Col.3:15-16)

But there's something in here beyond the gratitude part, and that's because the healing goes deep. The healing of the Samaritan had an outcome that was not exactly expected.

Some scientists think they understand healing, sort of. Yet that incredibly complex and mysterious process seems woven throughout the fabric of our lives, touching us at many, many points: we treat cuts and scratches with bandaids, headaches with aspirin, and a myriad of serious and not-so-serious conditions with all manner of technology. But the welcome restorative change comes as a mysterious gift.

That precious gift appears in so many everyday ways: the regeneration of our bodies and spirits after a good night's sleep; the uplift that comes in getting out-of-doors into the fresh air of a gorgeous sunshiny day; or the mellow coziness of a hot cup of coffee (or tea!) on a drizzly, gray day; the excitement of an unexpected phone call from a friend we haven't heard from for a long time; being in touch with our children, our husband or wife; the stirring of our spirits in hearing the pleasant sound of our favorite kind of music; a dish of our favorite ice cream; something that happened that put our mind at ease. Maybe that something was simply a prayer that we might let go of some worry. All of these can be very healing, and they're all good gifts. The healing may or may not "go deep."

The leper who was a Samaritan entered a new dimension. He came back to thank Jesus. That's nice. But what gets our attention here is that he did not return to life-as-usual. His life was transformed, not just his body.

In the French Academy of Science there's a prominent display of a very simple tool, an old shoemakers awl. The shoemaker uses an awl to make holes in leather, usually before sewing the pieces together with thread. The awl on display is special because one day while it was being used by a shoemaker it fell from the workbench and into the eye of his nine-year-old son. The son went blind in that eye, and soon became blind in both eyes. Eventually, to continue his schooling, he went to a school for the blind, and at this school he learned to read by handling large, carved wooden blocks.

As he grew older, the blind shoemaker's son thought of a new way for the blind to read by feeling dots that had been punched on paper, and he developed his new system using the same awl that had blinded him! His name was Louis Braille, and his new reading system for the blind was called, of course, "The Braille system." (Story from Guideposts, by Patricia Houck Sprinkle, 1978).

While he was not able to regain his sight, Louis Braille experienced healing in a deep and miraculous way, and he became a blessing to many people.

Many of us have had some kind of awl fall into our lives. When it strikes, we could ask, "How could God allow this to happen?" Or, "How can my eye be made to see again?" Or, "Is there transformation waiting in the wings through this unfortunate happening, if only I will claim it?"

Some say that deep healing requires that we humble ourselves; that we be willing to be changed; that we have confidence that we don't have to stay the way we are. Surely it also requires that we accept that physical healing is not always a part of God's answer.

Bandaids and aspirin are great! I use them. A lot. I really don't know if Antonia was healed, or if the white chicken helped. At least she got so she could sleep. But deep healing is about transformation. The 9 lepers in this story were healed of their disease, and that's wonderful. They probably went back to their everyday lives—to their work, their families, and that's good too. Maybe to carry on life as usual. But to carry on life as usual might not always be so good.

The tenth leper, a Samaritan, went back to Jesus, gratefully, and began a whole new life. His healing went deep.

Papuan Priest

55

MY HOME TOWN

October 21, 2001
Jeremiah 29:1, 4-7, 11-14

"Build houses and live in them; plant gardens and eat what they produce. Take wives and have sons and daughters; take wives for your sons, and give your daughters in marriage, that they may bear sons and daughters; multiply there, and do not decrease. But seek the welfare of the city where I have sent you into exile, and pray to the Lord on its behalf, for in its welfare you will find your welfare . . . . When you search for me, you will find me; if you seek me with all your heart, I will let you find me, says the Lord, and I will restore your fortunes and gather you from all the nations and all the places where I have driven you, says the Lord, and I will bring you back to the place from which I sent you into exile."

Jeremiah 29:5-7, 13-14

Do you presently live in your home town? It's interesting to see how many people have been "transplanted." I have. Ask preacher kids or missionary kids THIS question! And the moving still goes on. Most of us move many times. Our brothers and sisters who have moved here all the way from Tonga have. The people of Israel have. I'd venture a guess that most of us here have been transplanted. Statistics say that we pack up our bags, on average, as a nation, every six years (*Homiletics*, Oct 2001, p. 57). In 1900, they say, about 8% of the world's population lived in sizeable cities. A century later, in the year 2000, over 50% (or more than 3 billion people) live in cities. (Urban missiologist Ray Bakke, quoted in *Explorer*, Aug. 14, 2000)

In any case, the idea of "my home town" is very real to me. You ask me what's my home town, and without blinking I'll say, Waukegan, Illinois, just north of Chicago, right on Lake Michigan, you know, the home of Jack Benny, Otto Graham, Nat King Cole, and Outboard Marine, maker of Johnson outboard motors (although as of this writing, they've closed that factory, which is the story of many hometowns these days).

I've told some of you about my wonderful grade school class reunion last June, best class reunion I've ever had. Bonnie Brook Elementary School, class of '47. I met the girl who gave me my first kiss (I didn't kiss her this time).

Why is it my home town? I suppose because I spent my childhood and youth there. But I seldom go back there now, and none of my family lives there any more.

It IS nice to be able to romanticize our home town. but when I go back to Waukegan, it doesn't look the same. Everything looks smaller now, and quite frayed around the edges. The Genesee Theater, which used to look so grand, is just a wimpy little thing, not grand at all, even though it stands on the main street, Genesee Street (not far from *Grand* Avenue!). The homes where our family lived over the years look so small. As I say, it doesn't look the same, and I have no plans to move back!

Brad Edmondson, whose web address is "ePodunk.com" says that people would actually be better off if they'd stay put and get involved. Great hometowns have two things: people who stay around, and people who get involved. He mentions Sheboygan, Wisconsin, where people stay on the same bowling team for decades! Once known as the "City of the 4 C's" (churches, chairs, children and cheese), Sheboygan now boasts a Riverfront Boardwalk, a state park, a county museum, and a children's museum. Local foods include bratwurst, double brats, brats on a stick, brat gyros, brat tacos, and brat pizza. Pretty exciting, eh?

The Jews had home towns. They had a homeland. Jesus had a home town, Nazareth. In today's lesson Jeremiah sends a letter to the homesick Jewish exiles in Babylon. In this complicated history, which we won't go into right now, Jerusalem's best and brightest have been carried off to Babylon, where they're not sure just what to do. They feel stuck in a foreign, God-forsaken place, far from their true home.

Did God will that they be carted off to this foreign land? There's an inference in this passage that God had wanted that to happen. Whatever it means, my theology insists that God does not will what is bad for us or what will hurt us. In fact, we might justifiably say: "God does not will everything that happens, but God wills that GOOD will come from everything that happens."

So Jeremiah writes a letter to the exiles: "Thus says the Lord: Build houses and live in them; plant gardens and eat what they produce. Take wives and have sons and daughters. Multiply there, and do not decrease. But seek the welfare of the city where I have sent you. In other words, "For now, stick around, put down roots, and get invoved! Don't sit around nursing your disappointments or regrets!"

A great message for Seaview, a small church, rooted in a community. The pastor might well say, "Really BE where you are. Enjoy and build up your neighborhood. Seek the welfare of the place where you are. Seek the well-being of a diverse, confusing and often conflicted culture." Engage it, says Jeremiah, don't try to escape it. For in its welfare you will find your welfare.

As Christians in what many are calling a post-Christian culture, and during truly trying times, our challenge is to work and pray for the wholeness of the society with which our own well-being is tightly and irreversibly linked. This doesn't mean that we abandon the close spiritual fellowship of this congregation, and it doesn't mean that we become a social service agency or a public policy center.

Though we *are* engaged in those important things through other channels, it means that we will bloom where we are planted, seeking the welfare of the neighborhood and community where we have been placed. It's heartening that so many churches ARE doing and being in this mode.

We should never think that the size of a church or the size of its neighborhood is what really matters. Look at Sheboygan, Wisconsin! Look what came out of Nazareth!

It's true, Saint Paul wrote in Corinthians that we're like strangers in a foreign land. Somewhat like exiles. We are supposedly IN the world, but not OF the world. At the same time we believe in the central importance of God's forgiving, nurturing love, which became flesh: practical, concrete, visible. It happened in a radical way in Jesus, and it still happens through people like us.

And we all share a home town: PLANET EARTH. At the moment we have nowhere else to go. We cannot transplant ourselves, and had better take good care of the place where we have our roots!

Kathleen Dean Moore, in *The Sun*, March, 2001, a thoughtful journal of thoughtful articles, poetry and photography, speaks of kelp in the ocean:

> "A holdfast is the structure at the root end of a bull kelp that holds it to the ocean floor, even against the force of the tides. It's like a fist of knobby fingers that stick to the rocks with a glue the plant makes from sunshine and salt water.

"I'm fascinated by holdfasts, both for what they are and for their power as metaphor. What are our human holdfasts? As our children leave home and our parents pass away, what structures of connection will hold us together? How will we find an attachment to the natural world that makes us feel complete and fully alive?"

Take good care of your roots, and don't be afraid to put them down again, into nourishing ground. Wherever you are, be rooted and grounded in love. Build. Plant. Grow. God's promise in Jeremiah is: "When you search for me you will find me, if you seek me with all your heart. And I will restore your fortunes, and bring you back to your place."

56

REGARDING THOSE WHO ARE SURE

OF THEIR OWN GOODNESS

Pentecost 21, Year C
Luke 18:9-14

"He told this parable to some who trusted in
themselves that they were righteous and regarded
others with contempt . . . I tell you, this man, (the tax
collector) went down to his home justified rather than
the other; for all who exalt themselves will be humbled,
but all who humble themselves will be exalted."

Luke 18:9, 14

One of the special privileges I enjoyed as a young missionary
in The Philippines was serving as host to interesting church
visitors, some of them rather prominent, and it became
noticeable to me that, generally, the more important they were
said to be, the easier they were to be with. J. Manning Potts,
then editor of *The Upper Room* daily devotional guide, was
especially delightful, and one day as we met with a small group
in a local church, he shared some reflections on the Luke 18
text, and referred to the Pharisee as a "self-satisfied sweetie."

The term loses something in translation, but it works well in English!

People happily sure of their own goodness: if you're one of these, and serious about appropriating the spirituality of Jesus, you have a problem.

Typically, Luke shows us two contrasting characters. Each one described himself, and both were truthful. The Pharisee *really was* righteous by common tests, and the tax collector, apparently, *really was* guilty of graft and corruption. That's what they said. In describing themselves they were probably truthful.

And like he often did, Jesus turned conventional morality and wisdom on their ear! Those usually thought to be right and righteous are humbled, and the ones who are despised are lifted up. The "O.K." people turn out to be not so O.K. after all!

Here come the Pharisees again, and I'm beginning to feel sorry for them—always getting a bad rap. Let's not get into Pharisee-bashing. When Jesus talks about Pharisees, he is really talking about *us*. There were Pharisees known to be positive, fine examples of humility, and some who were considered the open, progressive people of their day.

The Pharisees *did* do acts of mercy—part of their understanding of the observance of The Law was doing acts of mercy. And so do we, and so our faith does direct us. It's said that the Pharisees were fascinated with Jesus' teaching approach, which often had him boiling things down to the central core of a matter, the few pithy things at the center of an issue, the "spirit" of a question. Pharisees could relate to this, and they liked to listen to Jesus.

The passage is clear about who is being addressed—those who trusted in themselves, whether they be Pharisees or not. Those who were self righteous, and who looked down on others. Persons who were quite sure of their own goodness.

This might well involve not only "nice" religious people, but nice, "politically correct" people, some of whom are religious, of course. Sure of their own correctness!

There's a fascinating documentary film, "First Contact" about the first visit of "white men" in the remote highlands of Papua New Guinea in the mid-1930's. It has actual film footage of the original visit of two Leahy brothers, along with interviews done in the 1970's of the New Guinea village people who had been present at the time of the unique 1930's interaction.

The village people were greatly puzzled and awed at these strange creatures who looked like humans and the flying machine that had brought them, at first wondering whether they were real, or were incredibly vivid ghosts. The question was resolved when one of the villagers secretly followed one of the white men into the bush. He came running back to the village, saying, (this is a polite translation) "They're human, they're human! They move their bowels, just like we do, and it stinks, just like ours!"

We have to note that many, if not most societies exalt the boastfulness and the arrogance of the proud. Sadly, modern psychology tells us that often attitudes of self-righteousness and arrogance are actually born of low-esteem, and that the macho attitude is often rooted in anxiety. In our own society, when things are not going so well for individuals outside the home, for example, we're more likely to see domestic violence. William Shakespeare said it well in *Hamlet*: "Conceit in weakest bodies strongest works!"

In our New Testament reading today, the tax collector stood afar off from Jesus—far from the altar, so to speak, knowing himself to be unclean. The Pharisee stood up close—confident in his righteousness, even praying, or at least thinking, "I thank you, God, that I'm not like the sinners!"

Jesus certainly wasn't praising or justifying the tax collector's way of life—surely he disliked it. And Jesus was not condemning the Pharisee's charity and honor. Surely he would have praised the actions. But the Pharisee, rather than saying "thank God, I'm not like one of those," might well have said, "There but for the grace of God go I!"

The scriptures are *not* calling us to a humility which

underestimates or depreciates our own worth. Genuine humility is evidenced by its spiritual power: people with a purpose, some famous, some little known, some almost "saintly," whose sincerity and humble goodness results in remarkable influence for good.

I recall situations where acquaintances have solved problems with humility, patience, and respectful listening, and have experienced healing, second chances, new possibilities.

I think of experiences with so-called "simple" people of the land, peasants in the Base Christian Communities in the villages of Mindanao, Philippines during the darkest Marcos years, studying the Bible in small groups, exhibiting profound theological and historical understandings which supported movement toward non-violent change.

I have recollections of pearls of wisdom coming from my own children, some humorous, some truly wise, some both!

I remember a scientist with unusual achievements who had a highly developed sense of awe, who acknowledged the marvelous role of the Creator, and who confesses the limitations of human beings in the process of knowing.

I have an organic garden. Compost and humus are central in the life of this garden. Out of lowly humus come delicious strawberries, tomatoes, and flavorful herbs! Out of the muck a pristine lily!

Christians hold that God's action in Christ is the prime example of humility. In St. Paul's words,

> "Who, though he was in the form of God, (he, Jesus) did not regard equality with God as something to be exploited, but emptied himself, taking the form of a slave, being born in human likeness. And being found in human form he humbled himself and became obedient to the point of death, even death on a cross." (Philippians 2:6-8)

Our journey as pilgrims of faith means moving from the anxiety of pretense to the peace that passes understanding; from self-deception to reality; from personhood locked up within itself to one that is honest and free; from the burden of having to be good enough to the release of being forgiven and accepted and empowered to live out a grateful life!

Ilocos Sur, Philippines

57

CHOCOLATE-COVERED WAFERS

Pentecost 22, Year B
Isaiah 53:7-12; Mark 10:32-45

" . . . but whoever wishes to become great among
you must be your servant, and whoever wishes to be first
among you must be slave of all.

Mark 10:43b-44

Just before the election of Pope John Paul II, a CBS
newscaster was roaming the streets of Vatican City posing this
question to people in the crowd: "What would you most like to
do if you were the Pope? How would you use your power and
authority?" The interviewer came to a 14-year-old girl, who
answered: "I'd cover the communion wafers with chocolate!"

Pretty amusing, but one of the problems of the church is
precisely that we've already "been there, done that." Some
call it "sweet talk" leadership and "sweet tooth discipleship."
Sometimes we make it appear so easy to be followers of Jesus
that the wrapper we've put around the gospel makes the Bible
look like a box of spiritual chocolates! Notice the consistent
public "Christian" appeals to identify with beautiful, rich,
athletic people.

Marcel DeSaulniers and Michael Grand produced a photo essay with the name, "Death by Chocolate, The Last Word on a Consuming Passion, (Rizzoli Int'l, 1992)." It might be a fitting title for the consequences of our seeming preference for sweet, chocolate-covered communion wafers over the plain bread of the Lord's Table! Our texts remind us that "Cross" is not a nice word. It's a harsh, splintery word.

The Isaiah passage anticipates the suffering and death of the messiah. No, we're not doing "Good Friday in October"—this is a recurring theme, one we find throughout the Christian year, and each Sunday we're to celebrate the day of resurrection.

In the Mark passage the disciples argue again about status! James and John come forward and say, "Teacher, we want you to do for us whatever we ask of you." Jesus asks, "What is it that you want?" And they said, "Grant us to sit, one at your right hand, and one at your left, in your glory!" They seem to be deaf to what Jesus is trying to communicate to them. Jesus replies, "You do not know what you're asking! Are you able to drink the cup that I drink?"

Sometimes the church becomes frighteningly like the society around it: people scratching and clawing to get to the top, to be the leaders, to be the greatest, to be the boss, to be the hero. We must wonder how Jesus relates to this. The Bible is clearly more comfortable with Jesus as "teacher," servant, healer, prophet, even Jesus the counter-culture man! I don't see this as a slap at clear, strong protective leadership, and I'm thankful whenever I see respected, trusted persons being given, and then taking up, accountable authority (in my experience our best leaders are not self-appointed, but drafted).

In this chapter Jesus seems to be patient with his followers, though this is not always the case. He tries to shift their attention away from the rewards that they're seeking, and to focus them on the path that leads to Jerusalem. If they had been expecting that their way was going to be "Easy Street," that the traffic lights were to be "green" the rest of the way, they were sadly mistaken.

Verses 43 to 45 reveal that being a disciple means a life, and maybe even a death, committed to humility and service, a message particularly important for leaders! Some of us, particularly those my age, went through youth fellowship singing "Are ye able, said the Master, to be crucified with me?" I think we sang it too much, and became too comfortable with it. Of recent generations we who sang "Are Ye Able?" may well be the most prone to "Decaffeinated Christianity!" It won't keep you awake at night in this troubled world!

Dietrich Bonhoeffer, the German theologian, spoke of "Cheap grace," in contrast with costly grace. Amazing grace is not cheap grace. Calvin Miller uses the term "Christaholic"— one who uses Jesus to seek highs and happiness as long as it suits his or her needs and purposes.

Let this speak to us across the range of life experience. There are no chocolate-covered wafers, for example, in the aging process! People who face this thoughtfully and reflectively know that even though each one of us is growing older day by day, most of us can still be fully alive in the ways that really matter. No matter how frail our bodies may become, most of us can pick up the spiritual challenge and expose ourselves intentionally, consciously, to new kinds of experience and stimulation. Even though we withdraw from some kinds of physical activities, we're able to put together new ways of being a real person.

I remember the valuable lessons learned from high school football: You keep going, despite the bumps and scratches and bruises! And now, years later, knowing that if I want to be fit, I must pay the price.

There's a story about a patient who went to his physician complaining of pain in several places. The doctor asked him to indicate where it hurt. He pointed first to his leg, then to his back, then to his side, finally to his head. "Every time I press on these places, it hurts." After a careful examination, the physician diagnosed his problem: "You have a broken finger." Could this be a parable about our spirituality?

One day I asked a friend who happens to be gay why it is that we see so many outstandingly creative individuals, artists, poets, musicians, playwrights, who have a same-sex orientation. Without hesitating he replied, "It's the pain and stress. You can not be gay in this society without experiencing enormous pain and stress, and the soul literally bursts with all form of expression." Artists and poets know this as they experience the connection between their pain and their creativity. Robert Bly, author of *Iron John*, wrote a chapter entitled "The Wound By The King's Men," in which he speaks of how from our wounds may come some of our greatest strengths.

The most perceptive, helpful Bible studies I've ever experienced were in the Philippines, when so-called ordinary people of God met in their humble thatched-roof meeting places to reflect upon the terrible forces that were causing death and suffering in their communities against the backdrop of the biblical drama. If you want to understand the Word of Truth in its sharpest clarity, don't go to those who are comfortable and self-satisfied. Listen, rather, for the voices arising from situations where there's pain and struggle. Those who struggle are more likely to understand the nature of "God's projects" for justice, righteousness, and peace.

In 2 Samuel, David said, "I will not offer burnt offerings to the Lord my God which cost me nothing." (2 Sam. 24:24)

In our text for today we're given a sense of what Jesus believes to be true greatness, and warned against trying to stay in the safe, pleasant places. We're pushed onward toward Jerusalem.

It's not really news that we *don't* have chocolate-covered wafers for communion! It is good news that we have the best "survival cookies" you can get!

58

STRANGERS IN A FOREIGN LAND—I

CHALLENGES OF THE SECULAR CULTURE

Pentecost 22, Year A
Matt 22:15-22; I Thessalonians 1:1-10

"But Jesus, aware of their malice, said, 'Why are you putting me to the test, you hypocrites? Show me the coin used for the tax.' And they brought him a denarius. Then he said to them, 'Whose head is this and whose title?' They answered, 'The emperor's.' Then he said to them, 'Give therefore to the emperor the things that are the emperor's and to God the things that are God's.'"

Matthew 22:18-21

A few years ago Hauerwas and Williman wrote a book entitled *Resident Aliens: Life in the Christian Colony (Abingdon, 1989)*. They've picked up a phrase from St. Augustine, "resident aliens," by which he meant "those who reside in the present world and have an interest in it, but whose home and citizenship are not finally of this age." Because, in a real sense, the church is an outpost, a colony of the new creation in the midst of the old.

We no longer live in a nominally "Christian Culture." We live in a society of unbelief. We are an alternative, a counterculture.

I have mixed feelings about defining my belonging in this way, because I love the world, this exquisite earth, with its rich diversity of life, and I believe that God loves it dearly, this beautiful, confused world. That's one of the key reasons why St. Paul's letter to the Thessalonians is of such great interest to us. It deals with the vital challenges that he saw for new Christian converts trying to live faithfully in a pagan culture.

Our reading from Matthew is along the same line, in the way that it deals with the question of paying taxes. "Give, therefore, to the emperor the things that are the emperor's, and to God the things that are God's." But which are which?! This is a lesson having to do with the issue: "Where do we put our deepest loyalty?"

The themes in this three-part series are especially meaningful as we approach the hallowed evening of All Saints Day, and Christmas, two of our most important festivals. These are now so laden with totally unrelated baggage that we sometimes find it hard to believe that they have anything to do with the Christan faith!

I don't want to convey the slightest idea of rejection of the world, or to infer that we're to separate ourselves from the world, because that's definitely not the point of Paul's letter, or of my message.

And I don't mean to infer that all Christians should resonate to the same tunes. Just like the Thessalonians, all of us Christians are like new converts, always seeking to lead new lives, always trying to put an old way of life behind. The experience of new life is basically one of joy, but it is in tension with the loss and the grief involved in putting behind an old life.

First Thessalonians is the first undeniably authentic letter of Paul. It was written in the early '50's, maybe only a few months after the first congregation was formed. We can cross-reference this with lines in the Book of Acts (17:1-10). If any of us needed "evidence," or primary material having to do with the very first congregations of the Christian Church, this is it! There's absolutely no doubt that it is written by Paul himself. Scholars note that the Book of Acts was written about 30 years later than this letter!

Paul, Silas, and Timothy had just founded the church in Thessalonica. It's hard to say just exactly how long they had been working there before this letter was written, but surely less than a year, and possibly only a few months. They had just come from Philippi, where they had suffered insulting treatment.

"Imitation" is put forward as the important method to help these "young" Christians to find their way. Paul looked upon himself as a model, even sounding arrogant at times (though his humility and sense of unworthiness comes through clearly at other points), saying, "Learn from my example." "See what kind of persons we are." "Use us for your models of nurture and growth." "Then *you* become an example, too!"

Works of faith, hope and love were lifted up as the essential elements to demonstrate their new identity as Jesus' followers. A different behavior is what sets us aside as people who are "special."

As we try to read between the lines of this letter we can surmise that the early Christians who took their faith seriously faced huge problems as they dealt with feelings of isolation, loneliness, even abandonment.

An increasing number of Christian theologians openly refer to our time as a "post-Christian" age. They don't mean that Christianity is dead, but rather that we are in a new and critical phase as a religion, where we're no longer the acceptable, popular, establishment religion or way of life. We are now, truly, a minority in our society.

Is this a post-Christian age, or is it a "post-everything" age? We see a major breakdown of trust in nearly all big institutions, whether they be governmental-political, church, business. We see the erosion of authority. "Out with the incumbent!"

It's the role of a local church to be a community of people

that can be clearly seen by the world, a community in which people are faithful to their promises, love their enemies, tell the truth, recognize and advocate for the poor, suffer for righteousness sake, and somehow testify to the amazing creative and redeeming power of God. I love St. Paul's words of blessing:

> "Grace to you, and peace. We give thanks to God always for you all, constantly mentioning you in our prayers, remembering before our God and Parent your work of faith and labor of love and steadfastness of hope in our Lord Jesus Christ. For we know, sisters and brothers beloved by God, that God has chosen you; for our gospel came to you not only in word, but also in power and in the Holy Spirit and with full conviction."
>
> *I Thessalonians 1:1b-5a*

59

STRANGERS IN A FOREIGN LAND—II

HOW SHALL WE LOVE?

Pentecost 23, Year A
Matthew 22:34-46; I Thessalonians 2:1-8

"When the Pharisees heard that he had silenced
the Sadducees, they gathered together, and one of
them, a lawyer, asked him a question to test him.
'Teacher, which commandment in the law is the
greatest?' He said to them, 'You shall love the Lord
your God with all your heart, and with all your soul, and
with all your mind. This is the greatest and first
commandment. And a second is like it: You shall love
your neighbor as yourself. On these two
commandments hang all the law and the prophets.'"

Matthew 22:34-40

This series addresses the dilemma facing the followers of
Jesus in the new millennium: That is, if the church is
increasingly like the world around it, are we, the church, in
danger of losing the vision of what it means to be "special?"
Today's Matthew text is the climax in the series of

controversy stories. The scholars and leaders were beginning to test and debate Jesus.

Jesus must have seen that this encounter with the Pharisees called for something sharp and clear: truth in a nutshell. That was what Jesus gave them! It's a powerful thing that Jesus said that upon these few lines are based all the law and the prophets!

The people around Jesus may not have been interested in learning from him at all—they were trying to trick him into saying something that would discredit him and make him less threatening!

Sometimes it seems as though the world is trying to test us! Clearly, one of the most urgent "test" questions facing the church is "how are we to love?" We know we're supposed to love, but HOW do we do it? That question "How, then, shall we love?" is found throughout the Bible. It seems timeless, and universal. It transcends religion.

We have the question in the story of Moses. After Moses had given the Israelites a review of how God had shown mercy to them, even in their stubbornness, he asked, "What then, O Israel, does the Lord your God ask of you? The answer was, "fear the Lord your God, to conform to all his ways, to love him and to serve him with all your heart and soul." (Deuteronomy 10:12)

We have the question in the story of the prophets. Micah asked, "What does the Lord require of thee?" (Micah 6:8). The answer was, "Seek justice, love, mercy, and walk humbly with your God." This was reminiscent of the admonition in Leviticus 19 to love the neighbor as the self.

We have it in the gospels. The gospel writers show Jesus responding to that basic question, "What should we do?," or "What is most important?" He combined the Deuteronomy answer of loving God with the answer of the prophets, of loving neighbor. In our Matthew text for today the question is, "Teacher, what is the greatest commandment?" Jesus' answer was: "You shall love the Lord your God with all your heart, with all your soul, with all your mind." The second is like it: "You shall love your neighbor as yourself. On these two commandments hang all the law and the prophets."

Jesus did not invent this, he was simply quoting Leviticus. But he was putting these two together in a new way, saying that this is the whole banana!

While I was reading in the *Interpreter's Bible* about today's lesson in Matthew, I learned that there are 613 commandments in the Old Testament (not just 10!). It said that 365 of them are negative and 248 positive. How would you like to live under that? Nice that we can stick with the "greatest" commandment!

This is not to criticize Judaism for legalism. Jesus was a Jew, of course! The sad thing is that many Christians, and Jews, and Muslims, too, seem to live under the weight of countless "do-nots," unclear about which things are the most important.

What comes across in this lesson is that our fulfillment is not based upon our intellectual prowess and scholarly knowledge—it is in our capacity to love. And that capacity is rooted in the fact that God first loved us!

One fascinating aspect of our modern technological culture is that while it is undeniably secular and even pretends to be anti-religious at times, it presses ever onward in its quest for immortality.

The culture cries out with the question: How shall we live, that we might have the abundant life? How shall we live, that we might escape pain and death? The shelves of the book stores have an amazing array of self-help books and $29.95 videos that encourage us to go beyond our limits to become winners! Books on diets or on exercise, on winning in business. These would seem to convince us that maybe we *can* live as though we're immortal. I wonder how many different kinds of "halls of fame" there are across America?

A positive thing in the self-help books is that they recognize the importance of loving self, and when Jesus says love neighbor as self, he recognizes this. So now we have a strong three-legged stool: love of God, neighbor, self. But stop and think of what we have without any one of the three. Leave out God and you have an atheist, with little power outside the self or the physical community. Leave out neighbor and you have an ascetic. Leave out self and you have a self-flogger with little self-respect!

A baffling aspect of our culture is the hi-tech hatred being thrown at us, particularly at our children. Some of the hottest-selling video games are seemingly developed by people who love to hate. Some examples: Ethnic Cleansing, Shoot the Blacks, and Concentration Camp Rat Hunt. The game, "Ethnic Cleansing" is promoted as "the most politically incorrect video ever made." Here we see that our urgent task is to challenge and remove root causes for haters, and to be "lovers!"

As strangers in a foreign land, in the tradition of the prophets, we must try to get first things first.

"You shall love the Lord your God with all your heart, and soul, and mind." The love of God, whom we cannot see, means reverence for life, and humility in the face of life! It means continuing conversation with God, or willingness to listen, to grow in love, and sharp commitment to the values we think our creator would have us pursue.

"You shall love your neighbor as yourself!" Why is neighbor love so challenging? How may we forgive? How do we put behind old resentments? How do we go beyond the gossip and backbiting and address our own need for forgiveness and growth? Why is it sometimes so hard to love? Why does hatred sometimes come so easily?

One of the amazing things about life is that love of neighbor is intimately tied to love of self! One reason some people have such a difficult time loving and accepting their neighbor is that they have problems respecting and accepting their own selves.

Some fine thoughts and questions have surfaced in our Thursday morning study group:

> "Loving is not a feeling. When you lose the feeling,
> that's the time to start loving."

"To love someone is to enable them to develop their potential."

"How do we discern between that which is destructive to one's self and that which protects one's self?"

"Loving does not mean having to put up with everything, but being willing to absorb some things. It's just not going to be ALL you."

The gospel tells us we can be O.K., by God's grace. We can love our own selves because God first loved us! We can love our neighbor with a self-giving love, because God first loved us!

How shall we love? Paul talks around this question in today's lesson from Thessalonians, but an answer comes through. Paul's deep affection and love for the Thessalonians is expressed frankly, honestly, unselfishly, in a gentle way. No deceit, no trickery, no gimmicks! Paul is not being manipulative—his only goal is to convey his own experience of the good news of God's forgiving love.

60

STRANGERS IN A FOREIGN LAND—III

WHAT DOES IT MEAN TO BE RELIGIOUS?

Pentecost 24, Year A
Matt. 23:1-12; I Thessalonians 2:9-13

"The scribes and the Pharisees sit on Moses' seat;
therefore do whatever they teach you and follow it; but
do not do as they do, for they do not practice what they
teach."

Matthew 23:2-3

As the holidays approach, we're pressed to define ourselves
more clearly as a people of faith living in a society of
indifference, cynicism, and doubt. Differentiating between our
core beliefs and mere fads and cultural baggage can be a
daunting task. So what does it mean to be religious?

Our reading from Matthew (23:1-12) is about people who
preach, but who don't practice what they preach, who do their
deeds in a way that they'll be seen by many people, and who
want to be seated in the places of honor at the feasts and in
the synagogue. People who love the salutations in the market

place, and want to be addressed with respectful titles. In this text "practice what you preach" is lifted up as being religious.

Our Thessalonians reading speaks of Paul's gratitude for the fact that even in the face of great difficulty in a hostile culture the Thessalonian church had responded to the Good News, had become imitators of the Christians who had brought it, and had then become the glory and the joy of Paul! Here "faithfulness" is lifted up as being religious.

These two passages pose a fascinating tension: On the one hand struggling to be faithful while living in a pagan culture, and on the other hand resisting having faith-become-deadened by rigid, institutional religion. We want to be an authentic community of faith, but we don't want to become stuffy-religious like the scribes and the Pharisees described in this passage.

I've been to impressive church meetings where you realize how easily that could happen! There's a beauty, grace and dignity present in the robes, the beautiful stoles and other garments, the scepters, and the lace. Here one picks up the feeling of status, dignity, protocol, titles. Who sits where, who is honored, mostly men. Stained glass windows. Brass plaques that say, "In memory of . . ." It has beauty and style. There are dimensions of it that honor God and honor those who have gone before us. But if we take the lesson for today seriously, these traditional practices do pose a serious spiritual issue!

Both lessons raise the question, "what does it mean to be religious?" The lesson from Matthew points the finger at the self-satisfied religious leaders who do not practice what they preach (23:3). They impose heavy burdens on others but do nothing to help in the carrying of them (23:4); their righteousness is one of show (23:5); and they are hungry for prestige and adulation (23:6-7).

Let's not construe this condemnation of certain Pharisees as Jesus pointing his finger at the Jews in general, as there were, and there are, many very humble Jews who would cheer what Jesus has said. We remember how Jesus lifted up the prophets, particularly Amos, Hosea, and the school of Isaiah, which said in Isaiah 58: "Isn't this the fast I choose? To loose the bonds of injustice, to let the oppressed go free, and to break every yoke . . . to share your bread with the hungry, etc, etc. If you do these things, you'll become like a watered garden, like a spring of water, whose waters never fail."

Matthew includes today's lesson very deliberately to be instructive to the young church. He does not show Jesus congratulating his followers because they are not like the others, because they were! WE, too, are the Scribes and the Pharisees!

The passage gets intensely practical: It is not good enough for the Christian leader to say, "Do as I say, not as I do." Those who tell others what to do but do not do it themselves are called into question. Those who do their good works so that all may see; those who love the best seats, the salutations, the honors, are challenged.

Matthew's gospel moves on to lift up a parable that speaks of ultimate and final issues: Matthew 25, the section entitled by scholars, "The judgment of the nations." Here we have the separation of people like the separation of the sheep from the goats, inferring that when we have healed and fed and clothed, and freed from prison the righteous poor, in effect we have done those things for Jesus. *That's* what it means to be religious!

Years ago, in his landmark book, *Future Shock (1970)*, Alvin Toffler noted that we live in a time of the "peril of over–choice." Oh, how that has proved true! We have cable T.V., and I don't even know how many choices I have when I watch TV. When I grew up, when we wanted an ice cream cone, we could get vanilla, chocolate, and strawberry. Now, how many are there? No wonder we stand befuddled before long lists, even the lists of brands of religion, brands of churches!

The ultimate word, the last word is one of joy and hope. But we cannot hear that last word until we choose to hear the first word of truth, which is the word that strips us naked. The Gospel is Good News, but before it is good news, it is the tough news that we need help! When we choose to listen to that news, we have a chance.

According to the *Handbook of Magazine Article Writing*, Alex Haley, author of *Roots*, has a picture in his office showing a turtle sitting on top of a fence post. When asked the meaning of that, he said, "When you see a turtle on a fence post, you know he had some help." That's us!

Before the Gospel can come to any of us as grace, it must come to all of us as judgment.

We need an answer that overshadows and outshines all other answers and choices, because the truth is that *we need help*. The reality is that we are people with staggering problems, personally, and as a nation, and as a world. Accepting THAT is being religious!

So, as a church, attempting to be a faithful community, we keep trying to be visible: persons and an identifiable place that can be clearly seen by the world, a community in which people are faithful to their promises, love their neighbor, tell the truth, respect and advocate for and with the poor, suffer for righteousness sake, and somehow testify to the amazing creative and redeeming power of God.

61

READING THE SIGNS OF THE TIMES

Pentecost 24, Year C
Luke 21:5-19

"They asked him, 'Teacher, when will this be, and
what will be the sign that this is about to take place?'
And he said, 'Beware that you are not led astray; for
many will come in my name and say, 'I am he!' and,
'The time is near!' Do not go after them."

Luke 21:7-8

I fondly recall pleasant hours of pointless chatter during
car games based on road signs as we took trips with the children,
and the extra chuckles we'd enjoy while driving on back roads
through places like Beanblossom, Fickle, Harmony, and Lapel.

While living in the Philippines I started a collection of
snapshots of creative roadside signs such as, "Don't Stop on
Both Sides at Once," "Sincere Lumber Company, Inc.," and
"Immaculate Conception Mattress Factory."

A Frank and Earnest cartoon has the two of them riding
along a road marked by an arrow: "Road to Success." But up
ahead is another sign: "Be prepared to Stop."

Signs make our lives safer and help us to make wise choices. They often save lives. We live out our days in the midst of signs: Road signs, warning indicators, caution lights, sparks, odors, and pains in our sagging sacroiliacs.

Years ago, coal miners would carry a canary in a cage down into the mine with them, as a means for knowing when there were dangerous gasses present, or not enough air. It was hard on canaries, but it saved human lives.

Some signs, the "frowns" and "nods" of life, are quite subtle, but they can be important. We spend time and energy sifting through the "indicators" around us as we try to live safe, meaningful lives.

When I was a young missionary, a bright but embittered Filipino pastor approached me at a conference and in a most direct, sharp way told me that missionaries should go home. He pointed out, correctly, that it cost about the same amount of money to send and support an American missionary as it would to support about ten Filipino pastors. I knew then, and I know now, that his admonishment, which hurt, was a sign of the times, and that I had something important to learn from it, even though the answer was not a simple one.

It may be totally empty of meaning that some kids wear their baseball hats backward. It's a dramatic warning signal, full of meaning, that mass shootings are occurring in our public schools, and that the resulting anxieties and fears are causing drastic changes in the nature of "community" in our schools.

We could go on and on with this, listing our back aches, and our heartaches, too. Jesus speaks of signs in the sun, moon, and the stars, and in "the roaring and tossing of the sea." Our text in Luke 21 is an interesting example of how Luke drew from Mark, and how he's concerned with signs having to do with ultimate and final matters. In a related Matthew text Jesus quotes Isaiah 13: "The sun will be darkened, and the moon will not give its light; the stars will fall from the sky, and the heavenly bodies will be shaken." (Matt. 24:39) We note that Luke's document, which carries Jesus' dire predictions about

Jerusalem, was written after the Holy City was besieged and destroyed by the Romans in 70 c.e.

There's strong reference to ignorance and indifference, and even hostility and betrayal by people who do not warm to Jesus' warnings. In the passage in Matthew Jesus mentions Noah and the ark. "People didn't pay attention then, he said, and it's the same now." With the early disciples, we witness and we're complicit in the massive faithlessness and skepticism about important signs.

As "Y2K" approached we heard about religious groups that believed that when the new millennium arrived we'd see the end of the age. It was reported on CNN that a group in Mindanao was digging caves and storing food and water, to be able to escape the "fires of destruction." They pointed to the Bible, claiming that we have all of the "signs of the times" mentioned in the book of Revelation.

Here the lectionary "calendar" has brought me squarely before a scripture passage that I surely would not have chosen otherwise! This is tricky stuff, and in my opinion it's badly abused in certain Christian circles. It's too easy to cop out by pointing our fingers at a wicked world out there, and to speculate as to who is "in" and who is "out." Wouldn't it be cool if we could get this over with once and for all, putting on our clean white robes and marching to the mountain top to wait for Christ's coming?!! Quite a few have tried that. I'm thankful for Matthew 24: "of that day and hour no one knows, not even the angels of heaven."

The New Testament speaks more to central truths than to calendar matters, insisting that Jesus is not simply a good man, a "special" teacher, but is God-with-us; that this age will not go on forever—it will in God's time come to a close; and that faithful discipleship, watchfulness, and readiness are our way to be connected with God's future.

Things *are indeed* happening in this world of ours of an ultimate and final nature, and we can be more aware of and sensitive to the signs. There *are* urgent needs and concerns to be attended to, and we cannot indefinitely postpone our commitments, either to God or to our community. We define ourselves, as individuals and as a church, in our response to urgent concerns and biblical values of faithfulness, justice, and compassion.

According to a study done in 2002 by the U.S. Conference of Mayors, homelessness in American cities rose approximately 19% during the past year, with 88% of American cities showing an increase. A sign of the times?

Is this a shallow, secular interpretation? I think not! My understanding of the total biblical witness says that God cares profoundly for the whole of creation, and that *all* of these things matter.

There's a serious tension found in this theme between the reality that we can *not* know the times or the seasons—and *knowing all too well* that there are crucial signs and symptoms which must be heeded—or else, including the dependable, relentless operation of God's physical, social, and moral laws! Therefore, as the Bible tells us, we must continually be "ready" (meaning *fully alive*), watchful, discerning, responsive.

Whether we like it or not, we cannot escape the fact that insensitivity, or inaction, or lack of readiness, can cause us to fall. Yes, Virginia, there *is* such a thing as being *too late*, and we can miss the boat. This can apply to matters ultimate and final as well as matters trivial.

Good News! God's calendar is not what we would make it. Our faithful and just God is always at work, with us and in spite of us, and our future is "blessedly" open!

62

MAKING AN IMPRESSION

Pentecost 25, Year B
Mark 12:38-44

"Then he called his disciples and said to them,
'truly I tell you, this poor widow has put in more than
all those who are contributing to the treasury. For all of
them have contributed out of their abundance; but she
out of her poverty has put in everything she had, all she
had to live on.'"

Mark 12:43-44

The tall man, barefoot and in shorts, slender, weather-
beaten, dignified, handed me a crumpled brown paper bag.
It held 6 smallish eggs of varied off-white hues. I was surprised
and touched. The unexpected gift was one that the giver could
ill-afford, and that I, a rich man, could not refuse.

Working out of New York City as a rural consultant for our
mission agency, I was in an African village at the edge of the
Sahara desert in northern Ghana, visiting rural projects
supported by our church. The area is not far south of
Uagadougu. I love saying that. Uagadougu.

The Christian Service Agency of Northern Ghana coordinated a number of worthy projects in that region, supported in part by the United Methodist Committee on Relief and Church World Service.

The area was so utterly dry that when I turned on the spigot in my humble sleeping room, dust came out instead of water! The people were among the poorest I've ever seen. At that time the desert was relentlessly edging south at the rate of about one mile each year.

Through the encouragement of an effective rural program of the churches, families were growing nutritious food crops during the dry season with water from hand-dug wells along dusty creek beds, and were leveraging their meager resources through savings clubs, credit co-ops, and buying clubs.

The generous gift of the six eggs had come from the heart. The translation of the brief speech was simple and clear: "Please tell your people that we are deeply grateful for their help." *I was impressed.*

In today's lesson from Mark, Jesus was in the temple compound. He was teaching. He saw scribes in their impressive white robes, greeted with respect wherever they went. But Jesus was painfully aware of how many widows whose property was managed by such men had been victimized, their assets unscrupulously taken. He saw the scribes in their handsome robes. *He was not impressed.*

Jesus had noticed how these self-contented leaders went for the best seats in the synagogues and places of honor at the banquets, and he cringed as he listened to the noise of their loud, long prayers. *He was not impressed.*

Jesus noticed how certain rich people would put large sums of money, often loud clanking silver and gold coins, into the temple offering containers. *And Jesus was not impressed.*

Apparently some other people were impressed. The so-called "up-country" people (in the Philippines they were called "provincianos") came from afar to witness the temple scene, and perhaps they *were* impressed. But Jesus, clearly, was not.

And then *she* came in. A "poor widow" is what the Bible calls her. In my mind's eye I see a shy, frail person mostly hid by the common homespun robe and shawl, coming slowly through the crowd to make an offering. She took what she had been concealing out of a small cloth, and making her way to the offering block, jostled by those with the larger bags of heavy money, put in her two small copper coins.

Jesus was impressed. He called his disciples over, and pointed her out. "Truly, I tell you, this poor widow has put in more than anyone. For those rich people gave out of their abundance. She gave out of her poverty, and has put in what she has to live on."

This lesson is one where I find myself straining to catch more of the original meaning. It would have been easy to simply pick up on the generosity of the widow, entitle the story "The Widow's Mite," and then preach a rock 'em, sock 'em stewardship sermon. After all, it *is* getting to be that time of year. But the deeper lesson here is about what it really means to respond to God's love.

The story of the widow's gift is Mark's way of lifting up simple devotion and generosity as an indirect indictment of a religious system that allowed the exploitation of defenseless widows. Some scholars believe that Mark was referring to the practice of scribal trusteeship of the estates of widows. The women of those times were not usually allowed to manage their deceased husbands' assets. Through their public reputation for piety and trustworthiness, scribes could earn the legal right to administer the estates of the widows. As compensation they would usually get a percentage of the assets, and the custom was notoriously subject to abuse. Let's be sure to note that this was directly contrary to the Law and spirit of Judaism, which is to "protect orphans and widows."

The New Testament often characterizes the scribes as symbolic of stuffy, formal religion, of outward appearance at the expense of the real substance of faith. The gospels show

Jesus attacking this again and again, until finally the religious establishment could no longer tolerate him.

The self-righteousness that Mark criticizes in this passage, however, surely involves more than a narrow religious spirituality. Notice the pious phrases of some politicians, and all that we do in the name of national piety! It seems that nowadays aspiring political leaders say "God Bless You" more than preachers do! I, for one, have felt it necessary to pull back from saying it.

My own conviction is that the widows in their cultural enslavement represent for Mark more than widows. They represent the poor and oppressed peoples of his world, those most vulnerable. But widows are an exceptionally helpful focus for us, as in nearly every local church there are substantial numbers of widows. If the widows were suddenly taken away, the life of our churches would be greatly impoverished in a number of important ways!

The story of the "poor widow" might stimulate us to rethink what it means to be an authentic human being. The idea of simply being a good and decent person on an open journey of caring relationships with God and neighbor contrasts with the other ways in which we commonly strive to establish our identity: acquiring and displaying more and more "goods," winning more and more "races," playing the games with ever-increasing stakes that we hope will make people say, "WOW, I'M IMPRESSED!"

But the passage confronts us, saying: In the final analysis the essence of true religion is not outward form, but the quality of faith and caring;

In the end the hypocrites and the exploitation that they represent will not prevail; and

In the end, it is the widows and their friends who will find salvation and release. Tribulation will have an end, and God will bring forth from it something good!

63

IF WE ONLY KNEW

Peace with Justice Sunday
Luke 19:37-42

"As he came near and saw the city, he wept over it,
saying, 'If you, even you, had only recognized on this
day the things that make for peace! But now they are
hidden from your eyes.'"

Luke 19:41-42

A little girl came home from her church pre-school, and as
she was putting away her coat, her mother called out, "How
are you doing, darling?" "I'm tired!," was the answer. "Why?"
asked mom. "All morning long, I've been folding little paper
birds and praying for peace!"

It IS enough to wear us out! Even though the Cold War is
over, the thorny issue of weapons of mass destruction raises its
ugly head in new and frightening ways. Conflict in the Middle
East roars on unabated. Terrible ethnic conflicts fester, and
the threat of high-tech terrorism increases. Injustice deepens,
and the gap between rich and poor widens.

Every thinking person knows that the "problem" is not just
something out there. We're a part of it, and it's something

with roots within us. Beneath the bitter conflicts are attitudes, values, fears, anxieties, selfish interests. Questions related to peace are a grave challenge to our spirituality, and they test our seriousness as a faith community. Dare we say, "If we only knew!"?

Two important peace themes from the Bible give us clues. Both reach to the depths of our private spirituality, but both are profoundly connected with the idea of community. The first is the biblical vision of "shalom," and the second is "Pax Christi."

The name "Salem" (as in Salem, Oregon, or Salem, Massachusetts) means "peace and prosperity." A predominant translation of Jeru*salem* is "foundation of peace." Traveling in Africa and Asia in the course of my work I've run across a variety of forms of the word, like salaam, or salaam alaikum," or in the Philippines, "salamat," found in many of the languages there, which means "thanks," or "bless you."

Above all, in the Bible, shalom means *right relationships*. It often infers relationships within the context of covenant, relationships characterized by righteousness and faithfulness, peace, justice, well-being, and prosperity. Note verses 10 and 11 of Psalm 85, where the psalmist says:

> "Steadfast love and faithfulness will meet; righteousness and peace will embrace. faithfulness will spring up from the ground, and righteousness will look down from the sky." (RSV)

Vivid metaphors are often the creative way used in the Bible to describe the conditions of Shalom: justice like the "just-right" rain (Psalm 72); justice rolling down like the waters (Amos); and from Isaiah 32, like a hiding place from the wind, like streams of water in a dry place, like the shade of a great rock in a weary land! Rich desert images!

When we ask what makes for peace, we address the most basic theological and moral questions to be faced by people of faith: "What does it really mean to be saved? What is salvation in all its fullness?" Not just for me, me, me. For me, yes, but for all people, for the whole of creation! "How shall we live?" "Who is my neighbor?" . . . "Just what do we mean by 'the Kingdom of God?'"

The journey to search for answers can turn our lives upside down, but then we ARE talking about conversion! In the course of my travels I met a Korean-American campus minister in Chicago. He told about how he first arrived in the U.S. when he was a little boy, trying to "make it" in his new culture. He experienced many difficulties, but being very bright, he did well in school, and knew he could "get ahead." He became a real achiever, got top grades in college, and finally joined a fraternity thinking that would help!

But one night at a party in his fraternity house, while listening to someone tell a racist joke, he became so overcome with grief and anger that he hurled a bottle of beer through a wall and stalked away. His grieving and searching led him to the Church, and as he reordered his life came to see that it wasn't enough for him to be saved as an isolated individual, not even enough for him to so live that his Korean-American sisters and brothers could "make it" (whatever success means in this context), and not even enough so to live that all Americans could have the "good life." He saw that he must live his life according to Christ's attitude of love and caring for the whole world! Shalom for all!

I find it fascinating that Jesus' life is framed by Caesar Augustus at the beginning, and Pontius Pilate, at the end. Rome and the so-called "peace of Rome" is the setting for the proclamation of the good news of Christ's peace! We find Christ's peace, "Pax Christi," in the context of the peace of Rome, "Pax Romana."

There seems to be a tendency to make Christ's peace, the peace that passes all understanding, an internal, individual, otherworldly peace. That's important, too, but in this context we must emphasize the social and economic dimensions of

"Jesus spirituality." There's the kind of peace which existed due to the firm control by the Romans over the whole of the Mediterranean world during the time of Christ, called "Pax Romana," and there's "Pax Christi," the peace that led the shepherds into a "great joy" which was to come to all the people."

The peace enforced by Rome involved a system of strict control. There was a center, Rome, and there were the outside areas, the conquered provinces. As a schoolboy I learned about the fine system of roads, the fact that one could travel freely and far during those times, because of the absence of political boundaries. I learned about the common use of Roman money even beyond the Mediterranean world. I'm sure that some might have thought, "Wow, great for shopping!" (I can imagine a Roman tourist asking, "How much is that in *real* money?")

In the center of this world, Rome, there was material abundance and an unending quest for new commodities and pleasures. We also know that there was considerable corruption, even decadence, and for many a severe feeling of meaninglessness. What I didn't hear so much about as a schoolboy was that on the outer edges of this Roman world, at the edges of the city of Rome, and out in the provinces, there was unbelievable misery—people lacking in food, water, shelter, work, and education. Hopelessness was widespread. The economic situation is clearly reflected in New Testament chapters like Matt. 20 in the parable of the vineyard, where workers stood in line all day just waiting to be hired. Sound familiar?

If we can get ourselves beyond a ROMANticized view of this time in history we'll see that many other texts of the N.T. talk of the large numbers of landless people, about their hunger, their diseases, and their lack of possessions. Mark's gospel probably gives us our best view of the underside of the history of Roman Palestine: crowds—pressing, following, interrupting; farmers, fishers, the sick and lame, lepers; marketplaces, the roadside! Scholarship by persons like

Norman K. Gottwald in his socio-literary introduction to the Hebrew Bible, and Ched Myers in his book on Mark, *Binding The Strong Man (Orbis, 1988)*, give us important resources for understanding the context of Jesus' life and ministry.

My own experiences in areas where there is widespread poverty make it easier for me to visualize the biblical images—and they're not the idyllic picture postcard scenes that our churches displayed in the white middle-class Sunday School. Understanding this context has really brought my own Bible study alive!

There were prophets and poets, and people's movements. There was a significant revolt just about the time or slightly after the probable time that the Gospel of Mark was written. These movements had to do with the practical everyday life of the people. Christ cared about these people. The good news of Christ's peace seemed to be especially addressed to people who were hurting, the people on the fringes, but it eventually reached the center, Rome, as well. It was a gospel for rich and poor alike, but it often confounded the rich.

The messengers of Christ's peace were not well-received by the rich and comfortable. Jesus' serious followers were (and still are), consistently, harassed, silenced, and in some places eliminated by government forces, as Paul was. We can't help but think of some of our contemporary saints who have taken sides with the poor—the late Bishop Dom Helder Camara of Brazil, for example, who said, "If I give charity to the poor they call me a saint, but if I ask *why* they are poor, they call me a communist!"

The Roman system had effective ways to silence people and make them support the Pax Romana, the Roman Peace. We hear in the Christmas story, for example, that Joseph and Mary had to go to be "enrolled." It was an organized system of domination, with the military force to support it. The system drew on the wealth and energy of the provinces and maintained the privileged position of the few in the center.

Pax Romana. We even find the word inscribed on ancient Roman coins, where Caesar is termed a "peacemaker."

For Jesus, peacebuilding did not allow for terrorizing people into quiet submission through military power. It had to do with basic well-being and reconciliation, beginning with the lowliest and least. It was built not on the threat of physical force, but on right relationships, on fairness.

We know that Rome fell. Other "Romes" have taken its place. People still yearn for the Peace of Christ, and that peace is still good news to the poor.

There are major pieces of this question that cry out for our repentance, though, if we're to claim that peace. I'm not just talking about a narrow repentance which has merely to do with our private morals or our individual, otherworldly souls. I'm talking about one which deals also with the way we order our life together—one which touches our corporate lives: our systems and institutions, our lifestyles!

Advocates for peace are sometimes accused of being too critical, of being unpatriotic. I say, what better way to love one's country than to participate in its redemptive change! This is firmly within the prophetic tradition.

We *can* know the things that make for peace. God continues to reveal them, if only we will ask the critical questions. God blesses our search by revealing faithful people, even little people who pray for peace and fold little paper birds!

Micah 6:8 says:

> What does the Lord require of us?
> To do justice; to love mercy;
> and to walk humbly with our God.

Isaiah 32:16-17 says:

> Then justice will dwell in the wilderness,
> And righteousness abide in the fruitful field,
> And the effect of righteousness will be peace.